Shepherd of the Hills
Country

Shepherd of the Hills Country

Tourism Transforms the Ozarks, 1880s–1930s

LYNN MORROW
AND
LINDA MYERS-PHINNEY

THE UNIVERSITY OF ARKANSAS PRESS
Fayetteville, 1999

LIBRARY OF CONGRESS CATALOGING-IN-PUBLICATION DATA

Morrow, Lynn.
Shepherd of the hills country : tourism transforms the Ozarks,
1880s–1930s / Lynn Morrow and Linda Myers-Phinney.
p.   cm.
Includes bibliographical references (p.   ) and index.
ISBN 1-55728-574-8 (pbk. : alk. paper)
1. Tourism—Ozark Mountains—History.   2. Ozark Mountains—
Economic conditions.   I. Myers-Phinney, Linda, 1954–   II. Title.
G155.U6M668   1999
338.4'791767'1—dc21   99-31450
CIP

Chapter 6, "'As a Health Resort Taney is Unequalled': The Game Park"
originally appeared in *Gateway Heritage* with the title "The St. Louis
Game Park: Experiments in Conservation and Recreation." Reprinted
with permission from the Spring 1998 issue of *Gateway Heritage*, vol. 18,
no. 4 © 1998 by the Missouri Historical Society.

To all of our pals in the White River valley, but
especially to Kristen Ann for our time on Celtic Slope,
and to Denis for sharing my White River niche

Contents

Illustrations

Preface

"Wish You'd Find Out 'Bout That"

Histories commonly have autobiographical significance as this one does, and like many narratives, it is the result of ongoing research conducted over several years until the authors finally paused to summarize their experience. The authors have lived in the Ozarks with kith and kin and are familiar with the social complexities of the region, especially the small number of professional monographs. Both of us came to stronger reflections about the Ozarks in work on the campus of Southwest Missouri State University, Springfield, and its Center for Ozarks Studies. Both of us earned graduate degrees in history and in 1990 became part of Missouri's national model in local government records management and archives services, the Local Records Preservation Program. This division of the Missouri State Archives, Office of the Secretary of State, served to increasingly stimulate our interest and awareness of the Ozarks in the state's history.

In 1987–88 Robert Flanders and I team taught a special topics course, the "Great Bend of White River in Historical Context: The Tourist Industry, 1900–1930." Two years later, Linda Myers-Phinney concentrated the substance of that course in her master's thesis, "The Land of a Million Smiles: Tourism and Modernization in Taney County and Stone County, Missouri, 1900–1930." Earlier, Linda and I had become regular members of the White River Valley Historical Society where we made lasting friends with a common bond in Ozarks history. Both of us, with our friend Dr. David Quick, an architectural historian at Southwest Missouri State University, participated in historic preservation surveys of resort properties for the Missouri Department of Natural Resources; and all three of us authored sections of successful National Register of Historic Place nominations of properties in the Shepherd of the Hills country. At the request of Robert Gilmore, I became the editor of the White River Valley

Historical Society *Quarterly* in 1988 and director of the Local Records Program in 1990, while Linda has served as president of the society and assumed the duties of an archivist with Local Records. All the while, we continued through work and avocation a sifting of public and private records that continued to suggest to us that the history of tourism in the Ozarks represented a compelling subject.

Formal and informal interviews in the White River hills proved to be a continuing source of inspiration and crucial to the success of this project. Newcomers and natives alike perceived a significant and usable past along the White River, but often noted discrepancies in oral and written traditions. Walker Powell, grandson of Stone County promoter Truman Powell, offered his questions and gave judicious reflections to us. He knew that there seemed to be more to what he had been told about Marvel Cave and regional lore and said, "Wish you'd find out 'bout that." We hope that we have fulfilled his challenge.

Our bibliography lists residents who gave specific insights on local history. We would like to recognize some individuals who were particularly helpful with materials or support to the project. They include Rick Boland, editor and computer consultant in Raleigh, North Carolina; the late Robert K. Gilmore, a great Ozarks promoter; storyteller Douglas Mahnkey; Robert Wiley, an attorney, author, and Ozarks preservationist in Crane, Missouri; Lynne Haake and Mary Stokes, interlibrary loan reference specialists at the Missouri State Library, Jefferson City; Coralee Paull, an exceptional researcher in St. Louis, Missouri; and John Bradbury, manuscript specialist at the University of Missouri-Rolla, a historian who always keeps a sharp eye out for appetizing documents. Dr. Robert Cochran, director of the Center for Arkansas and Regional Studies, University of Arkansas, and Dr. Robert Flanders, former director of the Center for Ozarks Studies, Southwest Missouri State University, Springfield, entertained questions and comments, and offered encouragement. Dr. Ken Winn, state archivist of Missouri, cheerfully responded to numerous spontaneous discussions, and Dr. Gary Kremer, professor of history, William Woods University, Fulton, Missouri, critiqued an important chapter. Dr. W. K. McNeil, folklorist at the Ozark Folk Center, Mountain View, Arkansas, provided archival help. The readers of the manuscript, Dr. Milton Rafferty, the Ozarks premier geographer, and Dr. Larry Christensen, Distinguished Professor of History at the University of Missouri-Rolla, gave us important editorial advice that we took to heart. James Denny, fellow Ozarks Arcadian and longtime historian with the state park system, Missouri Department of Natural Resources, provided professional insights that illuminated much of our history. Jim's insights were the most substantial of all. Kevin Brock, acquisitions editor with the University of Arkansas Press, cheerfully advised on the many mechanical and procedural aspects that brought the manuscript to Fayetteville. My wife, Kristen Kalen Morrow, former high-school teacher at Forsyth, and her students, who knew the legends of Bald Knobbers, cockfighters, and tourists, patiently endured our endless tangents in the Ozarks. Denis Phinney ran the family business in Stone County while Linda traveled the state for the Local Records Program and read history at night.

Institutions that provided advice and resources for this work through their professional staff are many. They include the Kansas State Historical Society, Topeka, Kansas; the National Library of Canada, Ottawa; the Missouri Historical Society, St. Louis; the Missouri State Archives; the Recorders of Deeds offices, Stone and Taney Counties, Missouri; Special Collections, University of Arkansas, Fayetteville; the Springfield-Greene County Public Library, Springfield, Missouri; the State Historical Society of Missouri, Columbia, Missouri; the Western Historical Manuscript Collection, University of Missouri, Columbia and Rolla; and the White River Valley Historical Society, Point Lookout, Missouri, contributed papers, maps, and photographs. Special thanks go to the White River Valley Historical Society and the Missouri Historical Society for use of material formerly published in their journals concerning the St. Louis Game Park.

We have employed a variety of sources in this work. We hope to encourage readers who are reflective researchers to consider the wide range of historical documents available for Ozarks history. Over time, writers have consulted far too few repositories and primary sources trying to write about the Ozarks. The general significance of historic and contemporary tourism to our society demands that foundational work be accomplished in all geographic subregions of the Missouri and Arkansas Ozarks.

Lynn Morrow
Jefferson City, Missouri
February 1999

"To the Heart of the Ozarks"

An Introduction

THE LIVING MEMORY of what the upper White River valley once was is now faint. The federal construction of dams after World War II inundated the broad, fertile valleys, family farm landscapes, and immense gravel bars that were frequented by campers and floaters. Instead of seeing a valley cultivated by agriculturalists, visitors and natives alike see one managed by federal regulations that promote commercial tourism and the generation of electric power. In high schools along the valley students grow up not knowing where the White River is, thinking that the lakes—Table Rock, Taneycomo, and Bull Shoals—have always been there. Such is not the case, though. At one time the White River's 120 miles within southwest Missouri were nationally known due to the extraordinary historical circumstances of the twentieth-century tourist industry. This examination of Ozarks tourism focuses upon an earlier generation that laid the foundation for Missouri's present seventeen-billion-dollar travel industry, whose motto is "Where the Rivers Run."

Stone and Taney Counties in southwest Missouri lie contiguous to each other on the Arkansas border, Stone County to the west and Taney to the east. Two counties to the west of Stone is the Kansas border. The city of Springfield, historically important as the urban nucleus of southwest Missouri, lies twenty aerial miles north of the Stone-Taney County border in Greene County, but forty-five miles from the White River, which traverses both counties.

Over the eons the ground water in the upper White River valley has dissolved limestone base rock, creating karst formations—caves, springs, and sinkholes. The dissolution of limestone plus the effect of surface erosion has created long, narrow ridges divided by valleys containing deeply entrenched streams. This gradual wearing-away has created a characteristic physical landscape of great relief (distance between bottoms and ridge tops) and wandering streams. Erosion has also resulted in only average-to-poor soils except in stream valleys.[1]

The White River begins and ends in Arkansas, flowing 720 miles from its source in the Boston Mountains and through a series of man-made dams until it joins the Mississippi River. Along the way the river runs through Branson and Forsyth, Missouri, and Cotter, Calico Rock, and Batesville, Arkansas. The upper bend of the White River provided the earliest route into southwest Missouri. Early nineteenth-century settlers poled keelboats and flatboats from the mouth of the White, where it empties into the Mississippi River, into Arkansas and farther north and west into Missouri, a distance of some 600 miles. Henry Rowe Schoolcraft, who explored southwest Missouri in 1818 and 1819, found the White River sparsely lined with cabins as far upstream as the mouth of Beaver Creek in present-day Taney County.[2]

Although in 1851 the Missouri legislature took the James River township of old Taney County to form much of Stone County, the territory of the White River where it arched north into Missouri retained its homogeneity. The physical unity of the counties was reflected in transportation routes. Even after wagon roads such as the White River Trace opened from the north into the upper White River valley in the 1830s, rivers provided transportation, especially commercial. Delaware Town, one of the earliest and largest settlements in southwest Missouri, was located in modern Christian County on the upper James River and utilized the river, in part, for the long-distance trade which was its mainstay.[3] In 1852 steamboats first reached Forsyth, the county seat of Taney County, and in 1858 a vessel went further up the White to the mouth of the James River in southern Stone County.[4] Among the products carried to downstream markets on the White were furs, pelts, cotton, cattle, grain, flour, and lumber.

Beginning about 1870 overland freight routes eclipsed the upper White River waterway as southwest Missouri's primary transportation avenue. In that year the St. Louis and San Francisco Railroad was built through Springfield. In 1881 the Kansas City, Fort Scott, and Memphis line crossed Springfield on its way east and south. The following year, 1882, the "Frisco" Railway extended a spur line south of Springfield to Ozark, in Christian County, and in 1883 extended the tracks to Chadwick. As the rail point nearest the upper White River valley, the Chadwick terminus was patronized especially by Taney and neighbor Ozark County settlers for agricultural and timber exports. With these lines completed, freight wagons took over much of the river's business, hauling merchandise from rail points in Springfield and Chadwick south through the upper White River area into northern Arkansas. Local products, especially livestock, were then transported north to the railroad and shipped out of the area on overland routes. Businessmen from Missouri's two urban centers—St. Louis and Kansas City—began to frequent the Queen City of the Ozarks looking for investment opportunities and/or recreational hunting and fishing.

The rail lines precipitated a decline of the perpetuated socioeconomic frontier conditions that had characterized the region until then: low population density; economic underdevelopment; poorly developed physical amenities such as domestic sanitation, health care, transportation, and public education; and relative isolation. The area did, however, continue to be rooted in a stockman's agriculture without concentrations of industrial capital or machinery.[5]

The rail corporations expanded the resident population with a rush of homesteaders. They also brought new economic development to Stone and Taney Counties by providing reliable transportation for exporting marketable goods out of southwest Missouri; the dependable rails contrasted with the White River, which was subject to seasonal overflows and floods. The economic awakening was evident in the growing exploitation of the region's natural resources. In 1890 a handle factory was established in Taney County near the mouth of Roark Creek to serve the needs of miners in Lawrence County, Missouri, and several saw and flour mills and cotton gins were scattered throughout both counties. In 1898 Missouri's Bureau of Labor Statistics disclosed that Taney County shipped out eighteen different surplus products and Stone County shipped nineteen.[6] While this report reflected commercialism, the products shipped indicated that agriculture, supplemented by hunter-gatherer extractive activities, were still the main occupations. Manufacturing and commercial production that utilized skilled specialization were to come later as the railroad economies matured in the early twentieth century.

Regardless of the kind of labor which produced the surplus products of the 1890s, increasing trade, however, represented the metamorphosis of perpetuated frontier conditions—a process of change that writers often

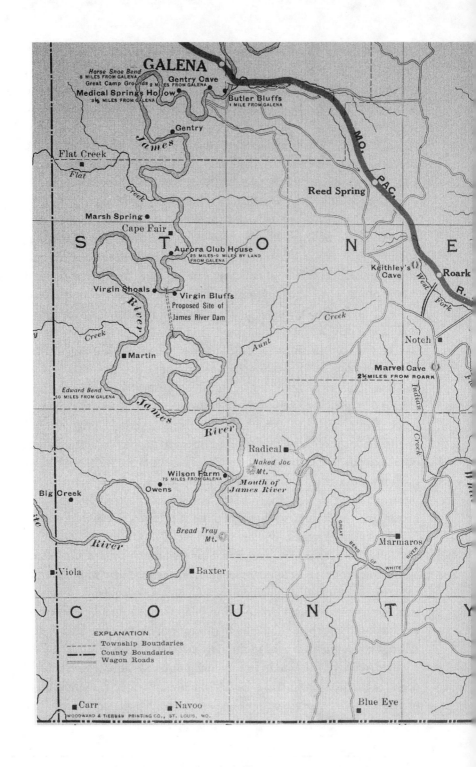

GALENA

Horse Snoe Bend
5 MILES FROM GALENA.
Great Camp Grounds 2 MILES FROM GALENA
Medical Springs Hollow
3½ MILES FROM GALENA

Gentry Cave
2 MILES FROM GALENA

Butler Bluffs
1 MILE FROM GALENA

Gentry

James

Flat Creek

Flat

Creek

Reed Spring

Marsh Spring

Cape Fair

S   T   O   N   E

Aurora Club House
25 MILES–9 MILES BY LAND
FROM GALENA

Keithley's
Cave

Roark

Virgin Shoals

Virgin Bluffs
Proposed Site of
James River Dam

River

Creek

Aunt

Creek

Notch

Martin

Marvel Cave
2½ MILES FROM ROARK

Indian

Creek

West   Fork

R.

Edward Bend
50 MILES FROM GALENA

James

River

Radical

Naked Joe
Mt.

Big Creek

Wilson Farm
75 MILES FROM GALENA

Owens

Mouth of
James River

te   River

Bread Tray
Mt.

GREAT   BEND   OF   WHITE   RIVER

Marmaros

Viola

Baxter

Blue

C   O   U   N   T   Y

EXPLANATION
------- Township Boundaries
-·-·-·- County Boundaries
======= Wagon Roads

Carr

Navoo

Blue Eye

WOODWARD & TIERNAN PRINTING CO., ST. LOUIS, MO.

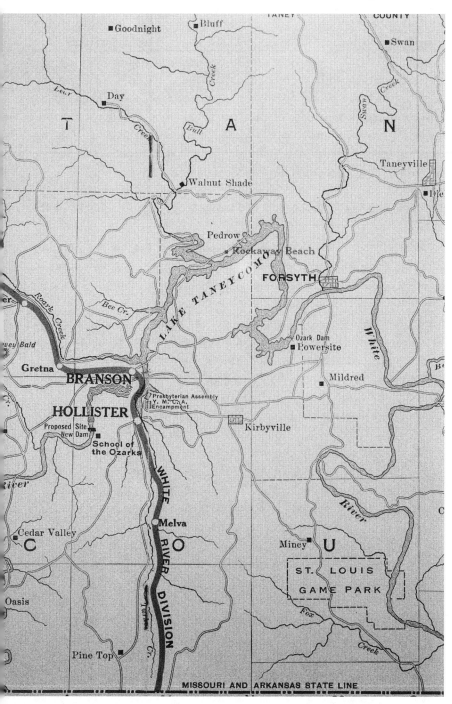

The White River/Shepherd of the Hills country, 1914 Bureau of Labor Statistics
Missouri State Archives

term modernization. Diversified trade signified economic development, brought money into a cash-poor area, and lessened the isolation surrounding the upper White River area by delivering an awareness of economic connections with the wider world beyond.

Thus, the frontier conditions in the upper White River valley began to erode as Springfield's railroad commerce activated change. Modernization began in response to stimuli outside the boundaries of Stone and Taney Counties—the rail depots to the north and markets in St. Louis and Kansas City vied for locally produced surplus. Modernization prompted by events *within* Stone and Taney Counties began in 1903 with the Missouri Pacific's extension of its St. Louis and Iron Mountain Railway's White River Division.

The White River Railway, built between 1903 and 1906, ran from Carthage, Missouri, southeast to Newport, Arkansas, generally following the valley courses of the White River drainage through Stone and Taney Counties. The railway acted as a catalyst, altering frontier lifeways more rapidly than ever before. The railroad brought Arcadian vacationers and urban entrepreneurs who recognized the potential for profits and prosperity, thereby infusing the area with new products and new ideas. Both by chance and by design the rail line fostered a more diverse economy, one which circulated money and modernization to the Ozarks as it disseminated information about the area, bringing ever more visitors and investors. In the service of tourism, amenities such as overnight accommodations, electricity, passable roads, indoor plumbing, nature walks, and attentive hired help were widely introduced into the upper White River valley. Souvenir postcards made by local photographers, for example, were sent far and wide, and johnboats designed and crafted by a Stone Countian were ultimately purchased by clients as far away as Canada.[7]

No one has determined when and where tourism actually began in the Ozarks, but the most significant and long-lasting change effected by the White River Railway was the tourism it facilitated and nourished in its service region. Tourism is about to become Missouri's number-one industry, and forecasters declare that tourism will be the greatest worldwide revenue generating enterprise of the twenty-first century. For Missouri and Arkansas the Ozark region is and has been the catalyst for a steady increase in visitors and investments that are significant in state economies.

As the twentieth century has waned, the tempo for both have dramatically spiraled upward to attract the attention of economists, geographers, journalists, novelists, politicians, real-estate brokers, and retirees. This short survey has selected the Shepherd of the Hills country, perhaps the best known of all places in the greater Ozarks, and focused upon themes, c. 1890–1930, that laid a historical and economic foundation for modern commercial tourism and changes in local society. It is a developmental story, one that Frederick Jackson Turner would have recognized. Turner, a historian of the Middle West, established the traditional paradigm a century ago for the closure of the frontier and the commencement of a new order of modernity. The early twentieth-century development of the upper White River valley, as the region shed its frontier qualities and joined in the larger national movements of urban and industrial transformation, fits neatly into Turner's theoretical structure. That is not to say that the Ozarks lost all of its agrarian flavor, only that its composition and direction in the early twentieth century was very, very different than just a generation before. Shepherd of the Hills tourism is a midwestern phenomenon with its principal boosters, actors, money and corporations, and critical mass of visitors, including Harold Bell Wright, hailing from the Midwest.[8]

The Shepherd of the Hills country, a name made famous as a literary device for the setting of Harold Bell Wright's novel, quickly became a permanent place name in Stone and Taney Counties, Missouri. The timing for the publication was perfect. Wright rode a partially completed railroad into the Ozarks and camped for a summer to write his tale, anticipating that modernization would soon change the land. In fact, Wright's book served as the first national promotion of the Ozarks, and boosters used it to institutionalize scenery and landmarks. Publishers released the book in 1907 as political discussions were underway for the impoundment of the White River, the major waterway through Wright's Shepherd of the Hills country. The successful completion in 1913 of Powersite Dam and Lake Taneycomo, the first White River reservoir, became the catalyst that wedded the novel and the region to commercial promotions in a generally agreed-upon space called the Shepherd of the Hills country.

Place names permeate the present and the past, carrying the power of cultural image; no named subregion in the Ozarks is any more recognizable to natives and visitors alike than the Shepherd of the Hills country.

Powersite Dam construction, 1912
Mabel Hicks Collection

Place names, however, are often imprecise, and observers will debate boundaries as the elasticity of names often depends upon its marketability. Histories of "naming the land" in any regional geography, however, are sure to capture the attention of folklorists, geographers, historians, genealogists, and general readers. In 1916 the statewide agricultural magazine, the *Missouri Farmer,* said plainly that Branson was in "the heart of the Ozarks" where Harold Bell Wright found the setting for *The Shepherd of the Hills.* The Missouri Pacific Railway used the "Heart of the Ozark Mountains" in the brochures intended for travelers heading to the James and White Rivers. While promoters have successfully built a tourist region upon the fame of Wright's novel, the literary name lies inside the greater Ozarks and, today, both are used interchangeably by millions of tourists. It seems that almost anywhere in Missouri and Arkansas tourists may encounter "a gateway to the Ozarks" as an invitation to visit and spend money. But the first "gateways" in regional promotions were those established by the Ozark Playgrounds Association during the 1920s. Greene County, for example, was the northeast gateway to an Ozarks of southwest Missouri and northwest Arkansas, whose center was the Shepherd of the Hills country, cradled along the James and White Rivers.

Wright focused national attention on the Ozarks, but the place name *Ozark* or *Ozarks* came from an earlier colonial past. In different usages speakers had applied the term to the Arkansas River, the Quapaw Indians, and the Arkansas Post. It was not until a trans-Mississippi expedition in 1819–20 that Maj. Stephen H. Long, in the employ of the federal government, imprinted the term *Ozark Mountains* on the region forever. *Ozark,* used as an adjective, gained ever-widening popularity in the late nineteenth century as applied to geological, commercial, cultural, and civic usages. Until the impoundment of Lake Taneycomo in 1913 journalists normally used two-word descriptions—*Ozark Uplift, Ozark Plateau, Ozark Mountains,* et cetera—but increasing attention to the region required a shorter, punchier term more suited to promotion—the *Ozarks.* The high-profile promotions surrounding the new Lake Taneycomo in the upper White River encouraged businessmen to culturally define the area as the "heart of the Ozarks."[9]

The urbanization of America, including the towns in Missouri and Arkansas, spurred a cultural competition between "the country" and "the city." Urban dwellers rejoiced in their accumulations of things, money, travel experiences, and institutional life, while country citizens still prized face-to-face neighborliness, the land, life in familiar circumstances, and spontaneous social events. Not surprisingly, voices from each area lauded their own virtues and criticized the other one, helping to polarize images of the two. Debates of the two views held in newspapers, books, and speechmaking gained momentum in the late nineteenth century and culminated in the country-life movement, a basis for early twentieth-century rural progressivism. The movement was a recoil from twentieth-century urbanization and industrialization; it was based on the belief that country life was more physically and spiritually nourishing because of its proximity to nature and the agrarian soil which had historically sustained American prosperity and success. Voices for the city and the country wrote unending newspaper articles that defended the quality of life in the respective areas.

Urban travelers who felt the stress of living in the city sought relief in the country, or Arcadia, as some liked to term it. The first chapter of this survey describes the Arcadian myth and identifies it as an important ideological context for understanding middle- and upper-middle-class Americans who desired a sojourn in the countryside. Many of these were inspired by Victorian serials like *Forest and Stream,* the leading sportsmen's magazine of the late nineteenth century, which published testimonials of successful outings from around the country. For example, one column from southwest Missouri in 1889 told readers in New York how to reach the fabled hunting grounds of the White River. The advice included the hire of dogs, guide, and camping outfits and where to stay in hotels at Ozark, Forsyth, and Bakersfield, Missouri. For these readers the Ozarks was a far and distant exotic place, but that was where Arcadia lay.[10]

The "priests of Nature," or farmers, were considered rude and primitive by city folk, but were generally a respected class of Americans. Corporations wooed agriculturalists to commodify all their activities for maximized profits until the emergence of an urban industrialized America, and its civilized denizens, became the model society for late Victorians. All the while, urban Americans, influenced by images from Classical educations, dreamed of a rural Arcadia where virtue, rest and relaxation, and the regeneration of the spirit was possible. This expectation of a regenerated temperament, explored in chapter 1, permeated the early sportsmen and tourist adventures in the Ozarks. Urban America sought mythological places and wanted pastoral playgrounds. Author Harold Bell Wright himself chose such a place near the Arkansas-Missouri border, expecting the Ozarks to restore his health. While there he drafted a morality play set among Nature's children, one that would define and change the very fabric of the area.

Whether late nineteenth-century travelers were urban or rural they all knew something about "curiosities" or attractions in their own locale. In the southern uplands of Arkansas and Missouri the curiosity was often a karst feature—a spring, such as Wolf Bayou Springs, or a cave, such as Marble Cave. City and country travelers learned about "relics" that were easily found at cave shelters and in deeper recesses of the caverns. Outings or "cave parties" included the discovery and exploitation of these prehistoric remains and the collection of them for souvenirs. Travelers looted hundreds of aboriginal settlement and burial sites in the Ozarks prior to 1900. Over time dry Ozark caves offered travelers and locals a sublime or

Pine Lodge at Marvel Cave
Postcard, Velma A. Bass Collection

secret setting for socials, civic and political meetings, dances, the storage of food, the manufacture of moonshine, and even use as brothels. Large caves warranted exploration.

Occasionally, investors imagined economic opportunities at these karst features. Some built mills at great springs; others in the 1880s tried to exploit the caves for their natural fertilizer to be marketed at railroad towns. For example, dozens of caves along the Gasconade River in Missouri were so mined for their bat guano. Promoters from the midwestern railroad town of Lamar, Missouri, assembled their resources at Marble Cave, trusting in mineral profits and real-estate promotion, but failed to replicate a vision for another Eureka Springs, Arkansas. Their energies, however, and the promotions of Truman Powell and Canadian W. H. Lynch kept an outside audience aware of its existence. In the twentieth century the grounds became a haven for artists and college and high-school groups who held annual adventures there. Boosters attempted to establish the great natural wonder as the Ozarks first national park, but negotiations failed. Its appeal as a natural landmark has been expanded for over a century; as the region's oldest, continuous tourist attraction it is now known as Marvel Cave. The development of this "bottomless pit" is examined in chapter 2.

The third chapter recounts the story of a St. Louis gentlemen's club which founded a new kind of site in the Ozarks—a recreational one designed to thrive within the bountiful natural resources of the area. St. Louis business cultivated an orientation to the southwestern states shortly after the Civil War; St. Louis investment capital and the sons of corporate St. Louis managers moved down the rail lines like any other immigrants. In Missouri and Arkansas in the late nineteenth century there really were no "historic sites" for tourists to visit—that is, outside of Civil War battlefields, a famous person's residence, or urban landmarks—but St. Louisans left Union Station for recreation at dozens of private places, owned or leased, throughout southern Missouri and northern Arkansas. Central to these attractions was the fauna of recently settled lands, whether they were prairies, uplands, swamps, or "the spreads" of lowlands. A goal for the society of tourists and sportsmen was to establish clubhouses in the country to entertain guests, and an emerging class of hunters and fishermen called "true sportsmen" came in significant numbers. Not far away, and sometimes together with the sportsmen, were resident and nonresident market hunters who became their "Natty Bumpos" or guides to successful outings.

The true sportsmen, parents of Ozarks tourism, brought real money into the Ozarks. In the fashion of the day, sportsmen traveled to the end of the railroad to seek adventures in the great outdoors. St. Louisans formalized their Ozark outings into long-term landholding, regular visits, and significant capital investments in buildings, fences, animals, and gala social parties. Their health resort, the St. Louis Game Park, like Marble Cave, became nationally known.

While Marble Cave and the St. Louis Game Park emerged as foundational sites in the history of Ozarks tourism, Stone and Taney Counties witnessed dramatic demographic change. Chapter 4 looks at midwesterners who joined the old southern population to seek homesteads or investments in legendary and newly advertised mineral lands. Although immigrants from the southern uplands still came to the Ozarks, the numbers of midwesterners was greater. Local hunter-stockmen commented about a notice-able influx of newcomers from St. Louis, north Missouri, the Great Plains, and the prairie counties of southwest Missouri. Many of these settlers adopted the open-range lifestyle available to them; they, too, had menfolk who wanted to hunt and fish and have an "easy living" in an economy removed from a capitalist structure that demanded work in measured time. Other newcomers worked to found small businesses and became strong voices for progressive agriculture and hopeful modernization through con-nections with railroads. These settlers, often hailing from railroad towns themselves and possessing marketable skills, came expecting change to take place in the Ozarks. The fact that St. Louis and Kansas City were the mar-ket and corporate towns for the Missouri Ozarks (as opposed to Little Rock and Fort Smith) and that immigration from the Midwest added signifi-cantly to local society accounts a great deal for a midwestern climate in the Shepherd of the Hills country rather than a southern one.

The social and environmental circumstances confronted by new-comers who settled with the natives and who competed for dwindling resources on the open range represented significant cultural challenges. Some, like Will Sharp and Ben Stults, became noted hunters, and suc-cessfully made the transitions into modern economies. W. D. Sylvester, a skilled mechanic, committed his fortunes with considerable difficulty for over a generation to possessing and cultivating a homestead in the Ozarks. Others, like the Gertens, Shamels, and Prestons remembered easier times in railroad towns, and after homesteading government lands, left the Ozarks for a more familiar life. At the turn of the century progressive journalists, proud of new Ozark towns, continued a city versus country debate by excoriating urban wholesale houses that marketed by mail. But Ozarkers, whether old or new settlers, saw much that they liked in Sears, Roebuck and Company, Montgomery Ward, and wholesale houses in St. Louis. The local export of products from mixed-farming economies gen-erated income that allowed Ozarkers to purchase manufactured goods from American industry.

By 1900 the tourist-sportsman, whether visiting the St. Louis Game Park or recreating on the James and White Rivers, had established a sea-sonal presence. All over the Ozarks sportsmen traveled the railroads to engage local transportation in order to take a float trip, described as

Jacob Goetz, a manager at Marshall Field's department store in Chicago, who immigrated to Taney County in 1898
Museum of the Ozarks, Springfield

"Nature's Own Remedy." This romantic image, a temporary lifestyle enjoyed by Harold Bell Wright in several seasons, became the common vacation experience for tourists, male and female, investors, artists, and writers and is discussed in chapter 5. The outing became popular before effective governmental enforcement of hunting and fishing regulations; the experience was very different from that enjoyed only a generation later. It was the urban sportsmen who initiated the float trip, so memorialized in Ozarks journalism and folklore. Tourists-sportsmen wanted to travel long distances on the waterways to hunt and fish, and guns—not fishing rods—were the most expensive items in the flat-bottom boats. The presence of sportsmen as tourists influenced the parallel development of conservation as well as tourism.[11]

A railroad engineer who sensed the commercial possibilities in float fishing was the first to promote the famous Galena-to-Branson float. Hosting out-of-towners for a float trip to hunt and fish did indeed become the first broad-based commercial tourism in the Ozarks and was the ultimate sporting adventure on the White River during the early twentieth century. Railroads had promoted scenic excursions, but scenery as a salable commodity really took root in the promotion of float trips. Moreover, the trade created the context for a flowering of Ozarks folklore told by skilled guides around campfires on a gravel bar and captured by journalists seeking feature stories. The reputations of Ozark outfitters and guides such as Charlie McCord, Vernon Todd, Charley Barnes, Tom Yocum, and others were made on the river. Barnes, a member of a family that came to Stone County in the late 1880s, gained considerable fame as a master craftsman for building the famed Ozark johnboat.

Chapter 6, "God's Great Natural Park," looks at the greater environment around the cave, the park, the float trip, and the commercialization of the sportsmen's and tourists' Arcadia. The many related businesses that intertwined around the new tourism industry and its small railroad towns rallied around Wright's novel, which provided a vocabulary and setting. To experience romance, legend, natural beauty, and local hospitality and to meet famous natives in the Shepherd of the Hills country were promises sold to rail passengers by the Missouri Pacific Railway. Middle-class Arcadians championed the outdoors and healthy living, but lobbied for amenities, too. Hotels, tea rooms, artistic bungalows, electricity, and good roads all became part and parcel of development in the Shepherd of the Hills country. With Lake Taneycomo established and electricity available, promoters could think in terms of large groups that could be attracted for extended visits. Surges in seasonal population led to demands for increasing services and supplies for urban travelers who wanted resorts in the country, but not too far in the country.

While the railroad brought tourists, it also carried economic possibilities for corporate investors. The Shepherd of the Hills region was a source of pride for St. Louis merchants. Urban businessmen sent capital and skilled personnel who carved places for themselves and positioned their interests for access to state and national markets. The forest industry impacted all of Stone and Taney Counties, while agriculturalists concentrated on orchards, grapes, strawberries, and tobacco near the rail lines. Canning factories, especially those that produced tomatoes, were significant not only in family incomes, but also in providing the first wage-paying jobs for hundreds of

Float trip on the James River, June 24, 1907
Postcard, Kalen and Morrow Collection

adult and young women. Stock raising remained the core economy for most farmers.

The 1920s was a decade of unrivaled boosterism in the Shepherd of the Hills country and a time that solidified the local area into a middle-class tourist destination. Resorts along the Lake Taneycomo shoreline abounded and owners of the institutional Presbyterian Hill retreat and the YMCA camp celebrated their success throughout the Midwest. New towns like Branson, Hollister, and Rockaway Beach became known among thousands of urban vacationists. The twenties was also a decade that witnessed a weakened attraction among business elites for an Arcadian repast on the White River. But the good-roads movement, the Ozarks Playgrounds Association, and thousands of automobiles brought more money and development to the locale than the economy of Arcadian elites ever did.

Journalists, geographers, and folklorists continued using the Shepherd of the Hills name in their writings. The region represented thriving business and the potential for more business. The area had to have an image, but Arcadia was an early one that eventually faded in favor of the "backwoods," and that image and its impact are examined in chapter 7. The backwoods was not all negative, however, but it was different. By the time of the Great Depression business elites and middle-class Americans had widened their travel to the Rocky Mountains, the Caribbean, California, and Europe. The Shepherd of the Hills country, in the mind of high-culture elites, faded into just another rural American landscape similar to many others, having lost its preindustrial ambience.

But the Ozarks had enduring features that attracted a regular clientele from Missouri and the Midwest. Middle-class vacationers still enjoyed the outdoors, lakeside resorts, and touring the Shepherd of the Hills sites. Facilities with electricity made resorting in the Shepherd of the Hills country different from other interior Ozark retreats. Meanwhile, national culture in the mediums of film, novels, and Sunday feature stories had made mountain whites, including those in the Ozarks, into "hillbillies." By the twenties, the pastoralism of Arcadia had eroded into the backwoods of hillbillies, but not without profit to the tourist industry.

Midwestern progressives like J. K. Ross put a positive spin on the term hillbilly, and by the depression regional writers such as Vance Randolph used "hillbilly" with both positive and negative implications, resulting in conflicting images. Randolph's journalism, and that of others, complained in an antimodernist vein that primitive culture was ending—a complaint with which the urban Arcadians of the 1890s would have agreed. The hillbilly term continued to be used, although boosters in the tourist and business communities muted its derogatory connotations. But before there were hillbillies on the White River there were urban Arcadians. These city folk were educated, were fully immersed in commercial culture, had traveled to many American places, and expressed themselves in books and essays. In hindsight, it seems like it was only a matter of time until their society found the White River, a locale of natural beauty that appealed to their pastoral imaginations.

"Priests of Nature"

Arcadia Comes to the White River Country

RCADIA was the name bestowed by the Greeks of ancient times on a rugged and mountainous region of central Peloponnesus. Centuries later, Arcadia fell to the Romans in 146 B.C., and the conquerors saw in the region the essence of the simple pastoral way of life; it was the abode of Pan, the Roman god of meadows and forests. The great Roman poet, Virgil, writing in the first century B.C. evoked Arcadia as the symbol of rustic simplicity and happiness in the *Ecologues*. In so doing, Virgil tapped even deeper sources of the pastoral myth; his work was modeled on the idylls of Theocritus, the Greek poet who is said to have originated pastoral, or rustic, poetry. Virgil employed the ancient Hellenistic region of Arcadia to weave a mythic landscape of rustic simplicity and happiness.

By this creation of a symbolic and mythical Arcadian place, Virgil devised a motif that has exerted a compelling pull on the Western mind over the span of centuries that lay between his time and our own. As surely as the violent and alienating business of building civilizations and nations has proceeded apace in those intervening centuries, there has grown the deep-seated longing for a pastoral refuge of primal simplicity—an unsullied Arcadia of the mind and heart.

Around the turn of the twentieth century an Arcadian ideal of rural happiness came to dominate one stream of American intellectual thought. The preoccupation with the Arcadian myth began in cities; it was not farmers who considered country life a blissful idyll, but urban dwellers. And working-class people hardly put their faith in country living as a panacea; they had neither the leisure time nor money to pursue rustic idylls. It was rather the urban upper and middle classes who embraced the symbol of Arcadia so thoroughly that they actually believed it existed in the countryside of rural America.

An increasing dichotomy between rural and urban lifeways led the urban middle and upper classes to romanticize and idealize rural life. They began to imagine, as they were increasingly separated in time from their own rural roots, that the country was imbued with the attributes of Arcadian happiness—simplicity, honesty, self-reliance, humanitarian ethics, and a spiritual and physical wholesomeness that stemmed from closeness to nature and God. The farmer is "more than any other man, the true priest of Nature, whose very occupation leads him, as it were, to the portals of her temple." So wrote a progressive agriculturalist in Missouri in 1884.[1] Urban dwellers wanted to emulate these "priests of Nature" and to imagine living their lifestyle, if only in musings of fantasy. Their Arcadia was Utopian, more literary than actual, but it spilled over into thinking about real life because of the changing social and cultural context of American life.

Between 1870 and 1920 the population of America shifted from predominately rural to urban. The population of towns and cities ranging in size from 2,500 to 50,000 rose by 7.7 percent, and the number of people in cities over 250,000 increased from 7.9 to 19.6 percent. Overall, the percentage of Americans who lived in towns of 2,500 or more swelled during this period from 25.7 percent to 51.2 percent, almost doubling.[2] This burgeoning urban population paralleled the emergence of what historians have called the Progressive Era, a period from 1896 to 1913 during which per capita wealth tripled. Simply put, Americans had more money and traveled more frequently.

America also became more industrialized; during the first four post–Civil War decades the United States surged to industrial greatness. This was partly due to the staggering technological advances driven by such nineteenth-century inventions as railroads, electric lights, telephones, steam heat, and flush toilets. The employment opportunities and certain wages of industry drew many workers from farms to urban centers, while those farmers who stayed on the land utilized the new technology to inaugurate a more efficient agricultural economy that grew more productive and was less labor intensive. Metropolitan growth and technological advances meant that Americans faced a world in which rural living was largely a thing of the past. This transformation was so momentous that it occasioned Cornell University educator Liberty Hyde Bailey to conclude that "the whole basis

"Hiawatha and Minne Ha Ha in the Ozarks" depicts children and "back to nature," c. 1910. *Ed Miller Collection*

of civilization is changing. Industry of every kind is taking the place of the older [agrarian] order."[3]

As America became more industrialized and more urban the feelings of Americans regarding the country, which became synonymous with nature, underwent a change. Urban intellectuals exhibited a form of culture shock which was evident in their perceptions of city versus country: as cities loomed ever larger the rural landscape appeared to shrink. And as the country (and nature) seemed to disappear before the onslaught of urbanization and industrialization, both became more desirable. The country, when viewed as a haven of Arcadian happiness, became a refuge for escape from the pressures of urban living, a retreat to a simpler, less-stressful way of life. To the increasingly wealthy upper and middle classes who were somehow ill-at-ease with their lifestyles, leisure time spent in the country seemed to calm the anxieties of urban life.

In the early nineteenth century outdoors activities such as hunting and fishing epitomized the sins of the idle rich and the unemployed poor—who both dared to violate the capitalist work ethic. By the late nineteenth century, however, the growing Arcadian view of the country as a source of restoration and happiness justified outdoor recreation for the middle class. Arcadian writers proclaimed that "Nature . . . was a hospital, particularly effective for those suffering from dyspepsia and tuberculosis . . . more important, nature was also a playground. Play could contribute to regaining health," mending those who suffered from the city's unwholesomeness. Prof. Charles Richmond Henderson, of the University of Chicago, pointed out in 1909 that "Many of our rich men, under expert medical care are living a rural life several months of each year for physical and mental health."[4] In Missouri, St. Louis business and industrial executives spent their Arcadian moments in hunting and fishing camps along the Mississippi River valley, the interior Ozarks rivers, and the lowland swamps of southeast Missouri and northeast Arkansas.

The growing social acceptance of outdoor activities coincided with technological advances that increased the opportunities for leisure pursuits. Expanding technology, by making work more mechanized and efficient, shortened working hours, but the pace of work accelerated as work time contracted. "As work grew more intense and driven, men and women cherished their leisure time as a compensation for the frenzied pace of their working hours. As such, leisure [time] had to be spent; mere absence of work was insufficient."[5] At the same time, technology provided the means of rapid and expanded travel—first by train and railroad systems and then by automobile. Country holidays became accessible to the expanding and increasingly affluent middle class.

Frederick Jackson Turner's *Significance of the Frontier in American History* fueled concerns over a fading rurality that seemed to vanish as urbanization engulfed it. Turner conjectured that because American society had been forged on a frontier, its vigor and character intertwined with and depended upon frontier conditions. Writing in 1903, Turner proclaimed that the 1890s was America's first decade without a frontier.[6] His observations caused thoughtful Americans to worry over the future: would America be irreparably changed by the loss of its vital frontier connection?

One important expression of the anxiety over America's frontierless future came at the National Conference on Outdoor Recreation, convened in 1924 by Pres. Calvin Coolidge. Regarding the need for a national outdoor recreational policy, the president stated that "from such life [in the open] much of the American spirit of freedom springs." Theodore Roosevelt Jr., the executive chairman of the conference, reiterated this fundamental tenet of the American Arcadia: "The spirit of America . . . is bequeathed to us by the wilderness tamers who made this country." "In building the country," he continued, "the pioneers also built our national character, for they gave to Americans of today the hardy self-reliance, simplicity of outlook, and the initiative which form the bedrock of our national greatness. This is the spirit bred of life in the open." Because of the fear, previously expressed by Liberty Bailey and others, that the consequence of "city industrialism is to make dependent men and managed men"[7] the Report of the Commission on the Citizenship Values of Outdoor Recreation decreed that outdoor activity constituted a "prime factor" in forming good citizens.[8]

For the expanding urban middle class, the changing nature of American life—attitudinal, technological, and demographic—exerted a profoundly unsettling influence and created an anxiety and distrust of the consequences of all those sweeping and pervasive changes, anxiety that expressed itself in an atavistic longing for a lost rural past. Modern life seemed too complicated, too burdensome, and too artificial; in essence, it seemed overcivilized. Rural America, by comparison, harkened back to a simpler, happier existence—an American Arcadia. At a time when too much modernity seemed the root of modern difficulties, nostalgia infused the rural past with a patina of perfection. Historian Jackson Lears termed this distrust of progress and the attendant longing for the rural past "antimodernism," a "recoil from the artificial, overcivilized qualities of modern existence." This trend, according to Lears, rested on the belief that "urban artifice and mechanical convenience had transformed the apple-cheeked farm boy into the sallow industrial man."[9]

The middle-class longing for an Arcadian past found expression in many facets of American life during the late nineteenth and early twentieth centuries. In architecture, for example, it became fashionable to build in a rustic style utilizing native materials left in a somewhat rough form to achieve a "natural" look. The arts-and-crafts movement eschewed the excessive ornamentation and overstuffed quality of nineteenth-century furniture in favor of more unadorned designs based on principles of simplicity and usefulness. Programs of nature study were launched that emphasized bird watching and plant identification. A trend in landscape architecture aspired to a wild, disordered, unplanned look, while a movement in urban park design attempted to bring a bit of the country to cities. In the field of education, knowledge of the outdoors and wildlife was stressed, and summer camps were established where urban children experienced nature firsthand. A new literary trend exalted and even sentimentalized rurality.[10]

Through all these manifestations of the back-to-nature movement ran the assumption that an urban environment was generally less desirable than a rural one. Cities were considered bad for people because they were manmade artifices; country environs, conversely, were thought to be naturally better because they were divinely created. Closeness to God seemed to give the country certain restorative qualities; the country eased the cares of weary urbanites and uplifted their spirits. In the tradition of the nineteenth-century Transcendentalists, advocates of the country viewed it as God's abode. Contact with nature brought a person closer to divine experience. This not only rejuvenated the soul but improved character.

America's Arcadians were bolstered by the fields of psychology and medicine, which blamed many ills on the tensions and pressures of urban life and prescribed periodic retreats to the country to restore bodily and mental health. Paralleling Sigmund Freud's hypothesis that repressive civilization caused many of modern man's ills, American psychologist Granville Stanley Hall recapitulated the theory of genetic psychology which held sway for a generation after 1890.[11] Hall, who received the first Ph.D. in psychology in the United States and went on to pioneer developmental psychology, believed that in order to attain vigorous adulthood, children must recapitulate the cultural stages of human development from the primitive to the modern. This reenactment could only occur in a natural setting. Denied the opportunity, urban children would develop into something less than fully formed, healthy adults. By the 1910s, Hall's theories were no longer in vogue among professionals, but prior to that time he no doubt inspired many urban couples to allow their children the opportunity to experience the character-building benefits of a rural setting.[12]

A faith in the wholesomeness of the countryside led more and more urban, middle-class people to spend time there. They sought, if only temporarily, to escape the oppressiveness of cities, to find spiritual regeneration in the countryside, to engage in wholesome outdoor recreation which would make them feel healthier, and to experience a simpler, less-complicated life. What they sought, in short, was a personal Arcadia in a place of pastoral happiness where cares did not exist.

There was, of course, an underlying irony in the quest for Arcadia. Arcadia was more the invention of a deep, unsatisfied human longing than an actual place. The Arcadian ideal had always been deeply imbued with mythic overtones, and this was as true in turn-of-the-century America as in the time of Virgil. Indeed, those who visited the country wanted a circumscribed Arcadian experience that was divorced from reality in many ways. Nature could be a very dangerous and unpleasant place, but urbanites did not desire the feral, the fierce, or the barbarous; those real qualities of the natural world were unpleasant, and unpleasantness was not part of the Arcadian experience they were seeking. Their quest for Arcadia was really a search for a particular emotional experience associated with a particular place that possessed "Arcadian" qualities.

Urban Americans wanted to play on an Arcadian stage which created the illusion of natural, unspoiled wilderness. The gritty realities and violent facets of country life that did not fit the Arcadian vision were either ignored or reinterpreted. The urban notion of Arcadian happiness required all the comforts of urban life. City vacationers sought refuge from the crowded and frantic pace of modernity, but they did not reject the conveniences of modern life when they repaired to country retreats. Most stayed in resorts, camps, and country clubs where nature had been groomed to an acceptably controlled level. As John Jakle pointed out in his study of tourism, "For most tourists, the quest for nature was an inclination to pleasure, and not a dedication to truly profound comprehension."[13]

The Arcadian vision found expression in a long tradition of American literature about man, nature, and civilization. This tradition can be traced back to Hector St. John Crevecoeur's eighteenth-century *Letters from an*

American Farmer. Crevecoeur perpetuated the Arcadian vision, as did Thomas Jefferson in his *Notes on Virginia* and his philosophy of agrarianism. In the nineteenth century Nathaniel Hawthorne, James Fenimore Cooper, Herman Melville, and others made use of pastoral themes, along with Transcendentalists Ralph Waldo Emerson and Henry David Thoreau. Naturalists John Muir and John Burroughs glorified nature near the turn of the twentieth century, as did a host of lesser-known writers.[14] Liberty Hyde Bailey authored several books exemplifying the Arcadian idea.[15] Dallas Lore Sharp, an ex-minister who turned to teaching English at Boston University, penned twenty-two volumes of essays devoted to living the Arcadian life. One important literary genre was nature-oriented fiction for adults. These works ranged from the jungle stories of Edgar Rice Burroughs to the sentimental and innocent adventures penned by Gene Stratton Porter. Intellectual historians term the emphasis on pastorality an "Arcadian tradition."[16]

One of the most celebrated turn-of-the-century Arcadian writers was bestselling author Harold Bell Wright. His Arcadian setting was the White River hills of the Ozarks Highland. It was in this wildly beautiful and primitive locale that Wright formed his Arcadian vision, expressing it in *The Shepherd of the Hills*. The genius of his achievement was that he succeeded in striking a responsive chord in Americans who longed for an Arcadian setting where the morality play of urban corruption and rural purity could be acted out. His White River setting suited this requirement perfectly. Its stage was a natural and unspoiled wilderness where spiritually troubled urbanites could come for regeneration. The novel was in many ways a metaphor of his own personal quest. He, himself, had been a sick man, and had come to the Ozarks to regain his physical vigor, and had later drawn on the region for the inspiration for his famous novel.

Harold Bell Wright, born in 1872, followed other callings, including the ministry, before finally achieving fame in the genre of Arcadian literature. In 1905, while living in Kansas City, doctors informed him that his precarious health would no longer permit ministerial work. Wright then relocated to the White River hills, a region with which he was already familiar, as he had enjoyed float trips and camping on the James and White Rivers since 1896. In the Ozarks he had temporarily supported himself by painting houses and barns and had worked on a farm. Now

Posed photo of Harold Bell Wright in his tent during summer 1905 at Inspiration Point
Postcard, Kalen and Morrow Collection

Promoter R. W. Wilson and "natives" near Powersite Dam
Kalen and Morrow Collection

he returned again to regain his shattered health and to write a second novel. He and his wife camped one summer in a tent on what was later called "Inspiration Point" west of Branson, and here he drafted his wilderness classic, *The Shepherd of the Hills*. He completed the novel that winter in Lebanon, Missouri, and the book was published in 1907.[17]

The Shepherd of the Hills exemplified the Arcadian fiction that was being written in the early twentieth century. A formulaic Arcadian melodrama, the novel tells the story of a celebrated but careworn and spiritually burdened city pastor, the Shepherd, who retreats to the wilderness of the Ozarks Mountains in an attempt to recover inner peace and heal his tormented soul. One of his trials there was finding the courage to confess to his hosts, the Matthewses, that the unprincipled artist who had earlier wooed, seduced, and then abandoned their daughter to die in hopeless despair was none other than his own son. His second challenge lay in summoning the moral strength to convince the mountain maiden Sammy Lane to remain in her Ozarks home rather than yield to the allure of the big city with all its decadence and temptations. The Shepherd, of course, rose to both challenges. By proving his mettle, the Shepherd restored his faith in God and regained the vigor of his mind and body. Predictably, Arcadia had worked its healing magic.

The presumption of the Arcadian myth, that rurality was intrinsically superior to urbanity, was the foundation of Wright's story. Wright portrayed the Ozarks as a sanctuary. Just as the Shepherd came searching for an inner peace that he could not find in the city, so had Jim Lane retreated from family trouble on a southern plantation, and Old Matt and Aunt Molly had left their kin and a "worldly" life behind in Illinois. Aunt Molly ruefully told the Shepherd, "We've forgot the ways of civilized folks"; nevertheless, she expressed no regret at their decision to come to the hills. The Shepherd voiced Arcadian sentiments which differentiated the pseudo-civilization of cities from the honest values of country life. He mused over Molly's plainness, sturdiness, and kindness: "This is the stuff . . . that makes possible . . . civilization."[18]

Wright further expressed a contempt for urbanity through his characterization of Ollie Stewart. Although a local boy, Ollie had gone to the city to pursue education and wealth. Still, the critical difference between Ollie and the other country residents lay not so much in his having gone

J. K. and Molly Ross
*Tourist brochure, Linda
Myers-Phinney Collection*

to the city but in his wholehearted embrace of the urban lifestyle. Ollie provided the novel's comic relief, albeit by means of somewhat scathing humor which portrayed him as pitiable and contemptible. Just as urban life was a man-made artificiality, so was Ollie something less than a fully formed, vigorous man.

The reader's first glimpse of him is revealing. He appears beside Sammy Lane, "the splendidly developed young woman" of the hills as "but a weakling." Poor, citified Ollie had narrow shoulders and he stooped. "His limbs were thin . . . his eyes dull," and his sallow appearance reflected his

Ross homestead prior to remodeling into the Matthews cabin for tourism
Hobart Parnell Collection

spiritual shortcomings. Sammy Lane, the country girl affianced to Ollie, summed up his character by saying, "He couldn't be a bad man . . . he isn't big enough." "He is," she concluded, "too little—body, soul and spirit."[19]

Sammy Lane's ambivalence toward Ollie reflected her own struggle to make up her mind whether to move to the city with her betrothed, presumably becoming sophisticated and worldly, or to remain in her beloved hills and live the simple, unpretentious, and innocent life of an Ozark maiden. The Shepherd understood the pitfalls of city life and warned Sammy Lane that it was nothing but a sham. He described the city as a place of "false standards" and "petty ambitions," and strove to make Sammy understand that the "glittering tinsel of that cheap culture" was only "froth and foam." Of course, Sammy made the correct and moral choice to remain in the mountains; her crestfallen lover, poor, shallow Ollie, failed to grasp the fundamental rightness of her decision.[20]

Wright's story illustrated the rewards that Arcadia offered. The Shepherd went to the hills because he was "sick and tired of it all." It was not a physical malady, but a spiritual one. Sammy observed that "when you look right close into his eyes, he does 'pear kind o' used up." The root of the Shepherd's affliction was that "in the cities . . . our lives have so little of God in them . . . we come in touch with so little that God has made." But in the Ozarks the preacher discovered "what he had not learned in all his theological studies. He learned to know God, the God of these mountains." In the Ozark Arcadia he gained calmness, strength, and closeness to God. Amidst the Ozark ridges and hills that the Shepherd described as "temples of God's own building," he was "born again."[21] True to the Arcadian promise, the simple country life cleared his spiritual sight and restored his peace of mind.

By critical standards *The Shepherd of the Hills* could hardly be judged good literature, but it proved a roaring popular success. Wright's biographer Lawrence Tagg attributed this largely to the book's timing—a public steeped in the back-to-nature ethos wanted decent, outdoor romances with a clear-cut, moral message, and Wright fulfilled this need. Historian Roderick Nash described Wright as "a dispenser of wholesomeness, optimism, and the Arcadian Myth." Nash also pointed out that "next to names like F. Scott Fitzgerald, Earnest Hemingway, and Henry L. Mencken, those of Gene Stratton Porter, Zane Grey, and Harold Bell Wright have stirred little interest among historians." Nevertheless, between World War I and the depression, "books by the latter three appeared sixteen times on the national lists of bestsellers, while the works of the first three never appeared at all." By early 1918 *The Shepherd of the Hills* had sold two million copies.[22]

For the White River country, *The Shepherd of the Hills* was more than a bestseller—it was a phenomenon that would transform the region into a commercialized imitation of the novel itself. Just as Harold Bell Wright drew inspiration from the region to produce his great work, once it became a runaway commercial success the region began to redefine itself to fit the book—the White River area was defined and transformed by tourist promotion into the Shepherd of the Hills country. Within three years of its publication in 1907, tourists started coming to explore the book's setting, and the impoundment of Lake Taneycomo in 1913 increased the numbers of the curious. The book's settings were place-specific and not fictitious; they depicted a particular area west of Branson, Missouri, near the Stone-Taney County line. Visitors could actually retrace the steps of the book's characters and could even find residents who "seemed to be" Wright's characters. As one writer commented, "Nobody expected to see Scarlett O'Hara in Georgia, of course, but tourists in the Ozarks did hope to see Old Matt and Young Matt, Uncle Ike, Sammy Lane, and other characters in 'The Shepherd of the Hills.'" And visitors, too, hoped to find the Arcadian paradise which the Shepherd had discovered in the White River valley. *The Shepherd of the Hills* prompted author Otto Rayburn, a midwest Kansan, to explore the Ozarks in 1920. Rayburn acknowledged Wright's assistance in helping him discover "a modern Arcadia" in the Ozarks. "I am deeply indebted to Harold Bell Wright," he wrote. "He opened my eyes. Without him I might have missed the Ozarks entirely."[23] The book became so closely identified with the locale that it came to define the district, creating a roughly outlined geographical region west of Branson known as "Shepherd of the Hills Country."

With all those city folks showing up carrying pockets full of cash to see the sites associated with the novel, there were plenty of savvy locals on hand to make sure they did not go away disappointed. Local people recognized and exploited interest in the book, using names and characters drawn from it as promotional devices.[24] A Branson boating company became the "Sammy Lane Boat Line" after Wright's heroine. And as the line's 1922 brochure indicated, "Residents of the city take pride in pointing out to strangers the places of special interest to those acquainted with that popular and tragic romance." Branson businesswoman Pearl Spurlock parlayed the popular fascination with Wright's setting into a lucrative occupation. Calling her cab "The Shepherd of the Hills Taxi," she drove a circuit through the Shepherd of the Hills country. She transported tourists along roads which were often little more than a series of ledge rocks and regaled them with tales of local color. The Lake Taneycomo Chamber of Commerce produced a brochure encouraging tourists to see the sights connected with Wright's book: "Take a trip over 'the trail that nobody knows how old.' You can drive over Dewey Bald [Mountain] and around the rim of Mutton Hollow, visit Sammy's Lookout and the Matthews' cabin. . . . You can visit Uncle Ike."[25]

UNCLE IKE, THE POST-MASTER AT THE FORKS.
339 HALL PHOTO CO

"Uncle Ike" Morrill
Hobart Parnell
Collection

When queried about his beautiful heroine, in response to questioning, Wright stated that, "Sammy Lane is not a portrait of any living person that I ever knew. . . . there was no original Sammy." But Wright did base other of the novel's characters on real persons. Uncle Ike, a k a Levi Morrill, was a real-life character who did indeed hold court in his Lilliputian post office at Notch. His good friends, the Rosses, were models for Old Matt and Aunt Molly. Other characters, however, were fictional composites. Such admissions on Wright's part did nothing, however, to prevent local tourism promoters from supplying real-life stand-ins for fictional characters who had never existed except in Wright's imagination.[26] In recent years, a local guidebook, *The History: Those Who Walked with Wright,* provided the full identities of local people reputed to be the models for Wright's characters. Perhaps the most bizarre instance of attempting to repackage a real-life person into a Wright character came with the Morrill family, who demonstrated that they would go to almost any extreme to capitalize on the Shepherd of the Hills connection. When Susie B. Johnston, daughter of Levi "Uncle Ike" Morrill, died, her family, recognizing that to be one of Wright's protagonists was to claim some Ozark immortality, memorialized her in the Evergreen Historical Cemetery by having "Sammy Lane" chiseled on her grave marker along with her given name.

The log cabin homestead of Mr. and Mrs. J. K. Ross, "Old Matt and Aunt Molly," has long been the best-known tourist attraction on the Shepherd of the Hills circuit. In 1910 the Rosses sold their home on Inspiration Point to a restaurateur whose business occupied it for several years.[27] By 1926 the structure had fallen into disrepair. In April of that year Lizzie McDaniel, daughter of a well-known Springfield banking family, acquired the property and completely rebuilt the house in the following two months. She then reopened it as Twin Falls Inn, complete with a dining room, gift shop, and filling station. There was also an art gallery, where tourists could purchase photographs of the Shepherd of the Hills country.[28] In testament to the fact that the fictional reality of the Shepherd of the Hills has vastly transcended the region's actual history, the Ross homestead has long become permanently fixed in the popular nomenclature as "Old Matt's cabin," while it and Uncle Ike's post office and homeplace are now enshrined in the National Register of Historic Places.

Uncle Ike was Levi Morrill, a white-bearded New Englander who graduated from Maine's Bowdoin College and went West. He practiced law in Kansas, fought for the Union army in the Civil War, and in 1881 married Jennie at the Lamar, Missouri, home of newspaperman Truman Powell. More than a decade later, in 1893, Morrill followed Powell to the Ozarks and settled at the Forks, a divide in the road not far from Powell's new house. Here he opened a store and the now-famous post office. Morrill's retirement to the Ozarks was the beginning of his career as a local celebrity. Although Uncle Ike was a minor character in Wright's novel, the fact that he was one of the few characters who was genuinely based on a real person was enough to ensure Morrill's enduring celebrity.

His tiny post office became a requisite stop on the Shepherd of the Hills pilgrimage, and Morrill went on to play an important role in the promotion of the region as a major tourist destination. In 1925, for example, the *Kansas City Star* printed an article on Morrill entitled, "The Postmaster at the Forks," and later that year *Pathe News* filmed a location feature on Uncle Ike and the Shepherd of the Hills country. The Kansas City Chamber of Commerce subsequently invited Morrill to a celebration marking the opening of an airmail line, and at his death in August 1926, Morrill was mourned as one who "has played a leading role in the publicity of this section." He died the day after his ninetieth birthday, on the second day of what was planned to be a ten-day festival in his honor. It was estimated at the time that "hundreds of tourists" were present for the merrymaking.[29]

The people of Stone and Taney Counties took both Wright and his book to heart. This is, no doubt, because he brought the area its first recognition and acclaim and helped to define the area geographically, culturally, and economically. A kinswoman of Wright toured the White River country in 1936, almost thirty years after *The Shepherd of the Hills* reached the public. She noted the esteem with which locals regarded Wright even then. "Really," she wrote to Wright, "you have no idea how you are almost worshipped in that section!" Pearl Spurlock, who crossed Wright's neighborhood for many years, summed up his influence—he "brought the world to our door with his book."[30]

The "discovery" of the White River country in all its apparent wildness coincided with the national middle-class back-to-nature movement. These few hundred square miles in the Ozarks—the Shepherd of the Hills country—would become a particular Arcadia for both its clients and its promoters. The railroad opened the area to outdoorsmen who wanted to float and fish the crystal waters and to journalists, artists, folklorists, travelers, college students, and others who wanted to visit the Arcadian place described in Harold Bell Wright's popular novel *The Shepherd of the Hills*. It made no difference that this "Arcadia" was not the product of some deep-seated Virgilian myth or even of a popular hunger for a haven of peace and tranquility far from the urban rat race; this "Arcadia" was pure fiction, the wholesale invention of savvy promoters trying to attract tourists and their money. This was the area's bread and butter, accelerated by the completion of Powersite Dam in 1913 which created Lake Taneycomo, the largest dam and recreational impoundment west of the Mississippi River, and one that attracted vacationers throughout the Midwest and the Great Plains states. The Ozarks rusticity and recreational opportunities made the Lake Taneycomo reservoir the "Playground of the Middle West." The development of the lake was accompanied by the expansion, diversification, and increasing sophistication of tourist-related enterprises. As the number of visitors grew and automobiles became more common, improvements in the rudimentary road system accommodated more traffic. This in turn attracted more visitors.

A combination of factors coalesced to make tourism a part of life in Stone and Taney Counties. First, the White River Division Railway provided access to an area rich in natural resources suited to and already used for recreation. Second, an ideological movement was afoot among certain intellectual circles which advocated the search for Arcadian happiness in the country. The Arcadian myth was perpetuated in literary and journalistic productions such as *The Shepherd of the Hills*, which presented wild regions like the White River country as an escape from civilization's anxieties. Third, Lake Taneycomo offered Arcadian travelers recreation in a natural, beautiful riverine setting which was touted as inspirational and wholesome while at the same time offering the amenities and conveniences of comfortable resorts and well-equipped outfitters. When many Americans were looking for a rural retreat where they might escape the problems of modern urban life the White River Railway opened the formerly remote area to these latter-day Arcadians and permitted them to visit a place where a preindustrial frontier still lingered in the hinterlands. For the first three decades of the twentieth century, to 1930, this region enjoyed a tourist boom. Then the Great Depression struck and began to hurt the tourist business, and in 1931, with the creation of the Lake of the Ozarks in central Missouri, tourism declined still further. But these setbacks were momentary; with the end of World War II the boom would start again and soar to unimaginable heights, and Wright's Arcadia would be completely engulfed by the glitz of Silver Dollar City and the garish music palaces on Branson's celebrated "strip." But long before all that, for a few brief decades, the White River hills, a k a the Shepherd of the Hills country, played a crucial role in the popular acting out of the Arcadian myth, American style, in the nation's heartland.

"The Bottomless Pit"

Marble Cave

MARBLE CAVE (or Marvel Cave after 1913), located in south-east Stone County, was the area's first "curiosity" and remains the single most influential tourist attraction in the White River hills. Marvel Cave is extraordinary even by the standards of a state that has over four thousand caves; its dramatic entrance through a deep sinkhole, its awesome verticality (at 383 feet it is Missouri's deepest cave), its gigan-tic rooms and underground river have long exercised a powerful pull on the imaginations of visitors to the White River hills. In this subterranean cavern tourists found primitive, untouched nature, experienced impene-trable darkness, and faced unexplored reaches reminiscent of man's early struggles in the dark forests of primordial wilderness. From the early years of its notoriety in the 1870s the "Bottomless Pit" was commonly compared with Mammoth Cave, Kentucky; as other caves were discovered in the Ozarks their degree of grandeur was measured against that of Marvel Cave.[1] Caves continue to play a major role in Ozarks regional imagery for their real or mythic association with Indians, outlaws, the Civil War, buried treasure, moonshine, tall tales, and great adventure. Situated 600 feet above the valley floor of the White River, atop Roark Mountain on an eminence with majestic views for twenty-five miles into the distance, Marvel Cave provided ample grist for the mills of major image makers in Missouri, America's number-one cave state.[2]

One of history's ironies is that Marble Cave's "discovery" by its first commercial investors was a result of early Ozarks tourism itself. Visitors to Springfield used the Queen City as a base to survey surrounding areas. The optimism of investors in railroad economies during the 1880s kept interest in new Ozark speculations at a historic high. The Springfield nexus of the Kansas City, Fort Scott, and Gulf (Memphis) Railroad brought com-petition to the established Frisco rail line in 1881–82, making Springfield a "tourist boom city" for several years. In fact, at Lamar, in Barton County, the local newspaper referred to the line as the "Kansas City, Springfield, and Memphis" connection. The Lamar City Guards was an active militia organization that paraded in its hometown, as well as Carthage, Pierce City, Springfield, and other southwest Missouri towns. The organization's spokesman and post commander Capt. J. B. Emery, postmaster at Lamar, served as master of ceremonies at numerous public celebrations. In May 1883 Emery led the Lamar unit on an excursion to Springfield for a May Day celebration. The members played in the band, brandished their weapons, visited the national cemetery, and were entertained at the local opera house. While there they made plans to return to an August memorial celebration of the Blue and Gray at Wilson's Creek battlefield.[3]

The August festivity included many dignitaries; Gov. John S. Marmaduke and former-governor John S. Phelps of Missouri were present as were Gov. James H. Berry and Sen. Powell Clayton of Arkansas. The Springfield Light Guards was the host militia for visiting units like the one from Lamar. The prairie dwellers from Lamar took a liking to the contrasting Ozarks environment. The guard members became familiar with the Springfield area, scouted the nearby neighborhood, and resolved to return yet again and expand their explorations.[4]

That fall the Lamar City Guards held a campfire retreat in Galena. These campfires were festive occasions of a fraternal nature and provided the occasion for singing, speechmaking, and patriotic drills before a community audience. One of the guardsmen, Truman S. Powell, later wrote about Galena and their Ozark outing. He described the town square of Galena as consisting of a few store buildings, a large barn, a blacksmith shop, and "several small buildings of a cheap nature all empty at the time." A man named Frank Carr put up a few travelers "from time to time" at his place. The fall weather was a perfect time for hiking, and popular destinations were karst curiosities such as Marble Cave. The militia men were guided to the celebrated "Bottomless Pit" by a local fifteen-year-old boy. The more enterprising of the guardsmen, as it turned out, were most inspired, not by nature's subterranean wonders, but by the huge accumulations of nitrate-rich bat guano they encountered; the spectacular limestone formations also struck them as a potential source of marketable "marble."[5]

Truman Powell,
c. 1884
*Walker Powell
Collection*

Before winter ended, on March 5, 1884, the Lamar militia men and associates created a new corporation, the Marble Cave Mining and Manufacturing Company. Their charter was for "mining and working the mineral and ores in the states of Missouri and Arkansas with power to sell and dispose of any real estate purchased or held" by the corporation. The Lamar group was well acquainted with the coal-mining industry in their home county and through their connections had access to a variety of extractive equipment. The major stockholders were Capt. J. B. Emery, F. D. W. Arnold, and T. Hodge Jones; there were also five minor stockholders. This group included Lamar Greenback newspaperman Truman

Powell, who was later to become one of the foremost promoters of Marble Cave and the White River region; he served as vice-president of the corporation. Although the initial corporate motivation was to realize immediate profits from the cave's rich supply of guano, they were not insensitive to the great tourist potential of the Marble Cave property. Wishing to take advantage of the popularity of spas that prevailed in that Victorian age, they platted a resort community christened "Marble City." This resort dream, with its fabulous cave and its mineral-laden spring waters, was to contain lots for fashionable homes and no less than three parks. The Barton County group could draw inspiration from the nearby commercial success of Eldorado Springs and Jerico Springs, resorts in Cedar County, Missouri, and the booming resort community at Eureka Springs, Arkansas. These budding tourism entrepreneurs hoped they had a potential competitor in Marble City. They, too, wanted their wilderness camp to become a city.[6]

W. E. Sharp, renowned hunter and stockman, was one of the locals hired to work at the site. When he was not busy extracting the guano and hauling it to market in Springfield to be sold as agricultural fertilizer, he spent hours exploring the inner recesses of the vast cave and was even known to pull out his fiddle and play for dances held in the underground cavern. He later recalled, "The first time I went down into the cave I descended on what is called an Indian ladder—long pine logs pinned together with holes bored through into which wooden pins had been driven. These pins stuck out on both sides of the log, and you went down straddling the log." Sharp and other local pioneers came to be friends with the sociable Truman Powell, who was by then already deeply engrossed by the White River hills and Marble Cave. He was shortly to forge an alliance with the area that was to have profound consequences for the subsequent development of Marble Cave and the whole White River region.[7]

Since 1874, Powell, a former Iowa Unionist, had managed the *Barton County Advocate* newspaper on the square of Lamar. By March 1887 he had made the decision to move his family to Stone County and commit his future fortunes to the Ozarks. During the move Powell became seriously ill, and Levi Morrill, his friend and fellow newspaperman in Lamar, temporarily ran the business for him. After Powell recovered, he moved the *Advocate* to Galena where it became Stone County's first paper. The paper reflected Powell's Republican politics, "classing all Democrats among those who wore the gray."[8]

Powell continued his involvement with the Marble Cave venture, working with major stockholder Dr. T. Hodge Jones, who soon moved to Galena to keep a closer eye on his investment. For the remainder of the 1880s the Lamar investors worked to mine and market their minerals and to promote the new town. They had much more success at the former undertaking than the latter. The exploitation of the bat guano was a laborious seasonal enterprise of hard work. The stockholders and hired help had to load wagons in Lamar and haul equipment overland all the way to the cave where they spent months setting up machinery. Later, Captain Emery and his associates rode the train from Lamar to Aurora and hired hacks from there. This made for shorter and easier trips to inspect their investments.

In addition to launching the extraction operation, the company generated an enormous amount of publicity about the great Marble Cave and its natural wonders. The Lamar press stereotyped the locale as a sort of Al Capp Dogpatch and compared it with the Rackensack of Arkansas[9] "where the manufacture of moonshine whiskey is regarded as a virtue, where tow headed children are run down every Sunday by hounds to be washed and dressed; . . . where they cover their shanties with bull skins and leave the tails stick up for lightning rods." As the White River hills was still largely a wilderness setting, without towns and railroads, cosmopolitan outsiders tended to typecast the local people as hillbillies. The marketing of that image by investors in the 1880s launched a stereotypical characterization of Ozark natives that continues to be exploited with great profit to this very day.[10]

There were Victorian-era Ozarkers floating past the mouth of Indian Creek and occasionally hiking to Marble Cave around the same time Truman Powell and his fellow investors purchased it. Sons and daughters of affluent Springfield business families made the voyage down the James River to sites along the White River and sometimes to Forsyth. In summer 1880 young people belonging to the Boyd, Milligan, Parrish, Smith, and other prominent Springfield families traveled in four flat-bottomed boats on such a trip. The local press took notice of this outing; former Yankee army officer and then photographer W. S. Johnson photographed "The

White River Crew." They repeated the adventure the following year. By 1883 the outing had become so popular with O. L. Milligan that he ascribed a humorous but joyful description to the adventure. "I don't think I will go to Saratoga or Long Beach this year, as is my custom," said Milligan. "About the first of August I shall take a flying trip to Galena, where I will spend a few weeks fishing and bathing in the raging surge of the James, and next winter go south to Ozark and Forsyth." The Springfieldian was defining the beginning of a distinctly regional pastime: the White River float trip. This was around the same time that the Lamar investors had platted Marble City. By then outsiders from much farther away than Greene County had begun to frequent the White River valley and the great cave. The cave became a landmark for hikers and floaters who were willing to make the three-mile trek from the White River. In the late 1890s, Harold Bell Wright walked a well-worn path to the great sinkhole when he made his first visit. For decades, tourists floating the White River hiked to the largest cave in the Ozarks from a campsite at Indian Creek.[11]

By 1889 the Marble Cave Mining and Manufacturing Company was at an unprofitable juncture; while the extraction of guano had played out and the "marble" proved to be not worth extracting, the hope of reaping profits from the harvest of tourists lining up to tour the cave and springs still lay unfulfilled. At this time, there was no easy route to get large groups of tourists to the cave; the poor to nonexistent roads made a "show cave" in the undeveloped region unfeasible. Although the infrastructure was not yet in place, there was hope in the region that that day was not far off. By 1887, surveyors from the Missouri Pacific Railroad were looking at Roark Creek valley, and the rumors of a new railroad coming to the White River country were starting to appear in the newspapers. Still, the actual construction of the railroad was in the distant future and would not come in time to save the Marble Cave venture.[12]

Facing that reality in October 1889, the Lamar company sold the property for seven thousand dollars to Arthur J. Lynch, a businessman from Jackson County, Missouri. The following month, he sold it to his brother, Canadian William Henry Lynch, for ten thousand dollars. At the time, W. H. Lynch (1847–1927) was in Spokane, Washington, apparently visiting relatives, but he was the manager of the Danville Slate Quarry in Canada. Planning his own cave development, Lynch became a natural-

William H. Lynch
Velma A. Bass
Collection

ized American in 1890 to better position himself for loans, although he rarely appeared at the cave during the next several years. Meanwhile, Truman Powell and his sons, who had by then purchased land near the cave, continued to explore it. In the fall of 1892 the Powells hosted a party of three men who represented the Missouri World's Fair Commission and the state geological survey. They were accompanied by photographer C. E. DeGroff of Warrensburg, Missouri. The expedition's ensuing report credited Powell and his family with nearly all exploration done in the cavern to date.[13]

The new publicity about the cave may have prompted Lynch to give it more of his attention. In June 1893 Lynch undertook steps to promote his own speculative cave venture. He enlisted S. Fred Prince, an artist and naturalist who had homesteaded south of Marble Cave, to make the first systematic survey of the cavern. Prince compiled his findings in "The Cave Book," a written and illustrated description of the cave's structure, formation, and composition. The manuscript included Prince's detailed drawings, which revealed elevation as well as layout. Prince made additional surveys throughout the cave and more sketches of the underground landscape. He also continued to collect botanical specimens for another four decades, some of which he assembled for the agricultural experiment station in Lincoln, Nebraska.[14]

William Lynch, meanwhile, living in Toronto and Ottawa, did not have much time for the Ozarks. During the 1890s he was in Canada researching and writing for the dairy industry, work he had begun in 1881. The Canadian government printed and distributed his work in dairy reform, *Scientific Butter-Making* of 1883 and *Scientific Dairy Practice* in 1886, the latter work circulated in French and English. He even lectured about his work in England and remained busy speaking and writing about dairying in Canada, eventually founding the *Canadian Dairyman*. His association with Prime Minister Wilfrid Laurier in the 1890s led him to the Klondike, where he investigated the strikes at the Canadian gold fields and penned a set of regulations later adopted by the government; these new rules earned Canada significant revenues for her precious ore.[15]

During the early years of the exploitation and mapping of Marble Cave, a number of scholars visited the site and published their findings. *Scientific American* featured articles in 1885 and 1893, the latter article by geologist Edmund Hovey, who had been taken through the cave by the Powells in the fall of 1892. Hovey was charged by the Missouri World's Fair Commission and the state geological survey to determine the truth of the sensational feature stories about the cave that appeared in local and metropolitan newspapers. Hovey concluded that the rumors, though exaggerated, did describe a "sufficiently grand" natural wonder and that when the "projected railroads from Aurora and Springfield pass near it, it will undoubtedly become a summer resort." Famous naturalist Edward Cope visited Marble Cave in 1892 and was apparently the mediator for sending "mummified remains" of animals to the Smithsonian Institution for study. (Any analysis of these remains that might have been performed has evidently not survived.) Luella Owen came in 1893; she met and relied

Exploring Marvel Cave with candles, 1913. *Standing:* Susie Morrill; *left to right:* unknown, Genevieve Lynch, C. E. DeGroff, Dr. Fred Prince, and Ethel Hall
Velma A. Bass Collection

upon S. Fred Prince, who was just beginning his explorations and drawings. Owen proclaimed that the tour underground was worth every minute spent, but "the suit worn should be one he [the visitor] is ready to part with." She concluded her observations with the caution that those who love nature should make plans for a similar excursion quickly "while yet no rail-road quite touches the country."[16]

Luella Owen (1852–1932), the talented writer, portrait painter, traveler, and Vassar-educated scholar from St. Joseph, Missouri, had a particular passion for geology and caves. She became independently wealthy after receiving an inheritance in 1890 and then spent several years exploring caves, especially those in the Ozarks that were "little known to the ever restless tide of tourists." In 1893 she explored caves in Stone and Greene Counties. Five years later she produced a landmark book, *Cave*

Car touring the Shepherd of the Hills country
M. F. Miller Papers, WHMC-Columbia

Regions of the Ozarks and Black Hills, a standard geological reference for the next fifty years. In this book considerable space was devoted to Marble and other Stone County caves. Much of this material was written by Truman Powell. Powell and Owen were the first of many persons to advocate that the Marble Cave property should become a national park. For the next forty years promoters repeated this challenge in the hope that politicians and power brokers could convince the federal government to purchase the property. In the 1920s when the Missouri state government planned the development of a new state park system the Office of the Secretary of State published a summary of important caves for "scientific study and the interest of tourists" in its popular *Blue Book.* The state featured Marvel Cave and the Powell family's newly opened Fairy Cave in Stone County. The publication evoked Luella Owen's vision of "The Wilderness" with a road leading to the grounds of "a magnificent park" with the "entire absence of underbrush, and a beautiful covering of grasses or flowering plants of all kinds and colors," the coverlet of the Ozarks open range, "trackless and endless."[17]

In 1894, William Lynch, Truman Powell, or Truman's son, William, may have guided the unidentified author of Goodspeed's introduction to the *Reminiscent History of the Ozark Region*. The promotional publications of the day devoted a good portion of any commentary about the Ozarks to the caves of the region, and Marble Cave received the lion's share of attention. The grandeur of its eternal darkness, sparkling water, huge rooms, spectacular formations, and endless passages astonished all who saw them. By this time, many rooms and passages in the labyrinth had names—The Battery, Blonde Throne Room, Gulf of Doom, Mother Hubbard, Powell's Room, et cetera.[18] Some of these names were conjured up by stockholders of the Marble Cave Mining and Manufacturing Company for the amusement of guests who toured the famous bottomless pit. One local even proclaimed that a professor from Kansas City had interpreted the site as an ancient volcano that had blown off the top of Roark Mountain.[19]

In October 1894, W. H. Lynch, with his teenage daughters Miriam and Genevieve, opened Marble Cave to the public. Hoping to attract investors, Lynch had a stage erected in the giant room that served as an auditorium. A piano was lowered into the cave, and tall ladders were built to afford an easier entry. Lynch then hired an orchestra for subterranean performances and even retained New York and St. Louis artists to illustrate a publication of "marvelous accounts" of the cave. All this hullabaloo was short-lived, however, and soon faded due to the difficulties of getting tourists to the cave; Marble Cave was still accessible only from the Wilderness Road or a three-mile hike from the White River. This initial show did not bring a flood of tourists or money to Lynch's coffers, and he returned to Canada to seek new adventure in the Yukon. Lynch and his family returned to the Ozarks but rarely; he continued to reside in Canada while local residents explored and toured his great cave.

Lynch had taken a capitalist's risk on Marble Cave and came up short. Instead of profiting from the sale of lots and parcels while remaining in Canada, he encountered debt and litigation. His 1894 cave gala, complete with orchestra, had stimulated more debts than investors. By then the state of Missouri had attached a lien on the property for several years of delinquent taxes. In April 1894, Lynch raised three thousand dollars and bought himself some time by mortgaging the property to two women in Chicago. To sponsor the cave party in October of that year Lynch indebted himself to ten merchants and businesses in Galena, Billings, and Springfield, Missouri, obviously anticipating that grand-opening profits would redeem his debts. After the celebration, however, Lynch sold some "goods and effects" in the Marble City hotel and house at the cave and gave power of attorney for his property to a lawyer in Lawrence County, Missouri, before returning to Canada.

There, the overextended Lynch sought solutions for his financial worries in Missouri and, adding to his miseries, became embroiled in disputes with the Canadian government over payment for his services. He did not have a regular government post, only a short-lived commission to the Yukon. His political connections allowed him to do considerable work and writing for the government, but he did not receive any royalties. Trying to remain afloat, by 1897 Lynch valued his Missouri property at fifty thousand dollars and mortgaged Marble Cave to an investor in Quebec.[20] This came on the heels of a Missouri mechanic's lien on supplies and construction for work at the cave filed by creditors in 1895 and 1896 with Justice of the Peace Levi Morrill; Stone County sheriff's sales of moveable property at the cave netted Lynch's former backers some money. To stall the suits, in January 1897 Lynch deeded part of the property to a trustee in Quebec, Canada, who apparently settled the rest of Lynch's Missouri debts.[21]

In the meantime, Lynch got entangled in a political argument with members of the Canadian Parliament over a proposed memorial that would have compensated him for his past services to the Canadian government. He wrote the prime minister in 1898 that for twenty years he had unselfishly labored without reward "at a sacrifice that I verily believe no other man in Canada has made."[22]

He persisted in his appeals and clung to the hope that a small portion of the famed Yukon bonanza would finally be his. By 1900 he was living in Danville, Quebec, and his memorial was still under consideration, supported by others who felt him deserving of "compensation for public service." This service included eight years in the dairy industry as well as his recent mission to the Yukon, where he had drafted a Code of Mining Regulations. Lynch claimed that others had reaped remuneration from his work while he had not. Government opponents had officially removed Lynch from his Yukon post, but he had not received notice for several months afterward. During the interim his expenses and work had continued. A Department of Interior official dismissed his claims and stated that Lynch was well paid for his services and was the instigator of "the most unmitigated nuisance that I have ever had anything to do with." The correspondence suggests that Lynch may have received some recompense in a compromise, but it is unclear how much.[23] And as if Lynch did not have miseries enough, he was also plagued with bouts of ill health.

While Lynch fought his battles up North, the movement of modernity into the White River hills continued apace. When the White River Railway was constructed through the Roark Creek valley in 1905, the press reported new efforts to draw investment to the surrounding region. Journalists urged Missouri Pacific Railroad officials to build a rail line to Marble Cave. Others hoped Springfield capitalists would devise a workable scheme for developing underground tourism, but commercialization of the great sinkhole continued to lie latent.[24]

Truman Powell, now a real-estate broker and newspaperman in Galena, continued his lifelong fascination with Marble Cave, remaining an indefatigable explorer as well as the foremost publicist of the celebrated attraction. After the turn of the century Powell could lay claim to twenty years of probing the seemingly endless depths of Marble Cave. In addition, he had discovered or explored other local caves—over a hundred according to his estimation. Powell was a shrewd businessman as well, and sensed that with the construction of the White River Railway, it was time to intensify his promotion of Marble Cave. In June 1905, he led a party of six men on a ten-hour underground survey that generated publicity concerning the extent and magnificence of the cave. According to the *Stone County News Oracle* the explorers took "matches in bottles, corked tight to save from water, candles large and small, oil torches, lanterns, rope, and food." The all-night exploration led them to conclude that the cave was actually a "system of caves," the grandeur of which was beyond anything imagined before. As William Lynch had been an infrequent visitor at the property since the 1894 gala fiasco, Powell was probably hoping that Lynch would advertise the property for sale soon and that he could finally become the sole owner. Whatever Powell's motives might have been, he continued in his role as an unfailing promoter of Marble Cave and its untapped possibilities.[25]

In Lynch's absence, Ozarkers in Stone and Taney Counties treated the cave as a community asset. Truman Powell took a steady stream of adventurers there. Other settlers, too, wandered about the caverns on outings that commonly included lunch on the grounds. In the 1890s, for example, the Muellers and Gertens, German-American immigrants from Nebraska and Illinois, came to settle near Cedar Creek, Taney County. The Muellers toured the cave, and later took their new neighbors, the Gertens, on a Marble Cave outing. They loaded their wagons with lunch and lanterns and rode for a half day to Roark Mountain. After lunch the first adventure was to negotiate the treacherous entry. A tall tree trunk with stubs of branches left on for steps was lowered into the deep sinkhole entrance. The descent into the chasm was slow and careful, as was the climb out.

The memory of this trip by one Gerten woman was tinged with awe and satisfaction in experiencing such a natural wonder. Light from the lanterns made formations glitter in wonderful and fantastic ways and rocks thrown into dark holes generated no sounds to indicate that these black pits had any bottom. To their surprise the visitors saw the setting sun as they ascended from the darkness of Marble Cave; their exploration had lasted five hours.[26]

After the White River Railway started bringing tourists to the near vicinity of the cave in 1906, locals took over and guided these new visitors through the unfamiliar woods and along the narrow ridges to the great sinkhole. Members of the Kansas City YMCA once hiked all the way from Branson to the cave and stayed overnight. The next day the young men explored the inner recesses and returned to Branson, where they camped above the railroad bridge for three weeks.[27] Guides to the cave sometimes included vacationers who had simply become acquainted with the area by repeated visits or who were summer residents attracted to the fledgling tourist area known as Shepherd of the Hills country. Garber, a flag stop on the newly constructed White River Railway, became a point of departure for tourists heading for the cave. The hamlet had a general store and a post office that was managed from 1907 to 1923 by J. K. Ross and his wife, the couple gaining fame as "Uncle Matt" and "Aunt Molly," in Harold Bell Wright's *The Shepherd of the Hills*. Ross was also one of the several depot agents for railroad stops between Galena to Hollister. He handled printed timetables that were appropriately labeled the "Shepherd of the Hills Country." Garber also had a blacksmith shop, cattle pens, a barn, and a scattering of settlers up and down Roark Creek.

Dewey Bald
Dorothy Roden Collection

One of those was William Rullketter, a German-born Drury College history professor from Springfield who, because of ill health, purchased acreage at Garber in 1906 and built a country retreat. The proximity of the Garber railroad stop to Marble Cave offered an opportunity for Professor Rullketter's son, John, to earn spending money. Born in 1903, John spent the summers at Garber from 1912 to 1917 guiding tourists to Marvel Cave. He later remembered taking several dozen groups each summer for "twenty-five cents per group whether there was one or a group" and he frequently received tips. The lucky young lad got to keep all the money.[28]

Guide Johnnie Rullketter led his guests on a two-and-one-half-mile hike from the railroad up, out of Roark valley toward the Notch post office on the ridge, and then to the cave. Sometimes he toured the cave with the tourists, sometimes he just waited outside. Not all tourists wanted to go to the cave. "Some just stood around [Garber] and took pictures, mainly of Old Matt, and [then] caught the afternoon train." Other tourists left Garber for Notch in the mail carrier's rig or headed to Reed's Spring on the railroad; once there they hired local transportation to tour the ridges toward the cave and Old Matt's cabin.[29]

During the same period that young Rullketter was guiding tourists to Marvel Cave, William Lynch's second wife passed away, and Lynch's attention turned again to Stone County. By that time Lynch owned additional properties north of the cave reaching into Roark valley. He sold some of it and granted a right of way to Missouri Pacific Railroad for a switch in the valley, which came to be used by hikers to Lynch's resort and cave. In early 1913 Lynch joined his two daughters Miriam and Genevieve in Chicago. In June, at age sixty-six and accompanied by his daughters, William Lynch returned to the Ozarks and his legendary cave. The Shepherd of the Hills country appealed to the aging Lynch, and he concentrated the energies of his remaining years upon developing the cave as a tourist attraction. Before the summer was out old friends of the family from Chicago visited the Lynches, encountering a now-steady stream of vacationists[30] to the region and the new Lake Taneycomo. Besides touring the cave, guests lunched and purchased souvenirs at Marvel Cave Lodge, part of the Lynches' home, or rented one of the five primitive cabins which surrounded the lodge.

In 1915 Lynch noticeably improved the rickety ladders that led into the cave by replacing them with stairways and platforms. He purchased a "new supply of fresh overalls for the ladies" to make cave tours more convenient. As the Lynch family upgraded their tourist site, increased automobile traffic traveled the Wilderness Ridge Road from Reed's Spring to the cave—the first had been a Cadillac from Kansas in 1914.

That same year the Stone County Court took notice of the increasing summer traffic and extended an improved road from Reed's Spring southeast to the county line in the hope that the neighboring Taney County Court would link a new road to theirs. The trail to the famous site from the Stone County side was no longer just a cow path through the woods from the White River or up from Roark Creek; it was now a full-fledged road that brought automobiles right to the doorstep of Marble Cave. (The approach from Branson, however, remained longer and rougher.) The Lynches changed the name from Marble to Marvel Cave in 1913 and began to promote the new place name by initiating a rural correspondent's column entitled "Marvel Cave" in the *Branson White River Leader*. The Missouri Pacific, always interested in promoting tourism along the White River Railway, changed the whistle-stop name of the switch in Roark valley—located on land granted by Lynch—to Marvel

Pearl Spurlock's taxi at Uncle Ike's post office, 1928
Walker Powell Collection

Cave. Lynch's goal, however, was always one of selling the property for a
nice profit; although potential buyers considered the enterprise, none
made an offer acceptable to Lynch.[31]

Due largely to the untiring promotional efforts of William Lynch,
Marvel Cave drew a public filled with curiosity. Located less than a mile
from Uncle Ike's post office at the Forks (Notch), Lynch advertised the
cave's association with Wright's bestseller, *The Shepherd of the Hills.* Under
Lynch's management the cave became a significant Ozark tourist stop.
The bottomless pit was the epitome of a natural cathedral, a spectacular
place for artists to paint, naturalists to study, and scientists to explore, and
for everyone to write about. Lynch staged festivities that included a
bronco-riding exhibition, a camping-out celebration featuring performances by the Ted Nestell players, a traveling vaudeville troupe, a production of "Mother Goose," a production of Shakespeare's "Richard III"
performed in the cave by the light of a Delco generator, and a fiddling
contest held in 1926 to celebrate Levi Morrill's ninetieth birthday.
Attendance at these events was encouraged by free camping at the cave's

entrance. The Lynches even composed and marketed "Ten Copyright Songs" as a souvenir, playing up the Shepherd of the Hills connection with the song "Sammy Lane, I Love You."[32]

Situated atop Indian Ridge, Marvel Cave offered sweeping vistas of Indian Creek valley to the west and Jake Creek valley to the east, providing a picturesque location for artists to set up their easels. The ever-resourceful Lynches publicized the scenic views of the famous White River treeless "balds" and of the cave's awesome beauty. One of their promotions involved holding contests to determine the "most moving picture scenarios" of the cave and surrounding countryside. They hosted an art exhibition featuring local artists and invited the Ozark Press Association to attend. They also sold works by local artists in the Marble Cave gift shop.[33]

The various artists drawn to the region helped to publicize the Shepherd of the Hills country by producing vivid pictorial images of the scenic and mysterious White River hills region. S. Fred Prince, always a booster of the White River region, left his homestead near Marble Cave in 1919 to teach at Kansas State Agricultural College in Manhattan, Kansas, but he periodically returned to the cave area to paint the many scenes of natural beauty he observed. One of these paintings, of Marble Cave's Cathedral Room, reportedly attracted much attention in Kansas and inspired its viewers to see the cave for themselves. Another artist, painter Joseph Froula of Chicago, an old friend of Miriam Lynch, spent much time painting the local scenery; he returned home from one visit with thirty-five canvases.[34]

Urban artists, especially those from Chicago, continued to frequent the spectacular vistas at Marble Cave and the Shepherd of the Hills country. Among the Chicago artists who came were Rudolph F. Ingerie and Carl Krafft, who did much to bring the area to outside attention through art. Krafft, a frequent overnight visitor at Hollister on the White River, put together an exhibition of paintings by local artists in 1914. He showed it locally before moving the exhibit to Springfield and St. Louis where it enjoyed considerable success. He subsequently displayed some of the paintings along with his own at the 1914 Panama Exposition in San Francisco. Later in Chicago, one of his southwest Missouri canvases received a prize at the Chicago Art Institute.[35]

In October 1915 Krafft and Ingerie joined St. Louis artist Frank B. Nuderscher to found the Ozarks School of Artists. This organization was rooted in its founders' common desire to interest American artists in the Ozarks and to "bring before the American art lovers the beauty of this almost unknown section of the country." They hoped to "build up a distinctive school of painters" in the White River region.[36]

Although this lofty goal never became a reality, artists continued to draw occasional attention to the southwest Missouri Ozarks. The Ozark Painters' Organization, formed in Springfield, Missouri, with Ingerie as president, exhibited members' works at the McCaughen-Burr Galleries in St. Louis. By 1925 the fame of Ozarks art had spread even further; five paintings out of three hundred exhibited at the National Academy of Design in New York received special mention in *Art News*. One of these was "November in the Ozarks."[37]

Patrons of Marvel Cave and the Shepherd of the Hills country also included educational institutions. By World War I The School of the Ozarks annually sent its graduating classes on a camping trip to the cave. They hiked around Dewey Bald, cooked breakfast at the mouth of Marvel Cave, and made the pilgrimage through the vast underground chambers. Caving groups from Pittsburg Normal School at Pittsburg, Kansas, and Drury College and Springfield Normal in Springfield, Missouri, were frequently

Sammy's Lookout on Dewey Bald
Kalen and Morrow Collection

noted in the local newspaper columns. In the summer of 1920 Springfield Normal students traveled to see the legendary sites of Wright's book. When they got to the cave, the Lynches outfitted them in the traditional old clothing for protection from rocks and mud. They then descended a stairway with candles and at the bottom extinguished their lights in order to experience total darkness. With the tour over, they discarded the "touring clothes" and dined at Lynch's cave restaurant.[38]

College and high-school students arrived regularly at the cave during the 1920s, traveling by any number of ways. In 1922 students from the Marionville Academy rented a Model-T truck and placed benches that could seat twenty people back to back in the bed. They brought along sack lunches and did not fail to include water for the radiator as well as for themselves. As usual on any overland trip through the Ozarks at this time, the students had to patch several flat tires. Two years later the girls basketball team from Aurora High School rode the train to Branson and then up Roark valley to the Marble Cave flag stop. Once off the train they walked through the woods to the cave for lunch. After an afternoon in the cave, the student athletes spent the night sleeping on the floor of the Lynches' screened-in porch. They toured the cave again the next morning, then made the return hike down Roark Mountain to catch the train back to Branson.[39]

The increase in tourism at Marvel Cave was greatly accelerated by the parallel growth of the resort industry that accompanied the construction of Powersite Dam on the White River. Resort clientele in White River tourism were sometimes associated with business elsewhere. Overbeck's Sunset Inn, a popular resort at Branson, had a St. Joseph connection. The Overbeck brothers in St. Joseph, Missouri, operated a beer parlor on Lake Contrary, a famous fishermen's resort in Buchanan County, and were officers in a sportsmen's club. After Lake Taneycomo attracted development, the Overbecks encouraged their friends to ride the train to Branson and stay at their Sunset Inn. Others, such as, the Ford family, had middle-class jobs in the cities. Like many participants in the growing automobile culture of the 1920s, the Ford family preferred to drive rather than ride the rails. Their auto trips to Hollister usually took two days from Kansas City, with an overnight stay in Carthage. About 1926, after spending a few days in Taney County, the Ford family took an all-day trip on the railroad to

Marvel Cave. There they met the aging William Lynch, put on the brown coveralls, and followed daughter Miriam and her father into the cave. Instead of viewing the formations by the dim flickering light of candles as most visitors did, the Fords had their own automobile spotlight, powered by an airplane storage battery that brightly lit the deep recesses of the cave—not all tours in Marvel Cave were the same! This tour, like many, was followed by a dinner with the Lynch family.[40]

The expansive economic outlook of the mid-1920s business climate was felt in the Shepherd of the Hills country, where visionary women played significant roles in promoting the region. The Lynch sisters were already well known. Springfieldian Lizzie McDaniel King, who became friends with the Lynches, purchased and remodeled Old Matt's cabin. May Kennedy McCord was born in Stone County but lived in Springfield, where she began a public career of writing and singing about her native hills. Journalist Lucile Morris drew upon such in the Shepherd of the Hills in her early writings. Morris and others rode in Pearl Spurlock's "Shepherd of the Hills" taxi from Branson to the tourist destinations and back to town; Spurlock, a performer and local character in her own right, did much to promote the Shepherd of the Hills country. These women, and McDaniel's Springfield friends at the nearby Twin Pines Inn, Marie and Bertha Haberman, toured Marvel Cave and socialized with the Lynch sisters. In the spring of 1925 the Haberman sisters, who owned a photography studio in Springfield, took nearly a hundred photographs of the Shepherd of the Hills country, including Signal Tree of local folklore fame on Dewey Bald, Sammy's Lookout, Notch post office, and Marvel Cave. They held a midsummer exhibit at Marvel Cave Lodge that showcased their own talents and provided publicity for the primitive resort. Primitive though it was, however, patrons could enjoy wonderful chicken dinners "with all the fixin's" including berry pie, ice cream, vegetables, and home-cooked bread served in the Tea Room at the lodge.[41]

In the summer of 1925 William Lynch improved the road that ran from Branson over Dewey Bald to the cave and added a bus service. Traffic to the cave increased immediately. The following year taxi driver Pearl Spurlock, only one of several adventurous commercial drivers in the region, made eighty trips over that route to Old Matt's cabin. The caretaker there reported more than six thousand visitors, many of whom also toured

Marvel Cave. A group of artists responded again to the inspiring site by staging another exhibit especially for the Ozark Press Association. Residents of the area took their cue and ignited their cottage industries to produce "hickory chairs, rugs, baskets, quilts, and similar souvenirs" to meet the increased demand for local crafts brought by autos rambling over the rough ridges above Roark Creek and Mutton Hollow.[42]

William Lynch died in 1927, hailed as a pioneer and legendary figure in Ozarks tourism. Lynch had become well known for his amateur poetry, inventiveness, and scholarly demeanor, and as a veteran traveler to European countries. In his final days, Lynch was hospitalized with gangrene in Carthage, where his daughter Genevieve was superintendent of nurses. Genevieve sent the first notice of his passing to her friend May Kennedy McCord in Springfield, Missouri.

The daughters buried their father in the Shepherd of the Hills Cemetery (now known as Evergreen) which was already a historic shrine in 1927. In death he joined neighbors who had received fame as characters in Harold Bell Wright's novel and who had worked for the betterment of their rural community—Mr. and Mrs. J. K. Ross ("Uncle Matt and Aunt Mollie") and "Uncle Ike" Morrill, postmaster at Notch. In death, the regional press remembered Harold Bell Wright's visit to Lynch a decade before. In 1918 Wright had traveled to Marvel Cave and spent an afternoon visiting with the elderly Lynch. Upon leaving, Wright presented a khaki suit to Lynch, the one he wore while writing his Ozark novel *The Winning of Barbara Worth*. The gesture by Wright bestowed an important artifact upon a significant promoter of the Shepherd of the Hills country.[43]

In the 1920s promoters claimed that over fifty thousand tourists visited the Shepherd of the Hills country, drawn largely to Lake Taneycomo and the numerous resorts along the White River. By the mid-1920s an estimated seven thousand of those tourists annually made the automobile trip or overland hike to the Forks, Old Matt's cabin, and Marvel Cave. By the depression the cave site was still "off the beaten path" on an Ozark ridge that for most of the year reposed in relative isolation and calm. Genevieve Lynch evoked this romantic Arcadian setting where she, as her father before her, lived out the last years of her life, in her poem, "The Call."

> All the sweet wild life of the mountains allures me,
> Waves to me, claims my thought, calls me incessantly;

As I follow the ways of men, the contours of cities.
Crowded, shoved, hurried and huddled,
Always my eyes long for infinite spaces,
For minaret-mountain-heights balanced
Above, up above and beyond the last tree tops,
Where outstretched hands can almost touch
The cloud-flocks slowly sailing.
Where winds are the voices of friends
And sunlight, a hearth fire glowing,
And even the gray wolves howling
But wilder and fiercer brothers
Whose keen teeth can be no whit sharper
Than this hunger which wholly devours—
The cry of my heart for the mountains,
The need of my soul for their silence.[44]

The Arcadian myth had captured one more poet and made her its own.

"As a Health Resort
Taney Is Unequalled"

The Game Park

THE GAY NINETIES society of St. Louis extended its interest far beyond the city limits. The remarkable growth of the city and its commercial reach into the Midwest and the nation sent its residents traveling the rails on business and excursions—pleasure trips to see friends, relatives, and new towns, or simply to enjoy the adventure of travel. Elites of the city had already established summer homes and retreats near the city, in the Meramec River valley, and southward down the St. Louis Iron Mountain Railway towns.[1] Sporting men in the tobacco industry, however, looked much farther away from home to found their sportsmen's gateway into the Ozarks.

St. Louis businessmen had known something of southwest Missouri, even if only by reputation, for many years. St. Louis brothers Henry and Peter Blow and their partners had made a fortune in Newton County at the Granby Mining and Smelting Company, before and after the Civil War. Their mineral surveys and those of the Missouri Geological Survey had included Stone and Taney Counties, where in 1869, three miles north of the White River, a reputed Blow party explored a great cave later known as Marvel Cave. St. Louisans speculated in mineral lands in Taney County throughout the late nineteenth century, where several still hoped to strike it rich. In 1882 Springfield became the nexus for both the St. Louis and San Francisco Railroad and the Kansas City, Southern, and Memphis Railroad, while a spur line extended south into Christian County, through Ozark and ended at Chadwick. From these railheads and along the several wagon roads leading south from Springfield into Arkansas came settlers, commerce, and a new immigrant—the corporation.

During the 1890s new faces arrived in the White River country who would forever change the look of the land and its reputation. Immigrants and visitors tried their luck in this region partly because it contained the largest block of government land left for sale in Missouri. The more famous of these new arrivals—Harold Bell Wright, J. K. Ross, Ike Morrill, and Walker Powell—are remembered in the romance and legend of Wright's *The Shepherd of the Hills*. Canadian William H. Lynch, owner of Marble Cave, became a legendary promoter. But Democrats and industrialists Moses C. Wetmore (1846–1910) and George H. McCann (1848–1920) are rarely remembered. They represented a corporate immigrant to Taney County whose founding of a Democrat Playground, long before the Ozark Playgrounds Association rose to champion the area for middle-class tourists, influenced the future of Taney County and Missouri conservation in general. Contrary to the traditional railroad tourists who hunted in the Ozarks, and to numerous resident hunters who shot game as mere targets, Wetmore and McCann were tourists-sportsmen who owned property and had visions for development. They were the new "true sportsmen," club members with an ideology contrary to market hunters, and champions for a conservation ethic that supported the propagation of big game in Missouri.[2]

In 1891, "a club of St. Louis gentlemen," officers of the Liggett and Meyers Tobacco Company (producers of Star Tobacco, the largest plug tobacco concern in the country), formed the St. Louis Park and Agricultural Company, known more commonly as the St. Louis Game Park.[3] Moses Wetmore, controlling stockholder in St. Louis, and George McCann, company representative in Springfield and owner of the Old Coon Tobacco Company, were ardent Democrats and the primary leaders in the enterprise. At the outset Wetmore and his associates had a vision to develop a large, fenced block of land for a private game preserve. Southerners and others had built deer parks since colonial America, but gentlemen sportsmen of the late nineteenth century had additional goals. Elites and their political allies all knew that the time had passed to save the large herds of buffalo and the passenger pigeon, and now deer and other big game were threatened across the United States. Affluent sportsmen across the country were interested in game parks that also experimented with propagating deer (for sport and food), exploring the recreational potential of the grounds, and developing amenities for social gatherings. This diversified approach set the St. Louis Game Park apart from the traditional deer parks.

The company purchased lands in south central Taney County, primarily on the west side of the White River, southeast of Mincy, a crossroads trading hamlet. The land contained all the representative topography of the region—creeks, caves, an oak-hickory-pine and cedar-glade forest of steep ridges and hollows, and three miles of riverfront along the White River. Taney County did not have any factories, brick buildings, electric lights, improved roads, or large corporate timber mills or mining towns. The population of nine thousand was dispersed, with a few hundred citizens living in the villages of Forsyth, Kirbyville, and Taneyville. George McCann, president and real-estate broker for the game park corporation, purchased dozens of publicly and privately owned tracts, much of it nonresident, including his own speculative investments for the company.[4] The park property, amidst a vast open range, was forty miles from the nearest railroad at Chadwick.[5]

Corporate secretary J. P. Litton announced in 1896 to the readers of *Forest and Stream* that the St. Louis Game Park had amassed five thousand acres for their preserve and resort. The directors managed several species of deer—native, red, black-tail, and fallow—and Angora goats. They purchased elk in Illinois from a national authority on deer and a pair of deer from owners in Wisconsin. Several dozen Mongolian pheasants were released that year to join the resident turkey and quail. Earlier in 1893, the managers had surrounded five hundred acres with an eight- or nine-foot deer-proof fence and enclosed the rest of the land with a stock fence.[6]

Moses Wetmore worked hard in planning a grand opening to follow the November 1896 elections. That spring, in April, eighteen wagons left Taney County for Chadwick to pick up nineteen head of elk. However, four elk were killed in the roundup at Judge Caton's park in Ottawa, Illinois, and four more died in transit, but seven wagons made it back to Forsyth carrying an elk apiece. William F. Hunt, the park ranger and guide who had originally taken the St. Louisans into the Taney woods, supervised the transportation and was the principal manager at the park. He protected the game from predators and resident poachers, gaining a reputation as a fearless enforcer. During 1896, the owners enclosed an additional twenty-five hundred acres with deer-proof fence.[7]

By fall, the company was ready for VIPs to visit their new experiment. In October George McCann took seventeen people, including several

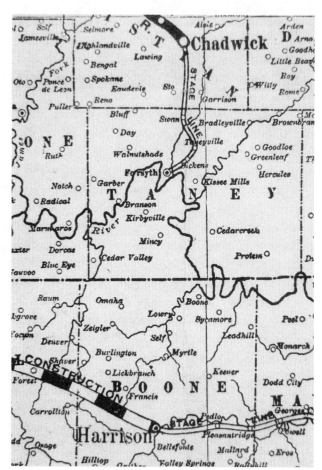

Stage line from Chadwick to Forsyth and railroad construction south of the White River in Arkansas, 1899

From Walter Stevens, Ozark Uplift, 1900

from Forsyth; one was Jesse Tolerton, the future Missouri game and fish commissioner under Gov. Herbert Hadley. They were able to witness the introduction of twelve new elk to the park, bringing the total to twenty-five. St. Louisans and Springfieldians joined Taney Countians, and many wives of the sportsmen participated in the deer feast and recreation.[8]

Wetmore, a great admirer and financial supporter of William Jennings Bryan, who had just lost a bid for the presidency, joined Bryan's party in Springfield. McCann arranged for the Bryan party to travel by rail to Chadwick; hacks were brought on rail cars for the overland trip to Forsyth. The Democrats held a supper and entertained speeches at the Hilsabeck Hotel in Forsyth on an overnight stop en route to the park.[9]

The White River landing at the St. Louis Game Park

From Walter Stevens, Ozark Uplift, *1900*

Wetmore had assembled an impressive number of political elites for this Democratic retreat into the Ozarks hinterland to show off his efforts in conservation. Joining Bryan were Gov. William J. Stone of Missouri, Missouri Democratic state chairman Sam B. Cook, Sen. James K. Jones of Arkansas, and midwestern political dignitaries from as far away as Michigan. A *St. Louis Post-Dispatch* reporter recorded the event, and his article was later reprinted in the state's *House and Senate Journals* in Jefferson City.[10] The more than ten square miles of fenced compound amazed the journalist. He christened it a "hunter's paradise of elk, antelope, wild goat, bear, squirrel, coon, 'possum, catamount, turkey and quail in greater abundance than in any place in America," and if hunting was too challenging, the fishing in the White River was superb. Urban sportsmen, hunting and fishing in the Missouri hinterland, had become the parents of Ozarks tourism.

The proprietors had constructed a frame, eight-room hunting lodge on top of one of the local balds, a knob overlooking the White River, where four hundred steps rose from the river to the lodge. Workmen removed the underbrush surrounding the grounds around the lodge, which allowed a large spread of grass to grow. The sportsmen arranged it so that one could purchase a flat-bottom boat in Forsyth and float down the White River, some twelve miles, and dock at the park. Standing at the lodge, a visitor could see the domestic cattle spread below in the parklands and peer southward into Arkansas. The St. Louis reporter concluded his description with a romantic poem entitled "White River," penned by Alonzo Prather, Taney County state representative.[11]

Nearby, a north-south country wagon road ran through the game park. Over time, the lands west of the road became the "cattle park," and those east the "game park." Wetmore continued importing elk, twenty from Jackson Hole, Wyoming, in 1898, and his herds grew dramatically. In 1906, however, the deer population suffered a decimating epidemic of black-tongue. The management later introduced controlled burning for woods pasture maintenance.

The proprietors relied upon local craftsmen for blacksmith work and traded at the general store in Mincy. The true sportsmen, however, did not readily invite locals into the park. But the Democrat Playground did allow for the usual playfulness associated with such informal gatherings for recreation. William J. Bryan, at ease with his friend Wetmore at the fall 1899 hunt, left a brief verse:

> O Wetmore, 'tis of thee,
> Wetmore of Missouree
> Of thee we sing.
> Long may thy path be bright
> With friendship's holy light,
> With stories of thy might,
> Let Taney ring.[12]

The fall 1899 hunt was the subject of a Sunday feature in the *St. Louis Republic.* A reporter accompanied the entourage of sportsmen, most of

Wetmore's deer at the St. Louis Game Park
From Walter Stevens, Ozark Uplift, *1900*

whom sported titles from their affiliations with state militias and their brief encounters with the Spanish-American War. Wetmore and Bryan bagged mountain goat, deer, turkey, squirrel, geese, duck, and quail, and they enjoyed fishing. On the return trip through Springfield, Bryan delivered a public address to raise proceeds for the local Confederate Monument Fund.[13]

Every fall, from the dramatic opening of the game park in 1896 until his death in 1910, Moses Wetmore and his associates held gala hunts and socials at the park. During the 1890s, Wetmore was president of the Liggett and Meyers Tobacco Company, the largest in St. Louis. He personally financed a regiment in the Missouri National Guard, gaining the sobriquet "Colonel." In 1908 he became W. J. Bryan's campaign manager and served as chairman of the finance committee of the National Democratic Committee; for several years he was a national committeeman from Missouri. Bryan's many trips to the game park with Wetmore became the occasion for various regional appearances of the great orator in the Ozarks.[14]

McCann, living in Springfield, had easier access throughout the year. He was a native of Ireland, settling in Springfield in 1867, where he soon chose the tobacco industry as his primary concern. His Old Coon Tobacco Works was affiliated with Liggett and Meyers. When Wetmore formed his own independent company in 1899, McCann became his vice-president, moving to St. Louis, until returning to Springfield in 1904. Then he founded the New Phoenix Foundry and Machinery Company, serving as president. In 1913 he and several game park associates organized the Southern Missouri Trust Company in Springfield.[15]

The Wetmore-McCann game park earned national attention from wildlife biologists and the federal government. Records kept by the owners and resident park rangers allowed scholars to include the game park in national surveys. For example, one pregnant pet doe in 1900 became the maternal ancestor for twenty-five deer by 1905, and in a survey published in 1910, Wetmore's efforts were acclaimed as among the most significant in the country.[16]

The publicity concerning the St. Louis Game Park may have encouraged other St. Louisans to establish another hunting-fishing-social club upriver from Wetmore's. In 1905 the Maine Hunting and Fishing Club moved the Maine Building of the 1904 World's Fair to a dramatic bluff site overlooking the White River. Passenger service on the new White River Railway opened in nearby Hollister in 1906, so visitors to the Maine Club could arrive easily, while those to the game park shortened their overland buggy trips from forty to only thirteen miles. Ten years later, the Maine Club building became the new home of The School of the Ozarks.[17]

The railroad brought other St. Louisans to invest in Taney County. The Bagnell Timber Company, the largest manufacturer of railroad ties in the United States, bought lands and began one of their many tie operations as a major employer in newly founded Branson. The Hobart and Lee Timber and Tie Company, the largest tie company in southwest Missouri, which was managed by another combination of St. Louis and Springfield investors, joined the famous Bagnell Tie Company in competition for the regional tie markets. These commercial timber companies, however, remained in Taney County for only a few years in the early twentieth century. The forests

St. Louisans at the Maine Clubhouse
Hobart Parnell Collection

of the White River hills did not have the marketable density that those in southeast Missouri had. The timber companies created no giant timber mills in Taney County nor did they invest in resort properties.[18]

The Bagnell company left Taney County on the eve of Republican Herbert Hadley's election to the governor's seat in 1908. The Hadley administration would become the most influential in the Missouri conservation movement until the Baker administration of the late 1920s. Hadley picked Taney Countian Jesse Tolerton as his game and fish commissioner, a man familiar with the St. Louis Game Park. This merchant and banker from the Ozarks became Hadley's close political confidant, and with the successful enactment of the "Walmsley-Hadley" game and fish regulations of 1909, Tolerton was pivotal in making the model game and preservation issues prominent in the Hadley government. The new benchmark laws that regulated Missouri game gave private investors in game parks a special exemption that allowed the shipment of elk or deer when raised in captivity.[19] Tolerton introduced Hadley to George McCann, and all hunted at the game park. McCann afterward sent boxed elk meat, elk head, and hide to the governor's mansion. In 1910, Governor Hadley established a state game farm near Jefferson City and built a much-heralded log cabin retreat of his own west of the city.[20]

Hadley's famous Ozark promotional tours on the railroads included returns to the White River. Government work in geology and agriculture had already established itself professionally throughout the state, and now the Missouri Game and Fish Department combined developmental visions in tune with growing commercial tourism. A locally famous publicity photograph, shot in 1911 for Missouri newspapers, was on a gravel bar near Forsyth where the ten-boat flotilla began its journey for the game park downriver. While there, the entourage dumped fish into the White River in an attempt to promote stocking Missouri riverways.[21]

The St. Louis Game Park, with its big-game populations, always provided a marked contrast for sportsmen who hunted elsewhere in Missouri and the nation, and the difference was not lost on Hadley. Even in Shannon County, famous historically for fall hunts, a Hadley supporter could only offer a local sighting of "5 or 6 deer out about 8 mile northwest of here [Winona] and also two nice bunch of turkey using the same woods."[22] A lawyer in adjacent Carter County wrote that we "have heard of several deer, also several turkey having been killed this fall."[23] Hadley supporters in Pettis and Johnson Counties also invited the governor and his game commissioner. Hadley jokingly wrote Tolerton that before he went to the trouble to make the trip he would require the hosts to "furnish a bond with a surety company on it that we can find quail after we get there."[24] All the while, Hadley and Tolerton were angling to attend the St. Louis Game Park with Maj. George McCann.

Where game used to be counted in the hundreds and thousands in outstate Missouri, a very few deer in 1910 gained local notice; however, at the St. Louis Game Park there were four hundred elk and one thousand deer.[25] Although Hadley left the governor's mansion in January 1913, he quickly joined Tolerton, McCann, and others in February to form the Missouri Southern Trust Company in Springfield. The Democrat park owner and his Republican sportsmen friends could play and do business together.[26]

Gov. Herbert Hadley on a gravel bar near Forsyth ready for a float to the St. Louis Game Park

Carl Moore Collection

Governor Hadley and a promotional group at the Branson Hotel, now a fashionable bed and breakfast

Herbert Hadley Papers, WHMC-Columbia

The Moses Wetmore funeral in November 1910 even prompted business elites to consider building an imitation of the St. Louis Game Park. Sen. William J. Stone delivered an emotional eulogy to Wetmore before representatives of the National Democratic Committee, Joseph Folk, Lon Stephens, James Reed, Edward Goltra, and a host of dignitaries. Perhaps reminiscences by Adolphus Busch, a game park devotee, encouraged major brewers to consider the White River country for a resort. A preliminary party left for Stone County to set up camp. Following was an entourage of wealthy sportsmen including August Pabst of Milwaukee, Edward Lemp of St. Louis, and others who wanted to inspect some five thousand acres for a game preserve. The sportsmen enjoyed their trip, but did not invest.[27]

George McCann did continue to host sporting parties during the teens. One, in December 1914, included executives and jurists from Cincinnati, St. Louis, and Springfield. They arrived by railroad in Branson and took carriages and guides to the park. After a week at the lodge they shipped deer and elk meat to their respective homes, a sure symbol of privileged access in a game-depleted Missouri environment.[28]

By this time, McCann was president of his new banking business and deeply involved in his quarry works, and his friend Moses Wetmore was dead. Perhaps these and other circumstances led to a decreased use of the game park, while a few Springfieldians and St. Louisans continued as guests in the fall months. For several years, however, the park went unkept. Fences were not maintained properly, elk and deer escaped, and locals managed to kill several of each.[29]

McCann, perhaps feeling his sixty-nine years, or the press of his business investments in Greene County, sold his game park in 1917. The new corporate owners were W. J. Clemens of Springfield and Paul T. Campbell of Kansas City, who later moved to Boston. The acquisition of the park, christened the Ozark Livestock and Game Company, consisted of 4,337 acres, all improvements, and "the deer, elk, cattle, feed, implements and other personal property belonging the company, and now on the premises."[30]

The name "Ozark Livestock and Game Company" never achieved popular currency. Locals and observers statewide continued to refer to it as the "Wetmore preserve" or "the St. Louis Game Park." E. Y. Mitchell Jr., prominent Springfield Democrat, enjoyed some use, taking allies on hunting and fishing trips, and suggested to Gov. Frederick Gardner that the owners would be willing to sell it to the state. Clemens and Campbell, however, used the game park much differently than the St. Louisans. True, it was an investment for the future, but it was also a personal retreat and ranch for the Clemens family, who lived at the lodge and the Colonial Hotel in Springfield. They stocked the land with hogs, mules, and cattle and did not entertain an active sportsmen's retreat, although resident gamekeepers continued to reside on the property. By 1920 most of the livestock was removed, and through the 1920s local stockmen leased grazing rights during the summer.[31]

During the 1920s the Missouri Game and Fish Department began to review properties for acquisition into its proposed state park system, and sportsmen recommended their favorite haunts. But popular places in any time command high real-estate costs, and it was no different with the old game park.[32] Nevertheless, in 1924, Dr. T. M. Sayman, a wealthy St. Louis patent medicine and soap merchant, launched his own campaign to encourage the state to buy the old "Wetmore preserve." Sayman, noted for his eccentric ways, observed correctly that there were several hundred deer and elk and that the state could sell brood stock to other game preserves. He admitted, however, that there were no "gushing springs" that so attracted park supporters, but Sayman claimed he could solve this problem by walking over the land to observe the proper place, and then drilling holes for springs.[33] St. Louisan Frank Wielandy, the governor's game and fish commissioner, suggested to Sayman that wealthy Izaak Waltonians in Kansas City might purchase the expensive park and donate it to the state, or better yet, Sayman could memorialize himself by doing the same.[34] Finally, Wielandy wrote a blistering letter to Gov. Arthur Hyde railing about the doctor's persistence. Wielandy had explained several times to Dr. Sayman that the state could not purchase the "Wetmore ranch" and concluded that "this illiterate ass" was a public nuisance.[35]

W. J. Clemens, however, kept the game park in the eye of the public and the Missouri Game and Fish Department. In January 1925 Branson opened a new tobacco market, and Clemens furnished an elk dinner for almost nine hundred people. In the fall of 1925 he donated fifteen deer as starter brood stock in the new state park system. Missouri, like other programs, was trying to establish game refuges and was encouraged by the recent success of Pennsylvania, where managers had reestablished deer-hunting seasons for the public.[36]

By the end of the decade, in January 1929, M. B. Skaggs, owner of the Safeway Grocer chain, purchased the game park property, paying forty thousand dollars more than Clemens and Campbell did in 1917. Skaggs, born in southwest Missouri, had a yearning for the Ozarks. He repaired the hunting lodge, constructed new buildings and fences, enclosed additional lands with a deer-proof fence, purchased additional bottomland farms to bring his unit to nine thousand acres, built and stocked a small lake, and added buffalo to the big-game park. Skaggs pastured hundreds of cattle until 1935, when they were removed in favor of limited grazing leases. Skaggs then began to rebuild the natural environment, concluding a management agreement with the Missouri Department of Conservation in 1939.[37]

M. B. Skaggs, unlike previous and recent corporate owners of the game park, became a friendly and visible neighbor to the locals and a patron to the county and state. In the autumn, Skaggs held drawings at the Mincy general store for the division of elk among all the customers of the post office. The modern Missouri Department of Conservation has long considered Skaggs instrumental in restocking Missouri deer herds and turkey populations. Skaggs allowed trapping of both species by conservationists, which included some seven hundred and fifty deer during the 1940s, a one-third contribution toward the state's total restoration program. Later, M. B. and Stella Skaggs endowed the Skaggs Community Hospital in Branson, while much of the Skaggs Ranch became public lands. In Taney County the game park lands have been known and are still referred to as the Skaggs Ranch.[38]

Travelers and temporary residents who have crossed the Ozarks have named the region and given it definition. Maj. Stephen Long's expedition named it in 1820, and Carl Sauer defined it in 1920; neither stayed in the region, but both left profound marks upon it. So it was with Wetmore and McCann. Their travel and transient residence in the White River country became a central force in its local historical transformations. Their brand of conservation in creating game parks as the area's first tourist attraction has long been passé, but it did represent radical departures at the time, a digression that molded the future. M. B. Skaggs fulfilled the Wetmore

Shipment of elk at Branson railroad depot
Hobart Parnell Collection

vision of making a lasting contribution in the conservation of Missouri's game populations, big and small. The forces of modern tourism have resulted in the opening in 1997 of a new game park, the Beaver Creek Elk and Cattle Ranch, encompassing three thousand acres and over one hundred and fifty elk. Locally, mobility in and through Taney County continues to give it a unique historical seasoning, a taste sought by ever-increasing numbers.[39]

"Cows Rather than Plows"

Newcomers Join the Natives

THE SOCIAL LANDSCAPE of the White River hills, prior to the town building along railroad corridors, was of a pastoral nature idealized by romantic minds. Arcadians interacted little with local life, but they nevertheless interpreted it, perceiving the social and cultural isolation of the Ozarks as a peaceful respite from the crowded, smoky cities. The same perceived isolation signaled quite another thing to prospective immigrants—a chance to start life anew on a frontier where they could achieve independence and a good living from the stockmen/agricultural economies. Some settlers sought to capture and prolong this interlude in the progress of civilization while others hoped to change it.

Taney County in antebellum times was much larger than it is today. Known then as the "Taney District" the county encompassed an area more than twice its modern size. As originally formed in 1837, Taney County took in the James River Township, which in 1851 was reformed to make up the bulk of present-day Stone County; a few years later another large portion of Taney was carved off to create Christian County, while in 1864 yet another section was incorporated into southwestern Douglas County. The original "Taney District" comprised over a thousand square miles and contained much of the Missouri White River hills. This vast region was a homeland for the "first families" of southwest Missouri; many descendants of these original settlers are still scattered among the same hills today.[1]

The first American families to enter the Taney District were attracted by the region's "range" and its economic potential as a livestock country. These settlers looked across an open range still owned by the federal government and situated distant miles from the nation's expanding railroads. Settlement was sparse and families largely squatted on the government lands; such settlers were slow to file patents for fee simple ownership in county courthouses or government land offices in Jackson and Springfield. Contrary to widespread myth, the land was not free, nor was it cheap; filing fees might equal a month's wages or more for the cash-poor backwoodsmen. The state of Missouri annually reported that hundreds of thousands of acres were available for homesteading in the White River country, the price at eighteen cents per acre in Stone County and in Douglas County at nine cents. As inexpensive as the price sounds, labor in Stone and Taney Counties commanded only ten to fifteen dollars per month as late as 1896.

The rugged, forested land was not of the quality desired by progressive agriculturalists who were used to fertile fields planted in neat rows of cereal crops. The settlers attracted to the Taney District were stockmen who pursued a different agricultural pattern from that of row-crop farmers. Some geographers have been led by their conventional prejudices of what constituted "good" farmland to define the entire Ozark region as being agriculturally inferior to adjacent regions with flatter relief and deeper soils. The Ozark attraction, however, was strong for families of modest means who could live off the land by pursuing subsistence economies, free from the obligation of paying for natural resources—especially grazing and timber lands—or from the need to maintain a large personal or real-estate tax base. For those who managed to accumulate herds of livestock, the Ozark range, however, did offer an avenue to the market economies of St. Louis or regional market towns. Substantial holdings by absentee owners and speculators did not interrupt the gradual population increase of settlers who cared little upon whose land they squatted, hunted, timbered, or ran their livestock. This situation changed imperceptibly during the course of the nineteenth century, although the myth of precious ores did stimulate speculation in mineral lands, especially in the years following the Civil War. The large-scale buying of timberland by outside corporations did not begin until the twentieth century.[2]

The immigrants to the White River hills were primarily southern uplanders with an Anglo-Celtic background who practiced "farming" that favored cows rather than plows. The Taney District stockmen's economy revolved around driving cattle and hogs to market centers, but families followed a variety of lesser economies as well, including corn whiskey production, raising cotton and tobacco in the bottomlands, timbering, and

NEWCOMERS JOIN THE NATIVES

the marketing of pelts and furs.[3] As the late nineteenth century drew to a close, a new group of settlers began to enter the White River hills and set up homesteads alongside the old-stock upland southerners. This group was primarily Yankee midwesterners and a few Germans. Their collective background was far different from that of old-stock settlers. They were flatlanders, by and large, not hill men. Their experiences were drawn not from the open range, but from associations with railroad towns, institutions, and commercial culture. As one journalist wrote, "Virginia leavened the land . . . later an influx of Iowa, Indiana, Illinois and other folk from northern states contributed to an entire new citizenry," one distinct from the natives, who were "a free people, not given to disciplinary measures and rather opposed to regulation."[4] This mixing of family backgrounds is representative of many regions in Missouri that can claim both a southern and a midwestern heritage. Printed references in Missouri to "this South" and "this West" are vague as to what precisely is meant by these regional terms, and although the federal census of 1860 declared that Missouri was in the Midwest, scholars are still at work trying to articulate the differences between the respective regions in this borderland state. One obvious conclusion is that the major Midwest market centers of St. Louis and Kansas City tied the Ozarks of the late nineteenth and early twentieth centuries economically to the Midwest. Observers can catalog stereotypes, myths, confusion, and contradictions concerning the old-timers and newcomers, but in the White River hills of the late nineteenth century it is certain that a new group of people with new values and a new vision of the future had arrived in the old Taney District. One fundamental characteristic of these newcomers that distinguished them from the original settlers was their commitment to boosterism and commercial development.[5]

The Civil War caused major demographic and social disruptions in the White River hills. Postwar accounts depict counties, including Christian and Taney, left nearly depopulated. In this border country, both pro-northern and pro-southern old families who had been forced to flee wandered back to their former homes and rebuilt. They were joined by other ex-Unionists, northerners, and easterners who moved in among the former antebellum settlers and established new homesteads along the rivers and tributary creek valleys. The great majority of these arrivals, both old and new, resumed the open-range economy and the "easy living"

Cowboys in Stone County
Postcard, Kalen and Morrow Collection

lifestyle based on subsistence and market hunting on the great government commons. Few postwar settlers brought with them any great amounts of cash to invest in building small manufacturing industries or opening mercantiles.

For such cash-poor immigrants the postwar culture of easy living transcended any generational or ethnic differences. In 1869 Nancy Sims, whose kin were from Tennessee and Kentucky, wrote her sister from Forsyth saying that "this is the best country for stock and fruit of all kinds and William says that he can make more lying flat on his back than he can there [in Tennessee] and work all the time."[6] A half century later in 1914, Isaac Workman, living on upper Swan Creek in Christian County, told the Branson newspaper editor that "We just had plenty in those days, when living was easier than it is now." Workman recalled making good money market hunting with his gun—as high as eighteen dollars a day. The easy living of the precapitalist hunter's frontier was still possible for male participants in the postbellum forests of the Ozarks.[7]

The Sims, Workmans, and others joined an arrested frontier far from the credit economy and labor markets that drove the Industrial Revolution in postwar America. Here the land was not yet commodified, or subdivided into farms, and the free-range stockmen's economy still reigned. The stockmen's wealth was mobile; owners and buyers drove bawling animals to markets in Springfield and beyond. Cattle drives seldom included more than 150 to 200 head. For such stockmen cattle was the chief source of wealth. The Ozarkers meat diet, consequently, was mainly pork, not beef; cattle values per animal were six to one or more over hogs, and besides, cattle drove to market much easier.[8]

Commercial marketing on a large scale had to wait for the White River Railway in the twentieth century. In the late nineteenth-century Ozarks, a pioneer made a living with fire, firearms, and an ax applied to large expanses of government-owned forest land. The plow was only selectively utilized in small places, usually the bottomlands of creeks and rivers or small upland prairies. These plain folk who became Ozarkers "overcame the agricultural limitations of the southern frontier by substituting woodlands and fire for scarce labor and equipment."[9] Management by fire was certainly more cost-efficient than hiring labor or leasing oxen to plow a wide prairie. As late as 1897 82 percent of the great commons of Ozark forest in this region was still owned by the government and was available for filing in the district government land office at Springfield. The White River hills was the last upland region in Missouri to offer the opportunity of open-range subsistence for migrants possessing little property, but who were skilled in living off the land.[10]

In 1890, as railroads steamed progress and commercialism across most other Missouri counties, Stone and Taney retained their frontier flavor. Settlers fabricated a built environment out of the most available material —wood; rarely was a brick or stone building encountered. Towns did not have brick mainstreets until the twentieth century. In an American migration that had reversed itself, the White River hills became a destination for families who fled the worn-out grazing lands and droughts of the Great Plains, drawn by huge blocks of government land. Families of little means could start anew by purchasing relatively cheap improved acreage. Homesteaders realized that failures in one great region did not discount the possibility of success in another. In the open-range Ozarks they could expect, with hard work, to achieve moderate prosperity and enjoy a freedom of

Oxen plowing in
White River hills

*Northwest Arkansas
Regional Library,
Harrison*

individualism. As Laura Ingalls Wilder put it, "No one who has not homesteaded can understand the fascination and the terror of it."[11]

The Wilders, who fled the Great Plains to seek a home in the Ozarks,
represented the general demographic trend. The *St. Louis Republic* reported
in 1896 that the recent influx of settlers had literally created what they
termed "The New Taney County." The press announced that since the
winter of 1893 new neighborhoods had appeared, peopled from the
Dakotas, Iowa, Nebraska, Michigan, and Minnesota. Joining these new
arrivals were "whole colonies" from Kentucky and West Virginia. The
influx started a building boom, and new schools and churches were constructed throughout the land.[12] A state government report concluded in

1896 that the natives of Taney County were old Kentucky and Tennessee stock, "but that Newcomers are mostly from Iowa, Kansas, Nebraska, and North Missouri."[13] In 1899 Walter Stevens wrote a promotional pamphlet for the Frisco Railroad reprinted by a St. Louis press. He observed that in September 1899 filings at the Springfield Land Office averaged six thousand acres per month and, that in Taney County alone, speculators and settlers, including a noticeable number of Germans, had entered over twenty-seven thousand acres in the last eighteen months.[14] This dramatic increase in the purchase of lands by new immigrants had a profound and transforming impact on traditional land occupation in the Taney District. As the new arrivals gained clear title for much of the available land during these years, the time-honored frontier practice of squatting on land without bothering to secure fee ownership or to pay property taxes succumbed to the modernizing trends at work in the Ozarks. Walter Stevens even titled one of his columns "Squatting No Longer Safe" in the south Missouri counties due to recent immigration and mineral speculation. By the dawn of the twentieth century the establishment of clear title by these immigrants and the corporations that followed cleared away many obstacles to future legal land transfers.[15]

Another major impact on traditional practices was the restricted exploitation of the public domain's natural resources; the great increase in livestock reduced the carrying capacity of the open range, creating a "tragedy of the commons." Stockmen's wealth increased with larger herds, but these herds required more range. More stockmen meant more competition for the ever-shrinking open range. In these prerailroad days, stockmen who favored sheep and goats had little appreciation for free-ranging cattle and hogs, let alone the deer hounds of sportsmen that bounded across their fields. But the lively public debates that culminated into political contests to close the range did not emerge until the 1920s. Until then, the newcomers in the 1890s ran their stock on old commons just as old-stock settlers had done for generations, joining the competition for resources in an increasingly depleted environment.[16]

Visitors to the White River hills encountered a region that was almost entirely forested, except for the hilltop glades that were the famous "balds" of the area. In such a landscape, wood was the most readily obtainable material for creating the local material culture of the region. Practically everything in the built environment—buildings, tools, and toys—was made of wood. The technology of wood craft produced the house and its furniture, spoons and buckets, wagons and wheels, barrels and hoops, split rails and posts, sleds and plows. Bark from oak and hemlock provided tannic acid for tanning hides. Wood ash helped in making soap and hominy and in tanning leather. Primitive mud and stick chimneys were still a common sight, but stone chimneys were becoming more frequent. When any old building had served one purpose, the frugal settlers recycled it to serve another purpose. An unused house or store could become a barn, a crib, or a chicken house. Movable fencing was vital in a culture whose settlers moved around, and split-rail fences were easily torn down and reassembled. Local craftsmen who produced this wide range of wood products were essential to the Ozarks frontier, but the demand for their services began to erode with the arrival of Rural Free Delivery in 1896, which ushered in another harbinger of modernity—the Sears, Roebuck catalogs. Consumers, even in the White River country, could now mail order phonographs, clothing, shoes, wire brush cards for straightening fibers prior to weaving on homemade looms, tools, prefab houses, and more. Ozarkers steeped in folk traditions of the forest were moving into the culture of industrial society.[17]

Another age-old practice of hill men began to decline in the face of all the late nineteenth-century transformations—they burned the woods to clear the forest understory to facilitate hunting and to rid accumulated leaf litter, thereby encouraging new plant growth for grazing. Geographer Carl Sauer, after a long career, concluded that man, throughout the world, managed his "mastery over the organic world with his employment of and experiments with fire."[18] Earlier, Osage Indian hunting parties and the migrating southern and eastern Indians set annual fires to keep favored areas in a prairie environment. Southern upland settlers who hunted for the market continued the established method of burning to control underbrush and open the woodlands so that hunters could sight and bring down game.

Post–Civil War immigration and increasing populations inevitably led to restrictions of the fires that had once played a central role in the settlement process. In one scientific study of the upper Swan Creek glades, scientists demonstrated that after 1870 the frequency of fires was dramatically reduced. The change was one of degree—less widespread, less intense, and less damaging to trees. Travelers to the White River hills commented on the open, park-like character of the land, a legacy of fire, as late as the 1890s. Grazing, however, not hunting, had by then become the premier activity on the glades, while combustible property such as rail fencing became a resource to be protected. Although new settlers complained about uncontrolled range fires destroying property, the traditional subsistence economy risked a great deal by not firing the woods. Without fire, travel, hunting, general visibility, and the gathering of natural fruits and berries would have been much more difficult. Without frequent burning fuel loads would build up and greatly increase the intensity and danger of unplanned woodland fires, "especially for a culture whose entire heritage was flammable."[19] The woods were becoming more populated, but Ozarkers continued to burn the range despite the increasing dangers to property and timber that fire occasioned.

While the use of fire was falling increasingly into disfavor among the newcomers, the pressure on the environment of their greater numbers and their livestock quickly began to have a negative and destructive effect on the landscape. Increased livestock resulted in overgrazing that in turn led to erosion. It was not so much cattle, however, as free-ranging hogs, by far the more numerous of the Ozark forest stock, that had the most deleterious effect on the environment. Hog wallows and bare ground where swine impacted the vegetation on thin soils were seen at every homestead. When widespread clear-cut timbering was then added to overgrazing, the result was significant environmental damage; erosion carried away not only the thin topsoils but also vast quantities of hillside chert and gravel which washed into the clear, free-flowing streams that the region was renowned for. These stream beds, in turn, became choked with gravel by the early twentieth century.[20]

The influx of newcomers also created a greater need for rural institutions, especially schools and churches. Outsiders had long reported on the absence of churches in the interior Ozarks. Journalists lamented in urban papers as late as 1892 that the Taney County seat was "without a church or place of worship."[21] But these observers were looking for churches in the wrong places; they did not understand that it was in the countryside, not in the towns, where Ozark institutions thrived. Prior to the immigrations of the 1880s and 1890s, the population lived in creek valleys, and later spread into the upland flats and finally onto the ridges. These were the settings for the area's religious activities. A church record book of 1869–72 reported the gatherings in Taney County by place names—Bee Creek Class, Bull Creek Class No. 3, Long Creek Class, Long Creek Class No. 4, Pleasant Hill Class, Righty Creek Class No. 6, Roark Class No. 8, et cetera. Check marks by names indicated attendance, the names of men and women were listed separately, and marital status was noted. Some meetings were held "at candlelight" (dusk) and the designated meeting places were often in homes of parishioners such as "Howard['s] on the Bend of the river below." To accommodate circuit-riding ministers, some preaching was held on Saturday while the clerk of the church scheduled first, second, and third Sabbath preaching for ministers of different denominations.[22]

By the fall of 1871, the Mincy Valley Baptist Church of Christ presented a full slate of issues for its congregation to debate and consider. Their rapidly growing congregation necessitated that several members be "dismissed by letter in May to organize a new church."[23] The remaining members concluded that the time had come to move beyond the practice of meeting in homes and to build their own house of worship. The minutes recorded the erection of a new eighteen-foot by twenty-foot hewed-log church building with windows, pulpit, doors, a ten-foot ceiling, and weatherboard siding. This house of worship was up-to-date by the standards of the Ozarks subsistence frontier.

The Mincy valley Baptists licensed one of their own number to preach and formed committees to hear cases of slander. Deacons and the church council reviewed candidates for baptism and met and discussed religious issues with sister councils in the area. As settlers moved into a nearby area the church voted to "extend an arm of this church into the settlement of the Bro. Layton School House." With population growth and the influx of outsiders and outside influences, new temptations inevitably crept into the wilderness Eden of the White River hills. Reports filtered in of the faithful attending "public places of sinful mirth," "making use of profane language," "hunting with a gun on Sunday," "attending dances," "adultery," "lying," "stealing hogs," and more. The church required straying members to come forward and make reconciliation or else face dismissal.

The growth and prosperity of the neighborhood led the church, by 1877, to erect a new building. This time it was a frame structure of pine

White River General Baptists at Hercules, Taney County, 1906
J. Ross Baughman Collection

lumber, twenty-four by thirty-six feet, with windows and doors and
weatherboard siding. (The sawn lumber probably came from the Layton
mill located nearby in the pinery along the Springfield-Harrison Road.)
This "modern" Baptist church was one of the first frame buildings in the
area. Despite the mistaken impressions of some outside observers, the
Ozarks of Taney County was certainly not without organized religion nor
a vision for modern facilities.

A recent survey of Missouri history notes a dramatic increase in
church membership during the 1890s; between 1890 and 1906 membership in churches increased from 27 percent to 36 percent.[24] This increase
dramatically changed the built environment; settlers intending to stay and
establish homes, farms, and businesses constructed numerous public
buildings, which included churches. Sometimes one structure might do
double duty as both school and church, but the faithful also erected buildings for churches alone.

In Stone County from 1886 to 1896 the number of Sunday schools
increased from a reported one to fifty-four, while the number of schools

increased from twenty to fifty-two; the situation was no less dramatic in Taney where the schools also totaled fifty-two, and churches could claim seventy-two congregations. Rural school and church buildings, in addition to serving their normal functions, were also available for pie suppers, debates, literary readings, and meetings of fraternal orders.[25] Ozarkers, like other Americans, were joiners, and these country buildings provided a continuous social setting for adults and children.

The growth in the number of public schools in the White River region during the late nineteenth century was matched by an increase in the quality of teachers as well. In 1891 the general assembly passed a compulsory county institute law that required a two-week minimum for the training and licensing of teachers. In this setting teachers acquired their teaching certificates. The local newspapers of the 1890s listed the programs and a roster of who attended. The thin institutional society of the Ozark frontier lost much of its sparseness during the 1890s as religion, education, and civic groups built community landmarks.[26]

Issues in the school districts were similar to those of today. In Taney County District One, where citizens had managed a school for several years, the directors in April 1892 organized and elected a board president and appointed a school clerk to keep minutes of their meetings. The board directed the clerk to take an enumeration of the district, awarded a contract to install a new stovepipe and ten new windowpanes, repair the roof, construct new seats and repair the old, purchase a new teacher's desk with a lock, and buy and paint a new blackboard. Like many schools of the period, the Taney County school was open for only four months out of the year and paid its teacher thirty dollars per month. The enumeration totaled sixty-eight school-age children, but only half of these attended during the year, with the average daily attendance only twenty-three. The ungraded school had a primary and five classes, and each class relied on the famous McGuffy readers.[27]

Districts formulated rules of behavior for both children and teachers. At Cedar Bluff school, in Stone County, no pupil could leave school without the consent of the teacher or a note from the parents, students should not write notes or throw paper wads or swear or use bad language on the school grounds, and "no one shall go to the creek without teacher's consent." (Nearby, across the county line in Christian County, another school specified that students would not throw rocks or clubs.) Also proscripted were courting or writing letters during school hours or whispering or laughing during study time. Boys and girls could not play together.[28] There were no restroom facilities as such; separate areas in the woods, where poison ivy was common, were designated for boys and girls. The success or failure in teaching and discipline depended heavily upon the personality of the teacher. Different teachers would structure the sequence of the daily curriculum on their own personal preference, and few teachers taught very long in any one school. Long tenures in teaching at one place, like the widespread appearance of privies, began later in the twentieth century.

Local historian Kathleen Van Buskirk examined the records of the Ridgedale School Board in southwest Taney County for 1892–1934 and described its evolution throughout that time.[29] The school was in a small township of only twenty-four rugged and mountainous square miles. The local settlers organized the school in 1892. The voters levied a tax upon themselves to pay the teacher's salary and to provide a building and supplies. The board hired a teenage teacher who had completed the eighth grade to instruct sixteen pupils for twenty dollars a month. In a few years the enumeration increased, but daily attendance continued at sixteen or less. In the 1890s a teacher reported, in spite of the tax levied by voters, that there was "no dictionary, no globe, chart or wall maps, no desks not defaced by cutting or writing, no blackboards, no library, and no building." The teachers and students met in the homes of residents, rotating from one to another. Finding citizens to serve on the school board, however, was always difficult. The small subsistence farmers and sawmillers, elected for three-year terms, seldom served out their full terms, and replacements were hard to find.

By 1897, increased population led the district to split in half. The west half retained the Ridgedale name while the east became Pine Top. The following year a school building was finally erected at Ridgedale; it consisted of a twenty-two-foot by thirty-six-foot frame structure built from sawn lumber of nearby mills. The district paid for the building in just one year. Class ended early that year, however, as the teacher, a young lady hired at sixteen dollars per month, departed to pursue other interests, leaving the school in the charge of a young student. The board canceled her contract.

Only four years after the first Ridgedale schoolhouse was built, the school board replaced it with a new structure that cost two hundred dollars and was financed by a bond issue; this time it required ten years to retire the debt. In accordance with the usual practice, the Ridgedale board allowed the building to be used for Sunday school. The Protestant services were held by lamplight as electricity did not come to the community until the 1950s.

Railroad construction in Turkey Creek from 1903 to 1905 created a brief population boom, but the transient railroad workers soon moved on. Then in 1905, the legislature passed a compulsory attendance law for children between eight and fourteen that increased school enrollments.[30] The press of new students strained the school budget; the board sometimes omitted necessary purchases for lack of funds. Over the next few years, the district survived, in part, from donations and fundraisers held at the school. Such efforts allowed a new school bell and furniture to be purchased. Still, changes at Ridgedale and other Ozark schools came slowly. It was not until 1913 that the first library, consisting of twenty books, was established, and in 1917 the district finally provided maps, a globe, and a manufactured blackboard.

The 1890s was a period of significant modernization that could be measured in part by the replacement of log schools with frame buildings constructed of lumber from the growing number of local sawmills. Modernization, however, came much more slowly to the local school system itself. Scarce funds made few of the contemporary teaching aids available. Young unmarried women, who could be paid less than their male counterparts, did most of the teaching and, predictably, turnover was high. The Ridgedale school, in a pattern that was probably repeated throughout the Ozarks, hired thirty-one teachers over a period of thirty-eight years, and most of these teachers were young women.

The prosperity that created new schools and churches came in part from the freighting business which flourished after completion of the Frisco Railway in the 1870s and the Kansas City, Fort Scott, and Memphis Railway through Springfield in the early 1880s. Springfield, a primary market for overland traffic that reached as far south as the Boston Mountains in Arkansas, was the hub of a network of wagon roads that converged from all directions. The Wilderness Road ran north-south through Stone County and the Springfield-Harrison Road wound its way through Taney County; both of these main highways had many secondary feeders. Roads were built

Covered wagons passing through Hollister, c. 1912
Viola Hartman Collection

on the ridges as much as possible. Travel accounts describe long and lonely journeys across ridges where houses were seldom to be seen; the settlements were in the valleys or on the slopes in easier reach of spring water or creeks. But the roads also traversed a rugged and rolling topography of creek valleys, low-water crossings, ferries, homemade bridges, and stump-laden paths that tested the strength of man and animal. Teamsters traveled in caravans, camping out along the way. During rains and high water freighters waited to cross swollen rivers, sometimes forming impromptu camps of dozens of wagons. In the winter the rivers could freeze; the ice had to be cut to enable ferries to cross and bring wagons safely to the other side. Teamsters were careful to have their animals ice-shod in order to safely maneuver frozen creeks and icy trails. The main roads also attracted a constant flow of men seeking work. Denver Hollars in southern Stone County remembered this forest near the Wilderness Road. He said, "There wouldn't be a limb on that timber up to maybe 15 to 20 feet. You could just see between, just like poles out there. All the underbrush was killed out and the forest was clean and pretty."[31]

The Thomas Welch family moved from Galatia, Illinois, to Kansas in 1880 and to Springfield two years later, setting up their household several miles south of town. Over the next several years, the Welch family moved many more times as Thomas Welch would relocate along the network of main roads in pursuit of his occupation as a teamster. Thomas Welch was one of a number of men who freighted from Springfield to various Arkansas towns along the Wilderness Road, across Kimberling Ferry on the White River, and southward. After one season the Welches moved to the mouth of Bull Creek, Taney County, on the Springfield-Harrison Road. One of the hazards of freighting was exposure to such diseases as malaria, still common at this time; both Welch parents succumbed to this disease at an early age—the mother at age fifty-one, the father at fifty-five. Recurring bouts with fever convinced the surviving Welches to move to Ponce de Leon, a fading spa town in Stone County. A few years later the family moved yet again, this time "into the woods" at Spokane near the main road. Here the family lived in a log house and enjoyed a characteristic Ozark subsistence lifestyle, running their stock on the open range and raising fruit trees. In 1893 son Thomas (1875–1959) managed to attend school at Marionville Collegiate Institute, where at age seventeen he earned a third-grade teaching certificate. He subsequently taught school for fifteen years in Missouri and Oklahoma and also engaged in other professions. At one time or another he worked as a "stenographer, banker, farmer, stockman, realtor, and insurance agent" living out his life in southwest Missouri.[32]

Freighting along the main roads was common from the 1870s until 1906 when the railroad began to contract for volume freight, cutting into the long-distance overland hauling. Teamsters, however, continued short hauls to rail depots well into the 1920s. While newspapers in the 1880s gave wide publicity to surveys for railroad routes, they still continued to mention the freighters, who in the meantime proceeded to serve the population. A Forsyth newspaperman proclaimed that "Rough roads and much mud and little money, and big loads and mad mules are among the daily experiences of the men who take the place of a railway in this county."[33]

Freighters earned a well-deserved living for a hard life spent in the open at the mercy of the elements and for nights spent in wagon yards far from the creature comforts of home and family.

Well-known wagon yards included the Linch Pin Camp Ground on the Wilderness Road and Free Jack Spring on the Springfield-Harrison Road. Linch Pin, about three miles south of Reed's Spring, got its name from the linch pin, a cotter key that slipped through the end of an axle to hold a wagon wheel in place. The unusual name of Free Jack was derived from the fact that the Taney County location had once been the home site of a freed black slave, a rarity in that section of the Ozarks. It became a wagon yard when Charles Mahnkey and his family, originally members of the large St. Louis German-American community, located there. The Mahnkeys had initially purchased a Cedar County stock farm, but soon relocated themselves astride the Springfield-Harrison Road in Taney County south of Kirbyville. Free Jack Spring was on their property and their hired hand, Jack, a black freedman, built his cabin near there and tended the Mahnkey's livestock, lending his name to the spring. In the meantime, Charles Mahnkey built a new frame house for his family, which he painted white with yellow trim. This brightly painted frame house was a novel sight in a traditional Ozarks neighborhood that otherwise consisted of unpainted log buildings. The Mahnkeys soon noticed the significant wagon traffic passing their farm and decided to speculate on the trade. Charles built a camphouse with bunks, equipped it with a stove and benches, and enclosed a large barn and wagon yard. He purchased extra hay, fodder, and corn from neighbors to resell, and his wife, Mattie Mahnkey, baked extra biscuits for hungry freighters. Charles was well-suited to this enterprise as he was an extrovert and master Ozark storyteller who entertained customers with his repertoire of tales. Free Jack Spring flourished for a dozen years until Charles Mahnkey's death in 1904.[34]

Mrs. Mahnkey's family then moved into Kirbyville where she and her children managed a small hotel and livery. Kirbyville, established by Springfield merchants after the Civil War, had a reputation as a service center and small manufacturing (grain and cotton milling) center. The town's general stores supplied settlers and freighters on the Springfield-Harrison Road which ran through it. In 1881 a Springfield newspaper reported that "Taney County has hauled enough cedar posts to Springfield which if sawed into lumber would furnish half the State of Kansas with pails, churns, tubs, etc."[35] The comment indicated the importance of the local timber economy, much of which came from Arkansas through Kirbyville, and signified the importance of the Springfield-Harrison Road as a corridor for traffic in raw, bulk resources bound for Springfield. For the return trip, or for deliveries south, teamsters loaded their empty wagons with value-added manufactured goods purchased in Springfield.

A wagon master near Kirbyville described freighting in the early 1890s as an honorable trade and one that paid above average for hard work and long hours. The men who became the freighters were "hickory tough, handy with tools," had extreme confidence in their horses or mules, and took pride in their work. They drove narrow-wheeled wagons painted in bright colors —reds, greens, and yellow striping. They carried waterproof tarps to protect their load; each wagon had a "jockey box" full of tools and grease. Freighters also stocked a grub box with mobile kitchenware and durable camp food. The only pretension that might be noticed in a wagon caravan was an extra touch of decoration on the harness such as good leather, brass buckles and rings, and occasionally pieces whittled from bone. The chime of bells fixed on the manes or harness alerted others of movement of the teams and helped locate the animals at night.[36]

Wagon trains typically consisted of a dozen wagons that could travel thirty miles on a good day. Freighters carried their own horse feed, but also relied on the roadside camps. Once in camp, the men indulged in storytelling, skygazing, and singing. If someone had a fiddle, the young men might perform a dance. A stopover in Springfield offered the opportunity to visit the city's many night spots before loading merchandise the next morning for the return trip. The freighters could be an independent lot, but their movement along primary roads in wagons loaded with trade goods helped to lessen the social and economic isolation of people who lived along the routes. The teamster made around four dollars a day, but he had to deduct his expenses and pay for the frequent repairs that had to be made. Local freighting in wagons did not disappear until the introduction of trucks in the 1920s.

Among commodities freighted out of the White River country was cotton. The upper White River valley in Taney and Ozark Counties had a climate that allowed for modest cotton production, and the crop was an important source of income for local growers and laborers. Small gins were scattered across Taney County, and the associated trade looms large in the romance of local history. Most settlers had a small cotton patch for domestic consumption (not baled or reported in economic statistics), but commercial growers who shipped their cotton to Springfield by wagon stood to make good profits. The local trade around the county always received notice in the newspapers, and the brisk seasonal cotton trade in small hamlets encouraged festive days at the mercantiles. After the railroad came, cotton still made for much conversation and provided seasonal jobs at picking time.

Cotton bales averaged five hundred pounds, and wagons usually hauled two, though some reminiscences report three. Cotton production for the export market fluctuated with changes in the weather, always a significant factor in a cotton region this far north. The aggregate cotton production in Missouri came primarily from the Mississippi lowlands in southeast Missouri, especially Dunklin County, where the climate and soil were more ideal, but small productions from Taney and Ozark Counties, where the yields per acre were the lowest in the state, were included in government reports. Wagons loaded with cotton grown in Ozark County headed for Chadwick, while most of the Taney wagons went to Springfield. A train of a dozen wagons was considered a large caravan, and before the railroad, farmers even shipped a few bales on cedar rafts downriver to Batesville, Arkansas, where both the bales and rafts were sold.

Taney County had a good cotton year in 1906; sales in seed and bales amounted to over thirty-six thousand dollars, although the 608 bales produced amounted to only one percent of the state total. In the years from 1903 through 1909 Taney exported an average of 700 bales annually, grown on two to three thousand acres. The labor-intensive nature of cotton growing involved family members of all ages and provided jobs to dozens of pickers and ginners as well as the teamsters. The cotton business had a brief, final flourish during World War I, but commercial cotton culture virtually disappeared by the depression.[37]

As late as 1900 the Missouri Pacific Railway and the Missouri State Board of Immigration still promoted Missouri lands, but especially the Ozarks, as a "land of independence and plenty for homesteaders and capitalists." Rural Missouri, during the 1890s, claimed 60 percent of Missouri's increase in population while a period of prosperity from 1896 to 1913 tripled per-capita wealth.[38] Although white settlers had entered southwest Missouri in the first decade of the nineteenth century, a near century of habitation had not brought an end to frontier conditions. Geographical barriers contributed to the area's physical isolation and its relatively low population density. Economic development in the Ozarks lagged far behind that of other regions, and there was a marked absence of skilled specialization. In every county there were notable exceptions, of course—Stone and Taney Counties had flour mills, and cotton gins operated in Taney. Milling and ginning were not full-time occupations though, but seasonal work which supplemented stock-raising agriculture. The lack of skilled specialization, along with the difficulties of hauling freight over the area's rugged terrain and poorly developed road system, inhibited the maturation of commercialized trade and kept these preindustrial counties cash poor.

Frontier conditions in the upper White River region had been somewhat mitigated after 1870 with the arrival of the Frisco Railroad in Springfield. The movement of people and products by rail increased the overland freight traffic from the southern hinterlands and stimulated commerce throughout southwest Missouri. Business lessened isolation, developed an outlook for trade and society beyond the neighborhood valleys, brought cash into more common usage, and encouraged a more cosmopolitan philosophy which valued modern communication, education, and institutions. The proliferation of newspapers, telephones, small public schools (that replaced the old subscription schools), churches, and fraternal societies within these counties was evidence of this more cosmopolitan attitude.

Changes that occurred later—between 1905 and 1930—brought to maturation those transitions that had begun slowly after 1870. There were, however, significant differences between the socioeconomic transformations that took place before 1900 and those that came after. The expansion in business and cultural outlook after 1900 came at a quickened pace. The gradual evolution in these areas up to 1900 lessened the conditions of a perpetuated frontier, while twentieth-century developments finally spelled the demise of the Ozarks arrested frontier. Exactly when "the frontier" ended in the Ozarks will be debated into the future and dependent upon the variations in definition for the term *frontier*. There is still no scholarly consensus on what *frontier* means exactly.

The modernization of the Ozarks spanned several generations, and the process by which this transformation unfolded can be illustrated in the lives and experiences of selected families as they struggled to adapt to changing circumstances. Ben Stults (1845–1930) was born in Kentucky, reared on the prairies of Illinois, and came with his family to Jasper County, Missouri, in 1866 to work in the lead and zinc mines. Ben was beset with rheumatism and asthma, but these afflictions did not prevent him from becoming a market hunter; quail and deer were his favorite quarry. As game became scarce on the prairies of southwest Missouri, he joined others in hunting trips to the Black and White Rivers in Arkansas. Ben worked in the mines, too, but bad health convinced him to move in 1883 with his wife and small children to Stone County, Missouri, where he settled on a high ridge along the Wilderness Road.[39]

The Stults family moved into a hewed-log house with a stick and mud chimney. "My women folks cried to see what a House they had to live in," said Stults, so he immediately hauled rocks to build a new chimney. He then turned to hunting, his first love. The first year in Stone County he killed forty-two deer and earned around thirty-five dollars for the hides. He compensated for his asthma by training a mule to carry him over the rough terrain. In the winter he loaded slain deer and dead hogs on wooden sleds that he pulled over the frozen or snow-covered ground to his cabin. Stults fondly remembered these pioneering years but admitted that the time was less than romantic for his wife, who longed for the conveniences in a railroad town.

Some big game such as bear, panther, and wolves had not yet been hunted out in the Ozarks, and these animals were still numerous enough to complement the available kill in deer, turkey, and squirrel. Stults enjoyed a reputation as an expert hunter; soon friends and their acquaintances from Carthage, Joplin, Webb City, and Oronogo came to Stone County for hunting trips and camped in Ben's barn. Ben said they brought "lots of Beer and whiskey. Some wouldn't hunt at all, Just Stay in camp and drink." Camp life, then as now, was a time for socializing and conviviality. Hunting and outdoor life were not traditions in all Ozark families, and neighbors to Stults asked him to guide them on nearby expeditions. Some newcomers to Stults's neighborhood had no familiarity with the wild denizens of the surrounding woods; one neighbor's son refused to shoot a deer because he thought it was a goat. By 1890 hunting and the changes in habitat wrought by agriculture were beginning to take their toll on the wild animal population, and Stults noticed the depleted numbers of game in Stone County. But he still accompanied wagonloads of hunters who came for fall outings. Stults told them where to position themselves while he and his deer dogs ran the game to his waiting clients.

By 1905, as railroad construction through Stone County progressed, Stults could look back on two decades of making a summer crop, feeding stock in the winter, searching out bee trees, and hunting for the market. He could recall the days when it was possible to go in any direction and find an abundance of game. But Stults also desired modern conveniences. He cleared timber to make a farm, traveled ten miles to get his mail and groceries, and went fourteen miles to vote. As new neighbors thickened the woods, they elected Stults as a justice of the peace, and the experienced hunter worked to establish a township and to get a mail route to within two miles of his house. Then local citizens built a school within three hundred yards of his house. Within two miles of his house was the new hamlet of Ruth that had been built beside the railroad that ran through Roark valley. Stults built a general store alongside the railroad depot and a frame twelve-room house next to his old log cabin. He witnessed orchards being planted up and down the Wilderness Road for commercial production. He started his own goat herd and watched "money changing hands" in times that seemed remarkably different from the frontier days and barter economy that had still existed merely twenty years earlier when he first arrived in Stone County. The old hunter, with his new store by the tracks, had now become a townsman in fact and spirit.

In 1883, the same year that Ben Stults came to Stone County, William E. Sharp (1868–1959) arrived there with his father and a family friend for a hunting trip. Thirteen years earlier they had left east Tennessee in a group migration that crossed into St. Louis with "sixty-five wagons and two-wheeled carts and four-horse, ox and mule teams." Some members of the party walked the entire way. Later, neighbors of the Sharps moved the one hundred miles from Dade to Stone County and sent back favorable reports which inspired the Sharps to scout the same country. The inexpensive land that was available for homesteading appealed to father W. G. Sharp "as he had always been a renter."[40]

In the spring of 1884 the Sharps moved onto a "run down farm" in

NEWCOMERS JOIN THE NATIVES

Will Sharp with a gray timber wolf, late 1920s
Walker Powell Collection

Stone County. On the way there Will Sharp noted the striking appearance of the Stone County Courthouse—it was pockmarked with bullet holes from the Civil War. When they arrived at Yocum Pond, W. G. Sharp purchased eighty acres of an improved farmstead and homesteaded a claim on an adjoining eighty. The price for this farm was five hundred dollars and his team and wagon. Will swapped two old guns for two sows who had fourteen piglets between them. Resident wolves, however, ate them all. Undaunted, Will fell in love with hunting in the Ozarks and reveled in the outdoors life. The previous owner of the Sharps' farm had built a deer lick thirty feet from the house, and he boasted of being able to kill deer by firing through the chinks in the logs of his house. The imagery fired the ambition of young Will.

One of the first changes the Sharps made was to move the deer lick three hundred yards from the house; they placed boards high in a nearby tree where at night they sat and waited above the scent of deer to kill the game. The farm had seventeen small fields, only an acre or two apiece, that were overgrown with thickets and thorns. The Sharps cleared and consolidated these patches into four fields. They straightened the fences to enclose small crops and then fixed up the barn and prepared to tend a small orchard. Mrs. Sharp did not like this new country where she could not easily attend church or send her children to school. After her untimely death, son Will learned the arts of sewing and cooking for his younger brothers. The family visited the markets at Marionville, on the Frisco Railroad, to obtain manufactured goods, although the Galena stores were much closer. The cash-poor Sharps resorted to the Ozarks tradition of barter to obtain their necessities. The Sharps dug roots—ginseng, golden-seal, and seneca—and in return these items secured flour, cloth, and general merchandise. When traveling, Will kept a sharp eye along the trails for wooden brake blocks that had fallen off the wagons so he could reclaim the metal nails for use on the farm. Both a hunter and a gatherer, Will traded deer saddles (hindquarters of a butchered deer), hides, and black-berries to merchants in Galena for staples to help support the family.

For forty years Will trapped, hunted, farmed, and eventually learned to hack ties. In later years, in 1924, his fame as a hunter landed him a new job. He was hired by the federal government to trap the remaining wolves in the Ozarks. Will and his fifteen-year-old son, June, packed up their camping gear, grub box, camera, fiddle, and guitar and went off to spend several weeks in south-central Missouri on the trail of the last generation of wolves in Missouri. Wolves, as it turned out, were not their only victims. In one county alone, they caught eighty-six dogs in traps. At the close of his famed wolf hunts, Will and his wife, Bessie (1873–1953), purchased Linch Pin, the old freighters' stop turned tourist camp south of Reed's Spring. The property had tourist cabins, a small store, and a filling station that allowed the couple to earn a living and to keep in touch with neighbors and the traveling public.

Sharp's legendary reputation gained additional stature in the 1950s. He hired out to talk, sing, and fiddle at the mouth of Marvel Cave for the entertainment of tourists. Travelers flocking to the White River hills hungered for local color and authentic hill folk, and Will Sharp filled the bill perfectly. The old hunter had successfully bridged the gap between the old Ozarks frontier and the modern age—his lifetime in the hills, his trove of experiences and tales, became a salable commodity that city folk lapped up avidly. Like many a personable old-timer, Will saw the opportunity and effortlessly tailored his lifeways to the cravings of commerce and tourism for the "real" Ozarks.

German-Americans joined the old-stock Americans of Anglo-Celtic ancestry in the White River hills. Dominick Ingenthron and his family arrived in the United States in 1854. He migrated to the Ohio River valley and fought for the Union. After the war he moved his family to Chicago, and then to Jasper County, Missouri, where he worked in a mercantile business. In 1873 the Ingenthrons homesteaded in Taney County. Skilled in masonry, he built a stone house in 1875. Young Joe Ingenthron, destined to become locally well known, married into another recently arrived German-American family. His bride, Eliza Ann Cornelison, came from a family who had also come to Taney after the Civil War.[41] The Ingenthrons located on the upland divide that separated the Bull and Swan Creek watersheds not far north of Forsyth.

In 1886, after years of pursuing a frugal subsistence lifestyle, Joe and Eliza Ingenthron began the building of their final homeplace. They hired Jessie Kenyon to build the rooms for the "big house," a fine hewn-log dog-trot with a dressed stone chimney and stone-walled cellar that included a

The Ingenthron dog-trot house, September 1982
James Denny Collection

drain down the hill to keep the contents of wooden barrels dry. Their homestead was distinctive for its cedar privy out by the chicken house, a privacy room constructed in the outdoors for the women. The Ingenthrons spent more than four years of meticulous work on the house before they finally moved in in 1891. In 1898 they carried their last pail of water from a spring. Their water now came from a well capped with a windlass that stood near the house. They planted an orchard and constructed an evaporator building for drying fruit. Their cattle, hogs, and sheep roamed the open range, but Joe Ingenthron was the first in his neighborhood to enclose his land with wire fencing. The Ingenthrons, like their neighbors, had a cotton patch for domestic use only. They took loose cotton to a gin and used all they raised to fabricate "quilts, comforts, saddle blankets, pads, cushions, and thread." By 1896 the neighborhood had grown to such an extent that Joe Ingenthron and his neighbors gathered together to establish Riverview School to educate their children closer to home. Their lifestyle combined a primitive plenty gained from the land with an enlightened outlook that embraced planned and progressive living at every turn.

Several miles south of the Ingenthrons lived the Gertens, another German-American family who arrived in Taney County not long after the Ingenthrons had moved into the new dog-trot house at their model farmstead. Father Gerten had learned to fabricate smoking pipes in Germany, before he immigrated to America in 1869 and settled along the Mississippi River at Fulton, in northwest Illinois. For two decades the Gertens lived in town until low foreign tariffs forced him to close his shop. Farmland in Illinois was beyond the financial means of the Gertens so they looked elsewhere. Daughter Margaret Gerten wrote, "The only thing to do was to go where the land was open for homesteading." Some Illinois neighbors had recently homesteaded in the Ozarks and sent back favorable reports, so in the fall of 1896, the Gertens liquidated their assets and by February of the following year were established on a claim near Cedar Creek, about four miles from the White River. Mr. Gerten soon learned that his former $1.50 daily wage shrank to fifty cents a day in the Ozarks, and he set about to master multiple economic strategies to maintain a living.[42]

The Gertens quickly discovered that their Illinois experience had ill-prepared them to live in the Ozark woods. In the Ozarks the "woods surrounded us on every side, as there was no clearing closer than a half mile."

They found themselves not only isolated but also broke. They spent most of their money in the move and were faced with the need to purchase farm-making tools. "So many things to buy," wrote Margaret, "tools from plows to hoes, picks, crow-bars, saws and nails. We needed seeds and other items to say nothing of staples. This took cash, without any hope of income before fall." As Margaret remembered, the family of six learned the art of living on the Ozark frontier the hard way. The immigrants hired a man and team to break new ground so they could plant cotton, melons, peanuts, tobacco, corn, cow peas, and other crops as soon as possible.

They learned that life on the open range had to be tackled one event at a time. They purchased a load of straw and stacked it on the ground preparatory to filling their sleeping ticks with straw. The range cattle, however, ate all the straw, and they had to substitute oak leaves. The "firey crown" of the woods set ablaze by cattlemen startled the newcomers. The Gertens kept tubs of water in readiness for wetting sacks should it become necessary to beat out fires advancing toward their rail fences; they learned from their neighbors that keeping a clean-swept yard also acted as a fire-break around the house. Clearing timber, splitting rails, burning brush, and picking up rocks in the rain took a hard physical toll on Father Gerten, who was more accustomed to the softer life of a shopkeeper. He learned that his neighbors joked among themselves about their property lines that "curved and twisted to take in every choice tree near their claim." Gerten and his neighbors selectively cut the cedar and walnut for export, while in the wintertime they cut cord wood to make extra cash selling firewood locally.

The children learned to set traps and catch small game for marketable hides. Mrs. Gerten kept her hens in a log chicken house and marketed eggs year-round, which netted modest spending money. Unlike many of their neighbors the Gertens did not have a detached kitchen. Mother Gerten had her cookstove in the house. In warm weather they moved it into the yard under shade trees; this arrangement worked fine except on rainy days. With the approach of planting season the family eagerly looked forward to produce from the spring garden to add variety to the winter fare of "salt pork, eggs, and corn bread." Neighbors taught the Gertens to plant by the moon and showed them how to make corn dodgers described as "baked meal, salt, and water, and bread that looked like a pale stepping stone."

The cows sometimes ate wild onions that imparted a strong onion taste to their milk and ruined it. Henry Gerten, Margaret's teenage brother, developed a skill in killing squirrels with rocks, or knocking them from trees so the dogs could catch them. The subsequent meal of squirrel and noodles was welcome relief from "pork and more pork." They dug a cellar and walled it with rock. All the while such intense labor amused the Anglo-Celtic settlers who scoffed at the backbreaking work of the Gertens.

The hard-working Gertens kept busy all the time, but found it difficult to produce much surplus for the market. The women could not purchase "ready-made clothes" and had to make their own. The family was hard pressed to acquire calico for homemade dresses, overalls, and shirts, nor could they buy shoes. The Gerten men needed all their discretionary money to keep the farming operation afloat. All the young stock born to the mature animals were sold for cash, and the revenues from their cotton crop was uncertain at best. Father Gerten, reflecting upon his former trade, and feeling increasing anxiety to make a better living, located red clay on his claim, built a log shop and kiln to bake pipes, and used the cane along the White River to fabricate stems. He produced pipes for several months to build an inventory and then ran a two-week route to sell them; this brought much-needed cash back to the farm. It seemed that the determination of the former shopkeeper to succeed in homesteading would eventually triumph.

The arrival of two other German-American families, the Muellers from Illinois and the Antons from Nebraska, made possible the first social life the Gertens had enjoyed since moving to the Ozarks. Before then they had not integrated into the local Anglo-Celtic social fabric. They had heard of the local fishfries and revival meetings, but "never went."

The three German families traded work and toured the countryside together; one of their outings was to Marble Cave. All three families grew fruits and vegetables, an activity "regarded by many [neighbors] as a sheer waste of time and energy." Margaret Gerten never ceased to wonder how her neighbors could live on one farm for several years but not establish any orchards, vines, or gardens to provide variety in their diet. She marveled over nearby "improvements" of several barns in various stages of decay, all filled with manure. Instead of the owner hauling the fertilizer to the fields, the old-stock Americans simply built another barn. Neighbors left girdled trees in the field for years to finally die and fall over. Margaret remembered them as "gaunt skeletons" that were eventually hauled from the fields and cut for firewood. These old-stock woodsmen, who had opened many clearings, followed a time-worn homesteading pattern. When faced with drought and bad times, they, to use Margaret Gerten's words, "just loaded the few possessions they had room for in the wagon, disposed of their stock, closed the door and left" for another claim. The Gertens never did understand what they saw as the wasteful practices of the nomadic stockmen.

Just as Father Gerten was nearing the date to finalize his claim in 1903 and receive his government patent on the land, he became ill and died. His widow traveled to Forsyth and completed the transaction. Her claim was denied, however, for some bureaucratic technicalities, and Mrs. Gerten and her son John had to continue living on the homestead another three years before they finally sold it to a northerner who never lived on the place. The surviving Gertens then settled their affairs in the Ozarks and moved to Puget Sound, Washington, where family members found work in the woods and mills. Margaret Gerten, in concluding her reminiscence of homesteading in Taney County, remembered what her father had learned about the land. "To possess a piece of land, even a small patch, was something to be proud of. It gave one status. The smaller the patch, the more it was treasured."

In 1898, the year after the Gertens came, a small group migration of four families left Vernon County, Missouri, for the White River country. John and Malissa Sylvester and the young families of their three children—Riley, Pleasant, and William David (W. D.)—were lured by the promotions of land for homesteaders and settled a few miles west of the James River on Flat Creek, just west of the Stone-Barry county line. Eighteen years earlier they had left Indiana in covered wagons for a new life in the West. During their odyssey they had worked in railroad towns along the Kansas City Southern and had become familiar with the commerce and society of modern towns. W. D. (1867–1938) had published a newspaper, managed a general store, and been postmaster of Worland, Missouri.[43]

W. D. kept a diary of his homesteading experience. He was not an outdoorsman who sought the chase, but a tradesman like Father Gerten, who wanted to farm. To accomplish his goal W. D. had to teach school, practice his master craftsman skills in carpentry, and commute back to

W. D. Sylvester's homestead
Edna Williams Collection

the Tri-State Mineral District to find work in a larger job market and
obtain some cash. It cost W. D. $18.00, plus an additional $17.30 in local
fees, to enter his homestead claim in 1903.

Sylvester's diary reveals that he undertook numerous building projects. He traded a horse for a fourteen-by-sixteen-foot log house that he
disassembled and moved to his claim, where he rebuilt it. He hauled rock
for a hearth and fireplace, built a stone fence, and constructed a stone
forge and lime kiln. He added a kitchen ell to his house, and built a hen-
house, a smokehouse, a fodder shed, and a carpenter's shop; he fabricated
a stable, a crib, and a hog pen for stock. He surveyed his property lines,
built a road, and fenced his yard. To obtain the necessary wood, W. D.
sawed logs, cut posts, split rails, rived boards, and hewed railroad ties to

sell. He worked on his house and that of his parents, John and Malissa, and spent many hours in his shop repairing tools and keeping his logging wagon ready for work.

Sylvester saw his pioneering experience as one of hard work and many disappointments. At first, tie buyers did not accept his primitive railroad ties; tree limbs fell on him and left him crippled for a considerable time. He chased his contrary hogs across the open range trying to get them home to feed and to butcher, and mules, too, ran off, requiring still more time-consuming treks through the hills. Sylvester learned the hard way that working in the woods was dangerous and that animals had minds of their own.

Despite their many hardships, the Sylvesters were committed to improving their claim. They planted shrubbery, grapevines, and fruit trees, and tapped nearby maple trees to make syrup. They raised stock, grain, poultry, and tobacco. The grain they hauled to area mills. W. D. and his wife, Nettie, planted a garden, gathered wild fruit, and burned the woods in accordance with traditional practice. Managing fires was everyone's business.

The carpenter's shop was a special place for W. D.; he took pride in creating domestic furniture, crafting bedsteads, bookcases, chairs, clothing baskets, coffins, and desks. He also made smaller items such as potato mashers, rolling pins, gun stocks, tool handles, and tools themselves. The Sylvesters were also community minded; W. D. and his father donated logs to make new seats at the Horny Buck school where W. D. taught a term.

But troubles continued. The older Sylvesters both died at age sixty, and cash money was still difficult to acquire in the barter economies of the countryside. In 1904 the Sylvesters moved to Pittsburg, Kansas, where W. D. could make $2.50 a day. He and Nettie had one son and reared three more of their own in Kansas. They held on to their homestead, but trips back to Flat Creek were rare until 1917 when they returned to the Ozarks for good.

The Sylvesters had leased their Ozark land for pasture in order to pay the taxes, but alas, someone had stolen their house. A neighbor evidently assumed the log house was abandoned and appropriated it for his own use. The Sylvesters borrowed three hundred dollars from a bank to build a new house on a ridge above Dry Hollow. W. D. used a popular pattern book available at lumberyards and constructed a bungalow. Though the house design was novel, the materials were traditional—he built of logs. Still the final result was a fashionable, rustic house that included a porch with native-rock veneer along the lower levels. Next he built a new workshop and then built new outbuildings for the farm.

By then, W. D.'s considerable building skills were in demand, and the expanding railroad economy created new opportunities. Fred Akin, a canning manufacturer, hired Sylvester to build two factories. W. D. and son Raleigh built houses and barns throughout the countryside and constructed their own brooder house for the family poultry business. The versatile carpenter also built a boat for Fred Akin. W. D. then bought a sawmill and resumed making and marketing timber products. In 1923 the *Crane Chronicle* in Stone County recognized his "rare talent of wood craft" and thereby helped publicize his custom work. "Billy" Sylvester, as he came to be known in his advancing years, fashioned highchairs, rocking chairs, cedar chests, clocks, dining tables, porch swings, and library tables, and sold furniture wholesale. His rocking chairs seemed to be a favorite in the Ozarks—in 1922 alone he sold forty-one of them. In time W. D. ordered his own letterhead stationery with the banner, "Builder of Fine Furniture." Billy died in 1938, but his descendants still continue to live on the original homestead.

Not everyone who tried homesteading in the Ozarks stuck it out, as has been demonstrated by the Gerten experience. There were hundreds of disappointments for flatlander families who left agricultural lands in the Midwest or the Great Plains for the hardscrabble existence on an Ozarks homestead; more than one homesteader later returned to more familiar lifeways elsewhere. But some of these short-lived newcomers in the White River country had children who as adults never forgot their formative and unusual years on the Ozarks open range. The reminiscences of the Shamels and Johnsons provide additional perspectives on the challenges of trying to establish a foothold in the Ozarks.

In the mid-1890s the Shamel family arrived at Greasy Creek in south Barry County, Missouri, a few miles north of the White River and the Arkansas line. The neighborhood they moved into was still rooted in the lifestyle and folkways of the arrested Ozark frontier. Harold Shamel, a youth upon arrival, vividly remembered the immense number of log buildings—

houses, barns, smokehouses, and farm dependencies—built in clearings of the forest. Some houses had no windows, admitting light only through open doorways. Women who had spent lifetimes on the forested frontier sat with men chewing and spitting into the fireplace and even wore boots. The children "could wander all day in the woods" without encountering barbed wire, and men spent the winter working in the woods. The fireplace and stove consumed cord after cord of wood.[44]

The newcomers marveled at the clean, open woods, managed by fire and grazing cattle and hogs. Pigs sneaked into fenced cornfields; and sometimes angry owners turned dogs on them to chase them away. Some neighbors fattened their winter's pork by keeping hogs in caves. The Shamel children received hand-me-down knitted underwear from city relatives. The incidental exposure of these store-bought underclothes at school was cause for schoolyard commentary; local children wore homemade underwear consisting of "white outing flannel that was fleece lined." The natives thought that the newly arrived Shamels were rich. The Shamels, however, knew better. The daily wage for labor was only fifty cents, and almost all commerce was by barter. Father Shamel tired of plowing through the rocks and longed for fields "where he would not hear the grind of the rocks all the time." The last straw came when a plow handle hit him in the groin and ruptured him. This incident drove him to write relatives in Kansas about joining them at a Santa Fe Railroad town. Years later, a grown Harold Shamel met a cousin in St. Louis who had lived across the creek from them in the 1890s. For her the memories of Ozark homesteading were too painful. She could not even bring herself to talk about the place.[45]

Preston Johnson, a child of southerners from Kentucky and Alabama and a diarist in the Ozarks, spent his teenage years during the mid-1890s in western Douglas County. His father went broke farming on the Grand River, near Chillicothe, Missouri, so he next chose homesteading in the White River country. His new farmstead consisted of an abandoned squatter's claim on 160 acres with a single-pen log hut and three fruit trees. The hut served as temporary quarters while the family built a new four-room house of sawn lumber. The inside walls of the new house had slats to cover the studs, but the ceiling was never finished and the house never was completely painted. A few years later an add-on room was started, but it was never finished either. Sometimes the men fled the house to sleep under the stars as chiggers and fleas kept them awake if they remained inside. Needless to say, this was not a tight house. Sleeping outdoors had its hazards as well—the family dog was kept near to warn of snakes.[46]

It seemed like Johnson menfolk were endlessly cutting wood—for fence rails, railroad ties, posts, clapboards, and fence paling. The father had wanted to expand his homestead and give eighty acres to each son, but the boys preferred working in town for wages to the unending, back-breaking labor on the homestead. The Johnsons scoured the woods for roots and herbs, but it was hard for newcomers to distinguish one plant from another. The family traded corn for medical service and bartered a heifer for a new carpet.

The teenage boys explored caves with pine torches, but spent more time trapping game and killing fish. They learned from the locals how to use bows and arrows to shoot fish in shallow water[47] and made pen traps for small game—their rabbits sold for three to five cents each. They made rawhide shoelaces from tanned squirrel hides. The boys spent their leisure hours in such sports as rat killing or playing marbles in the center of a dirt floor in a neighbor's cabin. The father groaned to his family that their old-stock neighbors "had no desire to go elsewhere or accumulate [property]." "They seemed innocent and freehearted and bore no malice. They had a wholesomeness that does not exist in densely populated districts." While Father Johnson developed a kindly tolerance for neighbors who enjoyed their easy living, and cherished his vision for his sons becoming landowners, Mrs. Johnson never held a warm feeling for the Ozarks. She said that "the Ozarks is a good place to die." She obviously never felt that the Ozarks were a good place to live. When she finally departed for the state of Washington to join relatives and left her husband, who wanted to remain and pay off debts in the Ozarks, she resigned herself to this decision by saying that "we came here with little or nothing and we are going away with less."

The Ozark woods dominated the lives of natives and newcomers alike. The woods, full of people, was the setting for work and play. Clearing the woods amounted to progress in a settlement and hope for the future. Corporate promoters clamored for forest products, and progressive-minded journalists applauded every effort to tame and exploit the woods—forest that could not be transmuted into profit stood in the way of capitalist boos-

Shooting fish in
shallow water
Ripley County Museum

terism. The act of clearing timber in the name of progress was perceived as
an essential step in the transition from wilderness to civilization. It fed an
exuberant confidence embraced by all pioneers on American frontiers.
Midwestern migrants who came to the White River hills, especially after
1890, wanted to accelerate the farm-making and settlement process. As we
have seen, some were successful and stayed while others left in failure or
frustration. In order to become a successful long-term resident in the
Ozarks, new arrivals had to learn, often painfully, to conform to a subsistence frontier economy that was not founded on the capitalist concept of
creating exportable surpluses to help drive the engines of a large scale market economy. Many immigrants of the 1890s, however, wanted to produce

---

marketable products for a cash return, but cash was constantly in short supply. The subsistence lifestyle, so loved by frontiersmen who knew only the pioneering culture, continued to flourish far into the twentieth century. Stockmen knew that "cows rather than plows" was an easier living, an easier living that is, as long as they had an unbridled access to a bountiful open range.

Rail transportation in the White River hills later created economies that inevitably moved families from their independent subsistence into cash markets, new consumerism, and cosmopolitan cultures. Frugal Ozarkers already enjoyed an easy living on the open range and a moderate prosperity, but the investments of logging and mining corporations would transform the social and economic landscape—for good or bad the market would change the lives of Ozarkers. The lumber and railroad work camps were the first signs that these changes were coming. Novelist Harold Bell Wright witnessed the embryonic transition when he rode the White River Railway to Galena and through Stone County on his way to Inspiration Point in 1906 to set about writing his great novel. In *The Shepherd of the Hills* he concluded the book with the "shepherd's" observation that the railroad and many new people would come down Roark valley and that the event would change forever the romantic respite that he had enjoyed.[48]

Native Ozarkers recognized the limitations of their environment and society and embraced the new opportunities of progress. C. C. Blansit, a veteran stockman in Taney County at Walnut Shade, became a realtor and advertised the properties that he knew the best—stock ranches for sale. He took pride in the fact that the land was cheap compared to northern prairie lands. They were "not level and our people are glad of it," he proclaimed, for the hilly Ozarks was a place for "good chances for the poor man to get a home." Blansit touted the open-range economy as a way to get a start in building a homestead.[49] Fellow realtor J. W. Blankinship, a former Arkansas schoolteacher turned rancher and businessman in southwest Taney County, also championed open-range stock raising, the poultry, fruit, and mineral industries, as well as mail service and phone lines. Blankinship asked of the travelers riding the railroad on their way to "the Heart of the Ozarks" to give the Ozarks a chance and to not condemn it on first sight. He warned newcomers that they could not "judge the merits of the country from the appearance of the premises of the average native farmer. He does not depend on the products of the soil alone for his living. That would require too much hard work. Neither does he appreciate the importance of having his farm 'look good.' True, he does some planting and goes through the form of cultivation. But his living comes more easily and more surely [on the open range]." Blankinship spoke to the midwesterners who were used to row-crop agriculture and unfamiliar with the easy living of Ozark stockmen. He concluded his pamphlet with an assurance that Ozarkers were just as interested in prosperity as anyone else.[50]

The notion of American mobility dominates our overall approach to demographic history, not the persistence of settlement in one place over time. The settlement experiences in Stone and Taney Counties is no exception to this generalization. Midwesterners by the thousands poured into Missouri in the late nineteenth century, and many headed for the open range and cheap lands of the Ozarks. At the same time old-stock settlers from the southern uplands continued their western migrations into the Ozarks, as their forebears had done for generations. While newcomers to the Ozarks appreciated the romance and the hospitality of the region, their presence had already set the future of Stone and Taney Counties on a new course. The 1890s peripatetic midwestern immigrants arriving in the 1890s were not seeking the perpetual ease of open-range lifestyles. Their approach to the land was different, and they wanted new and better schools and churches, volunteer associations, and middle-class affluence. One such newcomer, promoter Truman Powell, longed for the passing of the old ways and the introduction of new economies and more opportunities for money making in the Ozarks. Other recent arrivals included J. K. Ross ("Old Matt") and Levi Morrill ("Uncle Ike"), who would forever be associated with tourist-turned-author Harold Bell Wright in his famous novel. Each of them saw an improved future in an expanding economy. Ross, a multitalented man, was inspired by the boom town of Branson and speculated in his own townsite promotion, while Morrill enjoyed the daily society of a neighborhood constantly at his door for mail, news of local business, and gossip. W. H. Lynch, an anxious capitalist, would come back to his Marble Cave, always hoping to capitalize on the great natural wonder. And W. H. Johnson would welcome the timber and tourist industries by building Hollister, a whole new town whose very existence represented the future.

"Nature's Own Remedy"

Float Fishing and Ozark Tourism

A GUIDED OZARK float trip of the late nineteenth or early twentieth century was an event long remembered by sportsmen lucky enough to participate. For urban townsmen from midwestern railroad towns such an expedition was often their first outdoors encounter in the forested hinterlands of the Ozarks. The discovery by affluent and influential midwestern outsiders of an Ozarks region that abounded not only in fish and game but also with vast reserves of timber and minerals led to both appreciation and exploitation. The imaginations of many businessmen-sportsmen were sparked by the prospect of speculation in minerals and timberlands; they saw the possibility of developing agricultural and manufacturing markets in conjunction with rail export. Others perceived an environment worthy of conservation, but rarely offered more than journalistic musings. Investors and vacationers alike came to imbibe the shadowed stillness of enchanted settings; the float trip provided an exotic adventure to relax impatient capitalists and calm the anxieties, real or perceived, of urban living. The float-trip tradition begun by these tourists became part of a new middle-class Arcadian culture in the Ozarks. The following discussion introduces a regional context for the immediate success of float fishing on the James and White Rivers as the White River Railway was completed in 1906.

There were no travelers in the Ozarks who could properly be called tourists until after the Civil War. It was the advancing railroad construction in the 1870s and afterward that linked numerous towns and counties, allowing tourists to ride the rails on excursions to new Ozark boom towns to survey locally significant "curiosities." These sites were brought to public attention through the published survey work of geologists and other state-supported scholars and of journalists who provided reports and feature articles. Correspondents frequently made their own tours and recorded their personal experiences. Additional publicity came from railroad promoters who hired photographers to develop promotional brochures aimed at selling land, opportunity, and tourism. All of these sources induced men from an urban corporate world to explore the Ozark hinterlands in search of wilderness adventures and economic opportunities.

Caves and outdoor recreation were leading attractions in the Ozarks. In Nathan Parker's *Missouri As It Is in 1867*, geologist G. C. Swallow and Parker announced that there were "numerous spacious caves" in southern Missouri.[1] By the nation's centennial in 1876, tourists read about Indian mounds, springs, arches, and caves in Greene, Christian, and Stone Counties, which were considered "tourist resorts for pleasure-seekers." Caves near Galena were so well known that they were "visited annually by many tourists."[2]

The extension of the St. Louis and San Francisco Railroad (known as the Frisco after 1876)[3] from Rolla to the southwest Ozarks and Springfield opened new towns and economies to market and sportsmen hunters, tourists, and immigrants (including many ex-Union soldiers). Among the first destinations for tourists traveling to the interior Ozarks in the 1870s for recreation was Arlington, south of Rolla, for an outing on the Gasconade River. Charles Hallock, by 1877, advised sportsmen to bring their boats and camping gear and hire wagons at Arlington to transport themselves upriver. Later the St. Louis press described the conditions on trains for hunters who wanted to bring their dogs along for an outing.[4]

The ease of traveling on railroads which transected the wilds of the Missouri Ozarks gave rise to an episodic tourism supported by corporations who built and managed trunk and tram lines that connected with the national network. During these late nineteenth-century trips to Ozarks rivers and forests, sporting tourists took their gear and boats with them and hired teamsters and guides after they left the rail cars. The urban sportsmen initiated the float-trip adventures and introduced locals into recreation going downriver; eventually skilled boat builders who produced reusable craft for long-distance travel emerged in the Ozarks. The sale of local foodstuffs to the tourists attracted notice in the river valleys and in the local press. In 1879 the Missouri Fish Commission was established, and St. Louis sportsmen carefully noted where the Missouri fish commissioners restocked the rivers. Fish commissioners hired guides to show them springs and

Bird's eye view of Galena
Robert Wiley Collection

dumping points near strategic rail stops from where they could haul thousands of game fish from their hatcheries.[5] These Fish Commission dumping points became major destinations for urban float fishermen from St. Louis.[6]

During the 1880s a network of rail lines in southeast Missouri allowed sportsmen from St. Louis, Kentucky, Tennessee, and Illinois to make hunting and fishing safaris to the Black and Current Rivers in the Ozarks interior. Railroad and timber company executives and their guests journeyed to these rivers and occasionally built riverside clubhouses. Poplar Bluff became the nexus of rail lines in this region as early as 1872.[7] By the eighties, rail lines had been laid up the Black River valley across Butler County into Wayne County and to the timber hamlets of Mill Spring and Leeper. From there trunk lines led into Ozark timber camps; this rail network opened new areas of the southeast Ozarks to sportsmen, who made arrangements with corporate officials to be dropped off at a particular stop so they could float back to Poplar Bluff. This was the same route that outdoors writer Ozark Ripley

(James B. Thompson, one of the most influential outdoors writers) used in the early twentieth century. St. Louis and Memphis outdoorsmen established clubhouses on the Black and St. Francis Rivers near the St. Louis and Iron Mountain Railroad in northeast Arkansas. As the massive swamp drainage projects commenced in the southeast Missouri lowlands, sportsmen expanded their rail travel to this region and built new clubhouses in the swamplands.

The giant timber operations of Missouri Land and Mining, Ozark Land and Lumber, Himmelberger and Harrison, and other corporations in southeast Missouri opened a vast expanse of the Ozarks to sportsmen looking for Ozark float streams. Sometimes they received permission from tie rafters to float on a tie raft and fish or traveled on logging trains that took them ever further into the hinterlands to fresh hunting and fishing grounds. Ozark Ripley, for one, delighted in this form of travel into the southeast Missouri Ozarks backcountry. In his 1921 book, *Jist Huntin'*, a reminiscence of his travels in prior decades, Ripley wrote fondly of his "johnboat trips" on the Current and Eleven Point Rivers.[8]

The network of southeast Missouri tram lines experienced more expansion with the construction of the Kansas City, Fort Scott, and Gulf (Memphis) Railroad in the early 1880s and the subsequent extension of the Current River Railroad from Willow Springs to Van Buren. In 1888 two clubs incorporated—the Current River Fishing and Hunting Club in Ripley County and the Carter County Fishing and Shooting Club—that attracted many sportsmen to the Current River. In 1890 outdoorsmen from Johnson County, Missouri, rode the Current River Railroad to the end of the line and subsequently published a pamphlet of their trip, "Warrensburg Nimrods."[9] This classic account detailed the adventure of "True Sportsmen" from the city who engaged the romance of the backwoods. Their destination, the Current River Hunting and Fishing Club, included a boatswain among the directors and was representative of the dozens of similar sportsmen clubs constructed along the Ozark riverways as destinations for out-of-towners. Kansas City and Springfield businessmen patronized this club for more than fifty years.

Southeast Missouri never developed into a commercial float-fishing mecca, as happened so spectacularly in southwest Missouri. In southeast Missouri, exploitation rather than recreation was the principal pursuit.

Southeast Missouri sent the state's largest volume of marketable timber to mill in response to the national demand for railroad products; the industry reached its zenith during this time while southeast Missouri experienced a series of boom-and-bust company towns.[10] During this era, the Black and Current Rivers were the scene of giant timber rafts making their way to large sawmills. Some mill owners instructed supervisors to have lumber available to quickly nail together float boats on demand. By contrast, the James and White Rivers had a different ecology and a much smaller timber industry, one that lacked large river mills to produce float boats. The great tie and timber industry that characterized southeast Missouri had only pale cousins in southwest Missouri and northwest Arkansas. The tie and timber market in the White River country included some rafting, but it had numerous railheads at permanent towns situated along the twentieth-century railroads—the major tie traffic was overland, not on the rivers.[11] To these shipping points teamsters drove thousands of wagons loaded with ties. Consequently, the recreational float business on the James and White Rivers generally did not have to compete with the corporate timber industry.

Tourists and sportsmen continued their discoveries of different Ozark streams well into the twentieth century. By the late 1890s the *St. Louis Globe-Democrat* estimated that five thousand St. Louisans left Union Station and "took to the woods and waters" at the beginning of the fall season.[12] The traditional concept of river sport was hunting and fishing down the waterway. Late-model guns were the most expensive items in the boats, a crucial issue in the demand for stable, flat-bottom boats. The time was yet to come when Missouri game and fish would be considered community resources by statute. The only regulations were each man's conscience.

From southwest Missouri, Thomas Hart Benton described a rail trip taken in 1899 or 1900. His father took him from Neosho to Arlington, the Ozarks largest float boat depot at the turn of the century and a popular resort on the Gasconade River promoted by the Frisco Railroad. At the time, Perry Andres operated the outfitters' commissary. He had customers from throughout the Midwest and launched floaters in at least fourteen spots on the Gasconade and Big Piney Rivers. Typically, vacationers would step off a train, load their gear on wagons, travel overland

and upriver, and then float back in a "magnified skiff" to the railhead. Coming from southwest Missouri, the Bentons did not yet have convenient access to the James or White Rivers, as the commercial outfitting business had not yet blossomed in the White River hills.[13]

This situation was soon to change, however. The earlier construction in 1881 of the Kansas City, Fort Scott, and Gulf Railroad into Greene County and Springfield, the Queen City of the Ozarks, was a crucial event in tourist history. Springfield during the 1880s became a "tourist town" and a dynamic regional market center with rail connections to St. Louis, Kansas City, and the Southwest. This trade nexus significantly increased the overland traffic into northern Arkansas as freighters moved in and out of Springfield's markets while bringing not only goods but also their own lore of the sport to be had in the Arkansas hinterlands. Civic organizations from connected railroad towns communicated with their sister associations and took turns hosting community events. One active institution was the Missouri State Militia, with its marching pomp and ceremony, bands, flag-waving, and members who delighted in taking local excursions to see the sights.[14] It was members of a State Guard unit from Lamar who would purchase Marble Cave and become especially influential in promoting the Ozarks.

The press publicized popular activities for tourists in the Ozark outdoors. One such pastime was the search for Indian relics or burial sites, often a cave or rock shelter; another was to journey to a karst feature—a spring, a limestone arch, or, especially, a cave. The prevalence of karst features in the Ozarks was so attractive to settlers and visitors that early Ozarks tourism was truly "Karst Tourism"—and this is largely still true today.[15] Promoters in Stone County tried to mimic the success of Eureka Springs, Arkansas, by founding spa resort towns—some real, some existing only on paper. Examples included the fledgling spa resorts of Eau de Vie (1880), Reno (1881), Ponce de Leon (1881–82), Marble Cave City (1884), and Medical Springs (1884). Stone County lacked a railroad, but was accessible via the Wilderness Road and had river access from the Finley River into the James and White Rivers, and was thus able to attract these "spa experiments." Neighboring Taney County, however, proved too remote at this time; its resort foundings came at a later date after the completion of the White River Railway in 1906.

By 1890 Ponce de Leon enjoyed a brief prominence as Stone County's largest town, with a population of nearly one thousand. But the rural spa lacked a rail connection and gradually faded away.[16] By the 1890s, Taney County was beginning to experience significant outside investment exemplified by a game park. Wealthy St. Louisans brought their own journalists to advertise a southern mountain locale on the White River, the St. Louis Game Park.[17]

The visits by St. Louisans brought attention to the White River through feature articles in St. Louis newspapers. Close on their heels were a number of peripatetic Yankee midwesterners who were seeking an outdoors environment for better health. In their quest they "discovered the quaint survivals" of premodern America in the southern upland setting of the White River hills. Their travelogues helped "invent" a mythical Ozarks for an urban readership. Midwesterners came in such numbers to the White River region that they gained notice in the newspapers and government publications. Tourists to the rivers encountered more and more of their Yankee cousins. By 1896, Marble Cave was well established as Stone County's first significant tourist site, while the St. Louis Game Park became Taney's Arcadia for elite sportsmen. Floaters on the river spread the fame of these two attractions far and wide. The best hotels in St. Louis featured game from the St. Louis Game Park, gifts from urban travelers to the White River, and the urban press publicized the reputation of Wetmore's retreat "as a health resort" that was unequaled.[18]

Locally, resident boat builders and guides prospered from tourism and began to look forward to the influx of city folks in spring and fall. When the game park, amidst great fanfare, hosted William Jennings Bryan in November 1896, local promoters sensed that a new era was about to blossom. Float fishing as recreation was establishing itself at several points along the White River. Upstream at Eureka Springs, Arkansas, tourists put in boats at Beaver to journey down the White River. Near Galena, sportsmen sought out Jeff Scott, who had a reputation as an expert boatman able to guide a hundred-mile float on the James and White Rivers. At Forsyth, Charles Kinyon, a skilled mechanic, stone mason and carpenter, was also handy at boat building, and floated and fished with natives and tourists. The *St. Louis Republic* reported in 1896 that an "excursion" down the James River in a common flat-bottom skiff (the Ozark johnboat would come later) was a trip through one of nature's "wilder scenes." Local sportsmen from Greene, Webster, Christian, Douglas, and other counties established a tradition of traveling by wagon train to Forsyth and the White River to float to Buffalo Shoals, Arkansas, where they stayed at a regionally famous fishing camp. These expert anglers and gig fishermen were the harbingers of many more float fishermen to come. Recreation on the rivers by locals and tourists had become a common sight by the 1890s.[19]

At Forsyth young W. H. Johnson, son of the photographer of the "White River Crew" in the 1880s, had inherited his journalist father's interest in the Ozarks. The Springfield native had worked as a journalist, attorney, and small businessman at his father's photographic gallery, and was now engaged in promoting the area's "mineral lands" for potential investors and selling real estate to new immigrants. Johnson had a talent for sketching; he would demonstrate his artist's flare at Republican political gatherings and would accompany his newspaper columns with drawings. He loved outdoors recreation and learned the art of gigging fish from the natives. Gigging was another form of float fishing—although the floats were much shorter than those of the bass fishermen.

The great bend or loop in the White River above Forsyth afforded an easy and spectacular river outing. Locals and their visitors hauled their boats by wagon over the ridge to Casey's Ford, where the beginning of a ten-mile float back to Forsyth awaited them. Johnson wrote a feature article about this sport for the *St. Louis Globe-Democrat* in 1897 hoping to tempt members of the St. Louis fish and gun clubs to try their hand at gigging near Forsyth. He described the distinctive 24 x 2-foot gig boat with twelve-inch sides and no seats that took two sportsmen downriver for night fishing. In the center of this boat, near a hundred-pound pile of pine knots, was an iron and wire basket containing a flaming pine-knot fire that illuminated the river. Another iron pot filled with corncobs soaking in coal oil provided a quick light for dramatic occasions, such as gigging a big fish. The gig consisted of a yellow pine shaft twelve feet long with a three- or four-pronged barbed fork, or metal gig, on one end and a leather or paw paw bark loop for the hand on the other. This weapon was hurled like a spear at fish. The gig, sometimes called a javelin in the urban press, doubled as a pole to navigate the boat. Spearing fish for several hours was a skill that required much patience and practice to master.

Outsiders, consequently, did not normally learn to gig, and the sport ultimately became a target for criticism from twentieth-century conservation-minded true sportsmen, as urban float fishermen deplored the activity as one that wasted game fish. The true sportsmen were angered at seeing the scars and wounds on game fish, missed by giggers and finally landed by hook, while maintaining an indifference toward the larger "trash fish," usual targets of the giggers.[20]

Floating on free-flowing, pristine Ozark streams through beautiful wilderness settings provided not only opportunities for sport but also solace for the soul, and experiences to be long remembered. The famous author, Harold Bell Wright, while visiting relatives in Barry County, Missouri, went on a camping trip on James River in 1896 and in return visits to the Ozarks spent more time floating. *The Shepherd of the Hills* became a travel book for visitors who floated, hiked, and motored to see the legendary sites of his wilderness novel.[21] Significantly, Wright's book increased the number of floats and hikes from the White River to Marble Cave. George and Keith McCanse, father and son, took "many float trips with other boys on James and White River in 1901 and 1902, foundered on baked beans mixed with tar [?]; learned [that] eels [were] good to eat." These outings framed a point of reference for Keith McCanse in later years when he became an influential Missouri game and fish commissioner who envisioned the revitalization and conservation of the Ozarks wildlife resources through government intervention.[22]

Many floaters preferred an outing with a group. As early as 1890 the Mollyjoggers Fishing and Hunting Club on the James River, and many more to follow, provided a common way for locals and tourists to float, fish, camp, and enjoy the outdoors. The Mollyjoggers, an association of Frisco Railroad men in Springfield, took spring and fall trips. They loaded wagons with gear, employed a Negro for camp cook, took several bird dogs, and headed for the river to fill their days with hunting and fishing and their evenings with campfire entertainment. From newspapers and magazines they read aloud stories, dialect verse, and syndicated poetry to their assembled group. The all-male association enjoyed a sufficiency of liquor and sometimes more.[23]

Local residents treated the river and its bounty as occasions for festive events. The deep holes of water in the White River afforded a great opportunity to seine or gig fish. Win Jones told of catches under the bluffs at Branson. "Fishermen put seines on the bluff side and dragged both ends across to a gravel bar. It took two yoke of oxen to pull the fish out on the gravel bar." Men hauled wagonloads of fish to Springfield markets. In winter, the fishermen cut holes in the ice and gigged the fish, dressing and packing them in barrels prior to shipment.[24]

By 1903 the longtime rumors that a railroad was coming to the White River hills became a reality. The St. Louis Iron Mountain Railway, a subsidiary of Missouri Pacific, sent engineers to survey a right of way. Construction of the line, called the White River Railway, began at Newport, Arkansas, going northwest; the line from Carthage, Missouri, begun later, met the southern crews at Bergman, Arkansas. Charles Fulbright, president of the Branson Town Company and later a railroad immigration agent, and Missouri Pacific executives jointly invited three hundred editors from Missouri and neighboring states to ride the White River line's first passenger train. For a generation, the Missouri Pacific had transported sportsmen in and out of the eastern Ozarks. The new line, connecting the Tri-State mineral towns of Carthage, Joplin, Webb City, and other communities from the rugged Ozarks to the Arkansas Delta, was yet another lure for visitors and the parent of new economies. One spinoff would be commercial float fishing, but this time it was accompanied by the founding of permanent railroad towns which offered tourist amenities for the traveling public, service centers that continue until today despite the commercial demise of the railroad. The railroad opened up numerous access points on 375 miles of floatable river between Galena, Missouri, and Cotter, Arkansas. The result was vastly expanded opportunities for Ozarks float fishing and the local businesses that provided the boats, guides, and gear for these outings.[25]

Missouri Pacific advertisements promoted virtually every aspect of endeavor along the White River Railway access. This was necessitated by the great cost of building the line. Against advice from railroad surveyors, the Missouri Pacific built the expensive route through difficult terrain and was sorely challenged to make it profitable. Following decades-old tradition in the trade, railroad promoters drew the attention of tourists and immigrants to the Ozarks scenic wonders along its route. All the while railroad executives and stockholders hoped for the discovery of mineral deposits and subsequent commercial return.

As the construction crews and mobile railroad camps neared Galena, workers and businessmen, with the cooperation of the railroad subcontractors, used the partially completed right of way for overland travel during a float trip outing on the James River. As early as the spring of 1903 fishing parties from Springfield and Kansas City arrived in Galena ready for extended floats and camping. In May the *Galena Stone County News* reported that Jeff Scott had begun taking fishermen down the James and White Rivers to Indian Creek where they were met by teamsters and hauled back, sometimes with a stop at Marble Cave, then to Reed's Spring and Galena.[26]

By July 1904 the completed railroad progressed from Carthage to Aurora, reached Galena in October, and Reed's Spring by Christmas.[27] The Galena newspaper reported that city dwellers were coming to town for the pleasures of floating the James River. Just north of Galena stood the James River Club House, situated on the west bank by the ferry crossing. The club entertained overnighters, campers, and boaters. Included among the guests were photographers, hired by the railroads to take promotional views, and journalists who came to write feature magazine and newspaper articles. The press quickly championed the James River valley as an ideal location to develop "health resorts." Resorters on the river traveled in flat-bottomed boats, rowboats, canoes, houseboats, and occasionally in imported, manufactured gasoline launches. The Galena newspaper proudly proclaimed, "The James River seems to be the Mecca of the sportsmen of the southwest."[28]

The Missouri Pacific brought an experienced construction company to build several miles of track on the north side of the White River crossing. J. L. and Charles Yandell brought 125 men from a previous job in southeast Missouri to begin the work; they set up one camp at Lucia, the new post office on the White River that would later be known as Branson. The Yandells and others allowed sportsmen to catch rides back to Galena following a float trip.[29]

Railroad engineer W. H. Schriber saw the commercial potential in the embryonic, commercial float-trip industry. Schriber, who had surveyed the route for Missouri Pacific from Galena to Branson, had floated the rivers. He envisioned an efficient sportsmen's float, a "Galena to Lucia float trip," that began at a resort in Galena and returned by rail from Branson.

He purchased land in south Galena, sought St. Louis financing, and proclaimed his vision in the *St. Louis Post-Dispatch* as a "Six Day Trip in Thirty Minutes." He advanced the idea that tourists could come to his Bonita Hotel Resort, enjoy the amenities of a bathhouse, cabins, and pleasant socializing. The high point was a guided float trip for 131 miles to Lucia with a return trip to Galena of just 22 miles.[30] Schriber realized that most tourists who came to float were novices who needed the specialized services of guides. The rivermen handled the boats, cooked on a gravel bar, taught the inexperienced sportsmen how to catch fish, and made sure the entourage reached its destination. Thus the idea for what became the Ozarks most famous float trip was born.

As the commercial float business was only just beginning, even before rail track had crossed the White River, local citizens observed it with interest. Truman Powell, the tireless promoter for Stone County, complained about tourists who littered the clean gravel bars of the James and White Rivers with hundreds of empty salmon and clam cans. Natives immediately applied their local wit to the situation. One resident along the river told Powell that he wanted a calendar "so he could tell when them fools from Galena come down fishing. At such times he always caught some fish to sell to them so they could go home and tell the folks lies about what a string they caught." The littering tenderfoot tourist, however, was also bringing new money into the county.[31]

Floating became a warm-weather business for a few local men. Young Charlie McCord, son of a local physician and a strong Republican family, was the most prominent outfitter according to the Galena press. In these developing years of float fishing, McCord's services were sought by everyone from urban sportsmen from Kansas City and the Tri-State Mineral District to Missouri political dignitaries and even the governor of Oklahoma. Local boat builders, who had other occupations, manufactured and repaired McCord's flat-bottomed float boats. Missouri secretary of state John E. Swanger came often enough to become well known by several natives. The secretary came with Frank Wightman, the state railroad and warehouse commissioner, who had made a reputation in his business at Monett. Swanger and Wightman brought along Missouri attorney general Herbert Hadley, political and business associates from Aurora, and sportsmen who journeyed by river to the Aurora Club House at Cape Fair, or further downstream to Branson. The association with influential and prominent politicians on the river may have encouraged Charlie McCord to become a Republican candidate for state representative in 1906.[32] When McCord wasn't hosting VIPs, he took local businessmen, merchants, and Stone County Courthouse officials on float trips.

The Missouri Pacific Railroad continued to promote float trips in the media. In June 1905, a noteworthy month in the history of the new float business, railroad promoters at Carthage sent over forty fishing parties by rail to make the Galena-to-Branson float. McCord and others received the trade. The press reported that on one trip McCord and his five clients made the Galena-to-Branson float and caught 250 bass.[33] Obviously, the young Galena businessman, and other float-trip entrepreneurs, had their seasonal outfitting businesses well established.[34]

In 1905, Charlie McCord and Stone County circuit judge John T. Moore purchased a gasoline launch in Kansas City that they installed at the Galena Club House, formerly the James River Club House. McCord hired Albert King to build float boats. Galena restaurateur Charley Barnes

Barnes Brothers float party
Mary Craig Mappes Collection

(1878–1964), working in his spare time, began to learn from others and experiment on his own in building float boats. In the fall of 1905, such men suffered a setback when the White River Railway, which was behind its construction schedule, refused to return boats and baggage from Branson to Galena. The press announced a "spoiled season" for Galena-to-Branson float-trip operators, but optimistically stated that by the time the next fishing season arrived, regular trains would be running.[35]

By 1907, McCord was expanding his area of operations. North of Galena, he was hauling boats from the Oto area to the mouth of Crane Creek for service on the James and White Rivers. A hunting and fishing friend, Emery Boyd, helped him. Exactly who built McCord's boats is unclear. Boat builder Herb Barnes lived at Oto, and there was much visiting between him and brother Charlie in Galena. Did Charley and Herb Barnes, future legends in the float business, make some of McCord's float boats? Perhaps. Whatever the case, there were plenty of local boat builders around Stone County.[36]

As was the case earlier in the southeastern Ozarks, the railroad tie industry influenced float fishing. By 1905, the cutting, hauling, and marketing of railroad ties had become a brisk business in Stone County, and timber workers added a new twist to local float fishing. Standing upon tie rafts floated down the upper James River to Galena, rafters fished for bass, caught dozens of them, and upon arrival in the county seat sold the fish at a profit that matched or exceeded their regular wage.[37] Ozark men had long combined two or more economic pursuits and tie rafting and fishing was a good example of this practice.

Missouri's Fish Commission helped to promote recreation on the James and White Rivers. As soon as the White River Railway was completed in 1906, the commission included Galena and Branson in its program of stocking black bass in public waters.[38] Six years later the popularity of the two streams for float fishing led the commission to place these rivers first on the listing of public distributions from the St. Joseph hatchery.[39] The state-supported stocking of game fish on the southwestern Ozarks rivers further encouraged floating sportsmen-tourists to expect a good harvest of the finny tribe.

As soon as the Missouri Pacific Railroad crossed the White River in 1906 and gave impetus to the expanding float-fishing industry, other pro-

The White River Railway on a Stone County trestle
Hobart Parnell Collection

moters with different ideas about the outdoors began to lobby the U.S.
Congress to dam the James and White Rivers. No sooner had float fishing become profitable than certain powerful and influential capitalists envisioned more lucrative economies based on lakes and less on free-flowing
natural rivers. Such a vision ultimately spelled the downfall of float fishing. As far back as the mid-1880s the Army Engineers had surveyed the
White River above Batesville and concluded that the stretch from Forsyth
to Buffalo Shoals "can be rendered navigable at extreme low water in no
way except by the construction of a system of locks and dams."[40] Engineer
and lawyer William Standish advocated that prominent bends in the rivers
be tunneled and machinery installed that would channel the force of the
current to generate electricity. A congressional bill inspired by Standish
presented evidence that the contemporary tourist and commercial trade
of the river could not compete with the revenues that would accrue if the
river were dammed. To support this view, the bill included "a map, put
out by the railroads and those who furnish skiffs to induce people to come
to Galena and Branson and engage skiffs to float down these rivers." The

Famous river
guide Tom Yocum
Walker Powell
Collection

sample map, printed by the Branson skiff party (V. C. Todd) and the railroad, advertised the Branson-to-Cotter trip and a return by railroad in
three hours. Given the possibility of congressional action, it was not a fore-
gone conclusion that the newly established float business would survive.

Despite this possibility, however, outfitters on the river continued
their work. As the Mollyjoggers and others had earlier demonstrated, it
never hurt to have some home-grown entertainment on the outings. The
uncountable number of camps set up on gravel bars by skilled and personable guides and the local stories and lore told by them around campfires to thousands of clients formed the basis for a new strand of Ozarks

folklore. This genre was spun to excite the imaginations of tourists hungry for tall tales and mysterious legends. Any visitor who spent a number of days in the region would ask many questions about the Ozarks. Local guides, steeped in the knowledge of Ozark ways, stood poised to give them answers.

Local guides were proficient in identifying landmarks and relating them to tall tales and folklore. Caves, which had long served as both prehistoric habitation and pioneer shelters, were the sources of many interesting legends. Tales were told of treasure hidden in caves by Spanish conquistadors, or of gold and silver coins secreted there during the Civil War, or stashed there by desperadoes and bandits, or of veins of precious metals in lost caves that someone long ago had seen or heard about. The mid-1890s mineral fever along the Ten O'Clock Run in southern Stone and Taney Counties fueled a timely increase in the number of these legends. The potential for tourism of such legends was not lost on feature writers or the newly emerging guide service on the James and White Rivers.[41]

The James and White River valleys were endowed with rich historical traditions that provided much grist for the storytelling mill. There were

Branson-to-Cotter, Arkansas, float being towed across Lake Taneycomo
Postcard, Kalen and Morrow Collection

stories about the residence of the Delaware Indian nation on the upper James River in the 1820s; from the same period emerged the most enduring of all Ozarks legends—that of the celebrated Yocum Dollar. The Yocum Dollar legend perpetuated the myth about the existence of a lost silver mine (actually, the Yocum family were reminting the government specie provided as an annuity to the Delawares in a crafty money laundering scheme, and not mining it from a "lost" cave); still this tale capitalized on generations of precious-ore legends, and made for an entertaining story that is still told in many variants (and also immortalized in the present-day tourist mecca—Silver Dollar City!). The lead and zinc strikes at the antebellum Granby mines in Newton County and after the Civil War in the Joplin area further fueled the conviction that marketable minerals were still to be found "somewhere nearby." The Civil War and its often violent aftermath gave rise to still more legends. The region saw some of the greatest battles that were fought in the trans-Mississippi West—Wilson's Creek, Pea Ridge, and Prairie Grove. Postwar vigilante violence such as the Bald Knobber episode in the 1880s formed the basis for much sensational journalism in the urban, and later, local press. Moonshining was small scale, but ubiquitous, and was a much-cultivated theme in urban popular culture. Caves, mythical sites for their elusive treasures, became "living characters" woven into the backdrop of all these tales. Guides on the river pointed out Virgin Bluff, Breadtray Mountain, Marble Cave, Bald Hills, and other legend-cloaked landmarks to an audience eager for local color. The publication of Harold Bell Wright's bestselling novel, *The Shepherd of the Hills,* in 1907 could not have come at a more opportune time; passenger railroad service had begun and promotional optimism was in the air—in fact, Wright rode the railroad into Roark valley and got off to walk to Inspiration Point to write his book. As the guides' audience included journalists, feature stories helped proliferate variations of Ozark tales for regional and urban consumers. Journalist Edith McCall aptly described the opportunity embraced by Ozarkers who promoted numerous legends—the "story teller found a new sport in testing the credulity of these 'furriners.'"[42]

By 1908 some of the more famous guide personalities had begun their careers on the James River. Jeff Scott was a veteran, but newcomers Charlie McCord, Charley and Herb Barnes, and Tom Yocum became favorites. At Branson, transplanted St. Louisan Vernon Todd and his Branson Boat

Spend Your Vacation
at Cliff House, Powersite, Mo.
Lake Taneycomo. Fishing, boating and bathing. Rates $10. per week

Cliff House resort ad
Kalen and Morrow Collection

Company sent floaters up- and downriver. For the first few years floaters sometimes walked out several miles from the river following a trip, and a wagon picked up their boats later. Apparently this did not last long as early twentieth-century accounts tell of wagons, and later trucks, meeting tourists at the take-out point and driving them back to their camp or starting point. The local press published regular reports of dignitaries and groups who came for these outings, and combinations of politicians and businessmen received special notice.[43]

Outfitters located fishing camps along the banks of the James River. Their very number made it easy for tourists to plan a trip ranging from a day's outing to one of several days. The camps became community space—sites for marriages, religious sermons, alumni reunions, and banquets—

and were associated with a variety of agricultural enterprises. But floating was the primary business. Upstream from Galena, floaters could play and relax at Limberlost Camp (formerly the James River Club House and the Galena Club House)[44] or begin day-long adventures downstream. Generally, the first overnight camp would be at McCord Bend; the second at Bear Den Camp where, across the river, the private Aurora Club House was an urban sportsman's destination; and the third at Edward's Bend on an expansive gravel bar, termed "magnificent beaches of clean gravel" by the Missouri Pacific, or further down at Jackson Hollow. Tourists could then take out at Jackson Hollow or continue their float to the Kimberling bridge. Those that went on downriver floated to White Rock Bluff and reached a gravel bar camp. On the fifth day the float reached the mouth of Indian Creek, and vacationers could hike from the riverside camp to Marble Cave. The sixth day meant arrival at Branson and a ride on the train back to Galena.

Tourists also embarked from Branson and took boats downriver to Forsyth and beyond. Seventeen-year-old Charley Woodbury, his two brothers, and their three pals took an eight-day float in three boats from Branson in August 1907. Charley's diary recorded the trip, an adventure with a guide named Bill. The boys were awed by the majestic scenery, but spent a lot of time trying "to unravel the art of casting." Before the first day was spent, rains came and one boat capsized and sank. Crestfallen, they retrieved soaked baggage and provisions. The second day, the group reached Forsyth, populated with "bohunks and a few town-people," and spent the night feasting on sodas and candy. The third day, they traveled twenty-one river miles to Moore's Bend. Fishing was good, they purchased some watermelons to eat and had an enjoyable day. The next day they stopped at the mouth of Bear Creek, explored the countryside, and marveled at the hundreds of fish in the water.

The fifth day was Sunday. It had rained again the night before, and the youths barely escaped disaster. They awoke to discover water running through the camp and had a difficult time rescuing the boats. Unfortunately, Charley lost all of his photographs. One wonders if the guide was new at his charge. They loaded up and pushed on into Arkansas where they found a watermelon patch which they promptly raided (reminiscences commonly recounted the pilfered melons of late summer). Further downriver they stopped to visit a small house that sat back from the river. "The string of tousle-headed boys and girls . . . followed and stared open-mouthed" as the city boys looked around. The resident family sold them three dozen eggs, but "thought we were crazy when we asked them for canned fruit or preserves." The local residents displayed surprise at the appearance of tourists in their midst just as the city boys were astonished at the rusticity of the dwelling and its inhabitants. The vacationers journeyed on to camp at a gravel bar.

Charley's remembrance of Monday, the next day, caused him to reflect about the Ozarks. He wrote, "The locality we passed through is historic in a sense, and history about which nothing but guesses can ever be made." In a day when written local history resided primarily in newspapers and in a few scattered library books, Charley Woodbury had recognized that oral tradition played a major role in the countryside. He listened to stories told to him and recorded a brief tale in his diary concerning a southern patriot who had occupied a cave high on a riverside bluff. Continuing downriver, natives told about skulls and bones being picked up after hard rains in a nearby field and pointed to the stone relics strewn across the field as evidence of their claim. The Woodburys then saw "low mounds" near the water and wondered what race other than "moundbuilder" had inhabited the area.

The boys' next two encounters were with moonshiners and pearl hunters. They passed the "whiskey boat" about noon. The manufacturers told the visitors that they evaded the Missouri and Arkansas laws "by claiming that they hold a government license and that the county has no authority over the river." The diary had no further comment. The boys tried their own hand at pearl hunting and filled the boats with mussels, but no one claimed a pearl. The exploitation of fresh-water mussels actually began on the lower White and Black Rivers in Arkansas during the 1890s. Harvesters exported the shells to button factories, but occasionally found pearls on the inside of the mussels. A few rare discoveries of valuable pearls had made the harvesting a seasonal business and a hobby for natives and tourists along the rivers.[45]

On the seventh day, their luck changed. The youths opened more mussels and to their delight found several small pearls. These new experiences kept the party curious about the Ozarks. Charley, the diarist, marveled at the changing countryside and soon spied mistletoe hanging in the trees. A companion climbed up and cut some for the whole group. That evening, they tried to make pancakes, but "decided it was a shame to spoil such a good imitation of India rubber." Neighborly mosquitoes joined the group, and the guide Bill said that it was "the unluckiest trip that he was ever on."

Finally, on the eighth day they continued past more pearl hunters and were treated to a demonstration of gigging by local men. The boys enjoyed running large rapids and finally reached Cotter, Arkansas. On their last night in the outdoors they held another watermelon feast. The next day they took the railroad back to Branson and home to a city up north.[46]

The "early days" of the float business were transformed by the construction of Lake Taneycomo (1911–13) and the transportation of float fishermen by trains rather than wagons. Floaters used canoes, and the traditional flat-bottomed float boats with square ends, although some had pointed sterns. Gasoline-powered, manufactured boats that held several passengers joined the native craft built for three or four persons on the lake and on the White River. Locals and visitors still enjoyed canoes, some covered with canvas, and most boats on the James and White Rivers were locally made. The lake now occupied a huge spot in the center of a floater's map—125 miles of the James and White Rivers, while below it the White River extended another 250 miles. The lake's popularity caused all watercraft to be subjected to a much-larger public scrutiny that affected boat construction. Cumbersome, primitive flat-bottomed boats became uncommon while better-crafted boats, coated with paint, tightly jointed with sheer and rake, carried float fishermen in pursuit of their beloved sport. A goal of commercial float fishing was achieved with this new type of boat— a reusable, sophisticated craft that could be repeatedly rented for use on any kind of river outing. The celebrated Ozark johnboat had arrived.[47]

After Taneycomo, sportsmen still pursued the same great bass fishing, but journalists' glowing press accounts and romantic descriptions of float trips piqued readers' imaginations. The floater could journey through a "fairyland of backwoods hills and valleys," on an Arcadian odyssey where "civilization is left almost completely behind." The more intellectual commentators compared the experience to poetry and literature. The sentimental romanticism of *The Shepherd of the Hills* was constantly invoked. Tourists could actually meet the natives upon which Wright's characters were based and tour the actual sites mentioned in the book. "It is almost like floating into another land to glide into the mysterious blue and purple haze that makes the Ozark hills seem like some great painting, rather than a thing of reality." Thankfully, said one Joplin reporter, the flat-bottomed boats were almost "foolproof" for tenderfoot tourists.[48] The tourists chose from a generous range of commissary provisions that might include steak and eggs, one-hundred-pound cakes of ice, and plenty of beer.

The true sportsmen from the large cities were quite a contrast to Charley Woodbury's unassuming group and other urban middle-class floaters of modest means. In August 1914 Burt Loewenstein and Will Helman, members of the Valley Park Canoe Club and the Missouri Athletic Club in St. Louis, took an adventure to the Maine Club at Hollister. They journeyed not by train, but by water. They hauled a canoe and seven hundred pounds of baggage on the railroad to Galena and put in on the James River. These two men, according to a Branson reporter, "would cause more than a fleeting glance being both dressed for the sport." They carried a tent of silk texture, two air mattresses and a bicycle pump, a folding table and chairs, alcohol stoves, canvas buckets and wash basins, and a waterproof commissary box. One of them played a guitar for a "campfire jamboree." The two sportsmen stopped at Indian Creek and hiked to Marvel Cave, returned to the White River, and floated on to Branson. There they inspected the float equipment at the Walker Brothers White River Boating Company and complimented the owners on their gear. Then they spent a few days with friends at the Maine Club relating the events of their outing. The train, of course, returned them to St. Louis.[49]

Usually float trips consisted of small parties, but corporations and institutions often sent large groups to the famous float streams. Charley Barnes remembered his largest group in 1914. The flotilla for this trip consisted of thirty-one boats with guides chartered by the L. B. Price Mercantile Company of Kansas City. The party even brought several musicians. "Them fellers tooted around on the gravel bars a couple of times but after the guides didn't pay 'em any mind they put up their horns and didn't play any more."[50] Apparently, the urban visitors wanted to import some "high culture" to the backwoods.

While there were few reported clashes between the largely rural locals and the mainly urban outsiders, it was accepted that differences of appreciation would occur. City folk were not shy about stereotyping the native population with the sobriquet "hill billy," and locals in turn were not always sensitive toward the urban visitors or their recreational goals. Charley Barnes, for instance, hated to see "picture takin'" on the rivers. "Fellers used to drag their big strings of fish all over the gravel bars takin' pictures. They'd mess up the fish and let 'em lay. Sure spoiled a many a good camp ground that way. Kodaks sure spoiled a lot of fish in this country."[51]

While some individuals and companies came to the area solely for recreation, others who floated the rivers were inspired to invest in the Shepherd of the Hills country. Local tradition relates that in 1906 Rev. James Forsythe floated the White River in his personal quest for renewed health. Maybe so, but he also floated the river with a group of associates who shared with him the vision for a new mission to the Ozarks. Their party floated and boated from Branson to Forsyth, the county seat of Taney County. From this experience was born the inspiration that ultimately led to the founding of The School of the Ozarks. Leaders of the Presbyterian Synod of Missouri listened sympathetically to Forsythe's promising testimonials concerning the need for improved education in the Ozarks and raised money to found the new high school, the first in Taney County.[52]

The mission school experienced slow but steady growth, thanks to the generosity of donors from Kansas City, central Missouri, and St. Louis. Some of these benefactors took vacations to the region. H. T. Abernathy, a Kansas City banker who was also an avid fisherman and hunter, was one. On one of his trips to the White River Abernathy was moved to action by the institutional efforts and needs of the school. His patronage led to the construction of Abernathy and Stevenson dormitories, two of the first concrete and native-rock buildings on the campus.[53]

As the new hydroelectric Powersite Dam was being completed in 1913, R. W. Wilson built the Cliff House resort on a bluff above the dam. This was to be the first of many resorts on Lake Taneycomo. The Cliff House resort catered to urban sportsmen, especially Kansas Citians. It had a hotel with a dance hall, several small cottages, tents for camping in Spring Park, a tennis court, and horseback riding. All guests had access to a boat dock, boats, and supplies for floating down the White River. Wilson promoted group floats and hosted a variety of parties ranging from the Missouri Writers' Guild, the Audubon Society, the Izaak Walton League, to artist groups and businessmen. Burris Jenkins, a well-known Kansas City clergyman, author, and traveler, became a director and prime mover in this resort society in the years preceding the depression. High church officials from Kansas City accompanied Jenkins on his Ozark expeditions to the White River.[54]

The presence of cultural elites like Jenkins gave social status and prestige to resorting on the White River, and the local and urban press reported their appearances in the Ozarks. R. W. Wilson had envisioned that the Cliff House would serve as an anchor for a projected planned community, a picturesque real-estate landscape for investors in a new town, but it was a vision that never materialized. However, a contemporary Kansas City businessman, Willard Merriam (1864–1923), who also floated the White River while construction on Powersite Dam proceeded, came up with the concept for Rockaway Beach. In 1914 as Wilson continued enlarging his Cliff House resort, Merriam and his real-estate partners purchased land and developed the first Ozarks lakeside resort town devoted entirely to the tourist trade. At Rockaway Beach rowboating and canoeing were more localized recreations. Tourist boats loaded with passengers came from Branson for dancing, fishing, swimming, and relaxation. Vacationers at Rockaway Beach, however, observed many flotillas of float boats, tied together, being towed by a gasoline launch toward Powersite Dam for deposit on the other side and a continuing trip down the White River into Arkansas.[55]

The float-fishing business gradually became an ally and supporter of conservation and the newly reorganized Missouri Game and Fish Department of 1909. The passage of the first modern game laws in 1905 generated little enthusiasm in the vacationing public and none at all among the average Ozark outdoorsmen. However, the largest symbol for conservation in the region was the St. Louis Game Park which bordered the White River in south-central Taney County. It developed as a game refuge which was widely accepted as the contemporary model for the propagation of large game populations such as deer and turkey. As small local gentlemen's sporting clubs were being set up around this time, founders began to put the ideology of conservation in their charters. One example, in March 1909, was the Cedar Grove Bungalow Fishing and Hunting Club. This group of Springfield men stated in their charter that they would "establish a clubhouse and game preserve in Greene and Taney Counties for protection of fish and game," develop their real-estate holdings along the James and White Rivers for pleasure and for sale, and "enforce state game and fish laws."[56]

Gov. Herbert Hadley's administration (1909–13) used the new game law to launch progressive efforts in conservation. The just-completed Lake Taneycomo and undammed stretches of the rivers were obvious places to put into practice the new game regulations and the philosophy of conservation. A new alliance was forged between the Missouri Game and Fish Department, the tourist business, and conservation-minded outdoorsmen engaged in fishing and hunting, to champion a common cause that would benefit all involved. All of these proponents had a common stake in abundant natural resources for field sports and tourism. Resort owners and float-trip operators became early disciples of conservation, and later were founding members in Sportsmen Protective Leagues, especially the local Izaak Walton chapters after 1922. Governor Hadley's floats on the White River were highly touted Ozark adventures that brought press attention to the region and high visibility to the conservation partnership. Jesse Tolerton, game and fish commissioner, dramatized this new government and citizen coalition in his annual reports.[57] Tolerton chose St. Louisan E. T. Grether, coauthor of the Walmsley game law, as the deputy game and fish commissioner to manage the St. Louis branch office. Grether's connections with the St. Louis Game Park society continued the historic relationship of Taney's game park with St. Louis sportsmen, and helped strengthen the Ozarks' early conservation conscience.

Other branches of state government also took an interest in the southwest Missouri tourist boom. By 1914 Missouri's Bureau of Labor promoted the Galena-to-Branson float trips. They touted the picturesque scenery, the enjoyment for both men and women who could easily make the trip, and the cave tours. Tourist promoters aimed their appeals to both sexes. They equipped johnboats with camp chairs to not only make fishing easier, but to provide women dressed in hats and outing clothes a safe, comfortable seat while fishing or sightseeing.[58]

The companies in the commercial float business advertised their partnership with conservation, and the Empire District Electric Company knew it was good public relations to support popular recreation. At Powersite, the corporation kept a span of mules that hauled boats from Ozark Beach to the tailrace below the dam; later the company installed a lift at the dam to portage the boats. The Barnes Boating Company, in Galena, printed brochures that included, "We will be glad to send you a copy of the Game Laws of Missouri on request."[59] After 1919 the boating companies advertised that they could furnish Missouri (and Arkansas) fishing licenses to their patrons. As the river guides became convinced that fishermen who depleted the rivers by netting or gigging hundreds of fish represented an actual and potential threat to their business, they criticized these traditional sports and at the same time promoted a conservation ethic.

The float business in the Shepherd of the Hills country during the 1920s was as full of promise as most other local enterprises. More and more tourists wanting to float arrived in cars, and if they did not arrange for a return trip by rail, they expected to be hauled in trucks; bumpy wagon rides were becoming a thing of the past. The local perception of these visitors who drove in automobiles to the river was "Doctors, lawyers— big shots we called 'em—rich people would come in here," said Denver Hollars.[60] These affluent, city-dwelling midwesterners, filled with the pride of Progressive America, had easy access to the Ozarks by rail and automobile and the income and leisure time to take full advantage of the ever-expanding range of amenities being offered along the Ozark rivers of the White River country. In 1920 Joplin Rotarians founded the Ozark Playgrounds Association, a new regional organization that catered to the automobile tourist. They published a map of the Ozark playgrounds (southwest Missouri and northwest Arkansas) that was reprinted in newspapers and their promotional booklets. Their pamphlets highlighted such landmarks along the well-traveled James and White Rivers as Virgin Shoals, Jackson Hollow, Aunt's Creek, Bee Bluff, Table Rock, and other familiar attractions. The Ozark Playgrounds Association directed tourists to the major resorts, including those that specialized in float trips.[61]

Keith McCanse, like Jesse Tolerton before him, was a Republican from southwest Missouri who gave significant support to the float business in his capacity as Missouri game and fish commissioner. McCanse was a passionate outdoorsman and veteran floater who knew the rivers firsthand. In April 1926 McCanse published his first "Roster of Float Outfitters" in the *Missouri*

Game and Fish News. While tourists floated all the major Ozark waters by now, the James and White Rivers still led, by far, in the number of boats and guides. There were forty-seven boats and twenty-two guides at the Galena Boating Company and Barnes Brothers Boat Company on the James. Downriver at Branson, Forsyth, and Yandell Resort on the White River, over sixty float boats were available. By contrast, there were only forty boats for rent on the Gasconade and twenty-one on the Jack's Fork and Current Rivers. Outfitters of the White River country also kept the advantage of being able to offer rail service for boats and floaters; the Missouri Pacific Railroad continued to widely advertise this convenience in order to attract still more sportsmen to southwest Missouri.[62]

The railroads issued pamphlets for tourists that promoted specific locales. In the Shepherd of the Hills country the Missouri Pacific's "The White River Country in the Ozarks" was one of the best of these publications. It served up a full complement of descriptive text and photographs, train schedules, ticketing agents, daily and weekly rates for resorts and float trips, and an excellent map that showed local roads and tourist sites in relationship to the railroad corridor. The map provided detailed information on major camps and attractions on the Galena-to-Branson float: how far the hike was from Roark Station (the old Marble Cave switch) to Marvel Cave (2½ miles), proposed dam sites on the James and White Rivers, Dewey Bald of literary fame, and the St. Louis Game Park. Promoters represented the region as a "twentieth-century romance" enhanced by the modern amenities made possible with electricity from Powersite Dam. Electric conveniences of all kinds at the resorts made the visit to the Ozarks even more attractive. "The wholesome, democratic atmosphere would down-tilt the nose of the snobbiest snob on earth," crowed the railroad. Tourists stayed oriented by good advice and by using the quality map.[63]

Travelers who especially desired the Ozarks most famous float trip chose Missouri Pacific's folder, "James and White River Float Trips." As in its other brochures, the railroad explained that opportunities lie in the Shepherd of the Hills land "where characters of Harold Bell Wright's famous novel still live" and could be found upon inquiry. The reader viewed photographs taken along the famous float route and read descriptions of where the tourist could spend each night on the river. Of course, information on hotel accommodations were provided along with costs for the floats, including the two-dollar fare for returning each boat by rail from Branson to Galena.[64]

Visitors to the Limberlost Inn in 1920 could, for twelve dollars a week, rent a screened bungalow for four equipped with a spring bed, cots, tables, chairs, and oil stove, dishes, and cooking utensils. Those who wished to be pampered might enjoy a furnished room in the Limberlost Inn for $1.00 per day plus $1.50 for meals. These rates appealed to primarily an urban middle class. Few locals could imagine spending thirty dollars or more on a "camping trip" as urban "outsiders" commonly did.

Along the Galena-to-Branson float vacationers found many amenities. One enterprising businessman opened a cold drink and ice cream concession stand on the riverbank at the Limberlost Club, and Lon Earnest piped water to all of the cabins of Arnold Lodge. He installed lavatories, toilets, showers, and, in his own home, a bathtub. This fixture caused one astounded visitor to exclaim, "What left me absolutely dazed was the . . . revelation of a glistening bathtub with high-pressure running water. Imagine, a real, functioning bathtub at a river camp miles from where you'd

Tourists parked at Craig's Cozy Camp cabin
Postcard, Kalen and Morrow Collection

expect it!" Backwoods convenience did not stop at a hot bath: Dewey Short of Galena contracted to buy ice from the Lawrence County Water, Light, and Cold Storage Company of Aurora to sell to floaters. The company won Short's business with the claim that "our ice is in 200 pound cakes which . . . is better for fishing parties." Other merchants along the railroad followed Short's lead in seeing that tourists had ice.[65] Craig's Cozy Camp, sited on a hill overlooking Galena, was affiliated with the town's largest mercantile, which also contracted with guides for float trips. Patrons of the popular Bear Den Camp on the James River could enjoy a meal in the dining hall followed by a game on the croquet court. Oklahoma journalist George Evans was one who took advantage of the diverse riverside amenities. He wrote, "Gazing upward at the greenery or downward at the rippling water, who could help dreaming and feeling good to slow down and drift," he asked, "forgetful of all that irks and grinds in the far-away busy world?" "This," he concluded, "is the life . . . and you know it is nature's own remedy for a lot of real or fancied ills."[66] This was Arcadia indeed!

The fame of float fishing and river guides continued to speed through stories in the newspapers and serials of the 1920s. The postcard trade offered thousands of images of the spectacular bluffs along the float-trip route including Virgin, Centerpoint, White Rock, and Table Rock. Photographers also documented noted whitewater shoals in their repertoire— Virgin, Hitchcock, Jackson, Peach Orchard, and Ance Creek on the James River and Tombstone on the White River. The initial issue of *Ozarkian* magazine appeared in 1926, with a feature article on the White River float and guide Walt (Rattler) Guilliams. He was the epitome of the multitalented river guide. Equally adept in handling a float boat or tall tale, Guilliams attracted a clientele that included politicians, businessmen, and journalists. Guilliams regaled his audience with stories about Buffalo Bill, Jesse James, and Cole Younger (all of whom he professed to know personally) and tales of buried treasure near Breadtray Mountain (easily seen at the junction of the James and White Rivers). During the off-season winter months, Guilliams trapped bass for the Missouri Game and Fish Department to use as brood stock in the state fish hatcheries. Guilliams was a master at conjuring up the romance and mystery of the White River country. In his stories and in his deep knowledge of the ways of the rivers and hills he both embodied and exemplified that distinctive regional blend of truth and myth that formed the basis of such fictional romances as *The Shepherd of the Hills*.

Over the years a mixing occurred between oral traditions of the hill folk as passed on by guides like Guilliams and the local color journalism that transformed the real and imaginary locales of literature and folklore into "historical sites." So far has this process advanced that modern tour guides seldom attempt to make any distinction between literary, folkloric, and legitimate historical sites.[67]

By the late 1920s the prospect of more dam construction on the White River was once again in the news. In Joplin, the Empire District Electric Company had promoted the building of a dam across the river at Table Rock. Guides like Walt Guilliams believed the dam would improve the regional playground and even make fishing better on the many tributaries. Moreover, Guilliams was glad for the threat that the dam posed to gigging, a local sport he roundly criticized. During the years he spent trapping brood stock for state hatcheries he had seen many scarred fish wounded by the spears. He was especially incensed about giggers who slaughtered more than they needed and left piles of rotting fish on the banks. The Galena Boating Company, Guilliams's employer, finally refused to rent boats to gigging parties.[68]

At the beginning of the Great Depression floating in general was more popular than ever. The southwest Missouri outfitters began to offer new float trips on the upper James and Finley Rivers; the Galena Boating Company even transported sportsmen to the distant Current, Gasconade, Niangua, and Osage Rivers. The Galena outfitters also joined others at Forsyth to take fishermen to Cotter, Arkansas. By 1930 the Galena-based company stated that most of their trade came from Oklahoma and Kansas, with St. Louis and Illinois trade representing a strong second. They predicted that once Route 66 was fully paved across the state their business would multiply still further. Walt Guilliams, too, was optimistic. He believed that he would continue to guide tourists past Ozark scenery, share the secrets of bass fishing with urban sportsmen, and spend summer nights at the camps serving as the "official entertainer" of the float parties. He would continue to perform his "day job" of ensuring that his clients "saw the sights" and came away with a string of bass, and then, with a day of fishing and floating done, he would start his "evening job" of "amus[ing] his guests with Ozarks legendry and folk lore." His enduring reputation as a preeminent guide and storyteller guarantees for us that he was up to the task.[69]

"God's Great Natural Park"

The Railroad Transforms Resorting and Commerce

IN 1906 the Missouri Pacific was putting the finishing touches on the White River Railway route to Branson. That same year, in the state capitol, Jefferson City, a young and energetic attorney general, Herbert Hadley, was beginning the trust-busting prosecutions that were to generate national attention and catapult him into the governor's chair two years later. In this office Hadley earned an enduring reputation as one of the nation's most prominent exemplars of the Progressive Era of government reform. Less appreciated today is the fact that Hadley was a tireless promoter of the Ozarks. He joined others in advancing public faith in the economic possibilities of the region and was the first Missouri governor since the Civil War to spend any noticeable time in the Ozarks. His presence in and advocacy of the Ozarks received favorable publicity in local newspapers. His well-known float trips and appearances with local business leaders received wide coverage and helped to promote the new opportunities for investment and development that the railroads were about to usher in. Hadley touted the region to one national magazine by stating that "the Ozarks had none of the hardships incident to a Northern climate, and none of the depressing influences peculiar to a Southern one." The gates to this once-remote paradise were about to be thrown wide open. The rugged and beautiful terrain of hills, deep divides, and numerous creeks that had long impeded passage to settlers and travelers alike was now in the process of being bridged by modern rail transportation. A tidal wave of modernity was about to surge into the White River hills bearing a horde of tourists with leisure time and money to spend. A spectacular new era of economic development and expansion was dawning. The local businessmen and politicians of Stone and Taney Counties who hobnobbed with Hadley and his companions on their Ozarks junkets were quick to notice the profound change that was eroding their isolated and perpetuated frontier communities. Dozens of corporations were showing up on their doorstep, and a new class of business leaders arrived, bringing visions of a new and very different future for the White River country.[1]

The White River Division of the Missouri Pacific almost seemed magical in its transforming powers. Not only were the age-old difficulties of traveling in and out of the White River hills eliminated in a single stroke, but the instant economic impact on the surrounding region was equally dazzling. Even before the line reached completion locals beheld the modernizing effects of the railway that "changed the way most Missourians made a living."[2] The railroad, and later electricity, literally reshaped the Ozarks. Impending rail construction drove land values upward. "When rumors [of a railway] were substantiated by actual purchase of right of way by railroad officials," wrote one observer, "the value of the 'Old Fortner place' [on which Hollister later stood] tripled." Once construction started, "For the first time there was a market for everything that could be produced," recalled Mrs. C. W. Moore, who lived near the line in Taney County. The presence of work crews created such a demand, according to Moore, that "eggs went from three cents per dozen up and up, butter from ten cents [per pound] and up."[3] Besides creating a demand for local produce, railroad construction crews, composed of old-stock Americans, Austrians, blacks, and Italians, were themselves a novelty to locals, who would show up to view them in their segregated work camps.[4]

No sooner had the first train crossed the White River at the freshly laid out townsite of Branson than institutions and corporations commenced breaking ground for new facilities. Their success depended upon the ability of people to travel on a schedule and on time. Modernizers gazed at the great expanse of the White River bottomland, dotted with farms, and envisioned a market town and a mecca for tourists. Branson and Hollister may have had a new railroad bridge, yet there was still not one wagon bridge erected in Stone or Taney Counties; away from the railroad, travelers and commerce relied on low-water crossings and ferries. The regional commerce of the Shepherd of the Hills country would now find a center on the upstart railroad town of Branson.

Over the next generation the boosterism of things modern obscured major shifts in demography. Taney County lost 20 percent of its population to outmigration from 1900 to 1920 as Ozarkers, like other rural Americans, moved to the cities to find jobs and higher standards of living. Equally striking was the power of the railroad to concentrate the remaining population along its line. By 1914 more than half the population in Taney County had shifted to the southwest quarter of the county to be near the railroad and the towns it spawned. Stone County gained 14 percent in population during the decade of railroad construction, but showed no appreciable gains in the following decade of the twenties. During this period, cheap land was available for homesteaders who wanted to pursue a subsistence lifestyle, while larger investors bought up lands on speculation in the railroad economies. In 1914 less than 20 percent of Stone and Taney Counties was farmland valued at around ten dollars an acre or less. The indefatigable Truman Powell, a man who had hunted, mined, farmed, managed a newspaper, established Marble Cave school, and sold real estate in Stone County, claimed that the area had already demonstrated promise for immigrants even without the railroad. In 1904 he wrote that Stone County's population had tripled in the prior generation from four thousand to twelve thousand. The old population lived "plain and poor while all the current population lives better than they did then." Powell continued, "It is easier for a poor man to live here, keep his health and keep out of debt than it is in the prairie country."[5] True to Powell's forecast, a large percentage of the new immigrants were families of modest means. While outmigration of the old stock continued, new midwestern families from the flatlands took up residence in the Ozarks.

The editor of the *Branson Echo,* Frank Forbes, followed Powell's lead in promoting the region. Forbes had recently relocated to Branson from Pulaski County, Missouri, in hopes of discovering new business opportunities. In the rhetoric of perpetual challenge to urban dwellers, so common in small-town newspapers of the time, he proclaimed: "I can't see why people will wear their lives out in the cities, getting a bare living, when with a few dozens of old hens, a couple of brood sows, a cow and a calf, and an acre of two of grapes and berries, they could live like princes in Taney County and not work half so hard and have lots more fun. . . . Our whole county is a natural park, and we have more solid comfort and entertainment, live longer, die happier and go to a better place than many who pay rent, buy milk and scrimp and save and starve, in a vain effort to be in touch with the fashions, and the gilded palaces of sin."[6] This articulation of the Arcadian myth struck a responsive chord in urban areas. More than one city dweller cherished the belief that the White River hills could provide a setting for business and retreats that would foster robust and decent living.

One of the first of these Arcadian retreats was the Maine Club. After the 1904 World's Fair in St. Louis ended, a group of St. Louis sportsmen bought the state of Maine's exhibition building and incorporated themselves as the Maine Club. Next they acquired 207 acres of blufftop land on the south side of the White River, west of Turkey Creek. The following year they had the Maine building dismantled and shipped by rail to Branson. The railroad bridge had not yet been completed, so they hauled the logs by wagon to their blufftop site, and reassembled the clubhouse. The official opening of the club was scheduled for May 1906, which happened to be the same month that the developer and town father, W. H. Johnson, announced sales of lots for the new town of Hollister. One consequence of this happy coincidence was that the Maine Clubhouse proved to be a social hub for locals, perhaps more so than for visiting members, who did not always mix well with the natives. W. W. (Bill) Johnson, son of W. H. Johnson, remembered "the disappointment of the ladies who came from St. Louis with their husbands to the Maine Club, expecting something far different from the rugged hill country that they encountered. Some of them would arrive with trunks of clothes. . . . The women had no one to dress up for . . . as Hollister offered no entertainment or social life. Most of them were rather bored . . . for they did not share their husband's enthusiasm for hunting and fishing."[7]

In 1906, the year the rail line opened, the Presbyterian Synod of Missouri began construction of The School of the Ozarks in Forsyth. Conceived as a high school where pupils from southwest Missouri and northwest Arkansas could work to pay tuition, classes began in 1907. After its original building burned in January 1915 the school acquired the Maine Club property and relocated at the former resort. This proved a more suitable location than Forsyth because of its proximity to the Hollister depot and because the acreage could be used for income-producing agricultural enterprises.[8]

Burnett tie yards, Branson
Hobart Parnell Collection

Railroad construction created a thriving market for crossties. The Ozark forest, with its vast stands of oak, yielded for a time an endless supply of ties. The national demand for ties created cash employment for locals willing to put in the long, hard days of work required to produce them. Tie hacking was often their first job doing "public work" away from a subsistence farm. Ben Stults, who lived on the Wilderness Road in Stone County, wistfully declared that "them easy days [of hunting and living off the open range] are gone. There is not any more deer nor turkey for me. I am now in the timber business."[9] Ozarkers worked for tie companies or individual tie buyers, usually on a piecework basis; a few established their own small mill. The work required mobility and the tie hackers developed a reputation for rough and rowdy living. One newspaper, drawing attention to this fact, stated that "a jug of whiskey and the St. Louis *Globe-Democrat* will break up any tie camp in the world."[10] As the *Globe-Democrat* was so popular in the rural Ozarks, ads for timber jobs commonly appeared there.

The local boom in tie production for the railroad economy took place in a hinterland that remained primitive in terms of roads and other improvements. One citizen of Stone County wrote in 1906, "In 1860 when the Civil War broke out there was not a bridge nor a good road in Stone County. All the years since that time the people have been paying taxes, values have been increasing and the county revenues have multiplied over and over again, and in the year 1906 there is not a bridge nor a good road in the county. In fact no public improvements worth mentioning."[11] Despite the lack of good roads and bridges, the markets for timber products increased so rapidly that the same newspaper soon reported labor shortages on the farms because so many had turned to the new cash-paying jobs. Farmers who would have received but sixteen to twenty cents per tie in the 1890s now rushed to the woods to make ties for forty and fifty cents a piece. In 1907 Reed's Spring, in central Stone County, shipped 2,450 train car loads, or a reported 735,000 ties, and quickly became recognized as the tie-marketing center for the White River hills.[12]

The White River Railway also changed agricultural practices in Stone and Taney Counties. Farming and stock raising became more commercialized, diversified, and specialized in response to the opportunities offered by the railroad. Much of this transformation directly resulted from long-range planning by railroad corporate officials. They envisioned that new residents, when established as farmers, would ship their produce out by rail and consume the manufactured products brought by trains on the return trip. This stimulation of agricultural development also aimed at short-range growth by encouraging current residents to become more efficient producers and more avid consumers. The railroad's public policy was that "it is more profitable to build lines and develop agricultural sections which would produce tonnage, than to await the slow development of sections without adequate transportation."[13] Ozark farmers amply fulfilled the railroad's expectations. Livestock pens and loading docks at local railheads were crammed with the region's bountiful products.

The Missouri Pacific organized "exhibit cars" that featured lectures by agricultural specialists, displays of the latest farming methods, and machinery and stock that farmers could purchase at wholesale prices. In 1906 the railroad devoted special attention to promoting fruit production along the White River Division. The first Poultry Exhibit car also ran that

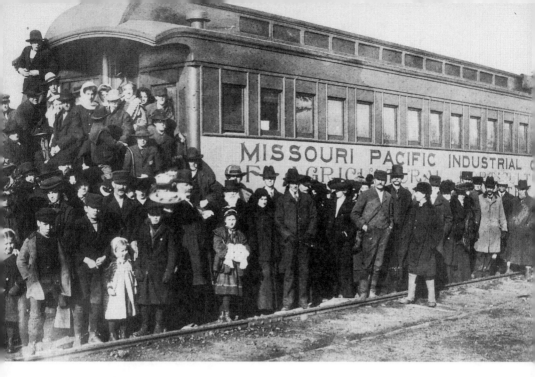

Missouri Pacific agricultural exhibit car
M. F. Miller Collection, WHMC-Columbia

autumn, followed in February 1907 by a Dairy Exhibit that toured southwest Missouri. Both the U.S. and Missouri dairy commissioners supported this project, which demonstrated the latest dairy appliances such as cream separators, pasteurizers, and refrigerators. The railroad also provided cattle feeding charts and ration recommendations. According to the railway, "milking machinery was new at the time, and created considerable sensation." Southwest Missouri became the leading dairy section in Missouri, and the Shepherd of the Hills dairymen found ready export to the Springfield processors.[14]

The Missouri Pacific Railroad set about in several ways to increase the number of immigrants to the White River hills. In addition to sponsoring float trips and agricultural promotions, officials began the development of a resort community adjacent to the rail line. This enterprise was Hollister. Unlike many villages which sprang up along the track, Hollister was a planned community, a collaboration between the railroad and William H. Johnson, a Springfield developer, former Forsyth real-estate agent and part-time journalist. Johnson owned a thousand acres on

W. H. Johnson's "thousand acres" that contained the upland Presbyterian Hill, the YMCA camp on lower Turkey Creek, and other resorts in the valley. Hollister is just upstream.
Postcard, Kalen and Morrow Collection

the south side of the White River that included the land between the mouths of Coon and Turkey Creeks. Johnson conceived the notion that the Turkey Creek valley would make an excellent resort location and persuaded railroad officials to join forces with him to develop the concept; by February 1909 the railroad appointed him an immigration agent for the White River Division. The infant hamlet of Hollister already could boast of a rustic Log Cabin Hotel, a building of twenty bedrooms and a dining room that drew a trade from train passengers destined for the Maine Club and nearby camps. Johnson's plan for developing Hollister revolved around the idea of an English village. He inaugurated his concept in 1909 with the construction of a Tudor Revival railroad depot. Next came a bank building and an English Inn, both built in the same style. This Tudor Revival motif was continued for many years in the designs of Hollister's downtown commercial buildings and imparted to the town's main street the singular architectural character it still retains, and which has earned it a listing on the National Register of Historic Places.[15]

The completion of the depot in January 1910 signified Hollister's rapid transformation from a whistle-stop to a resort town. It also demonstrated to Missouri Pacific officials that Johnson had a serious vision for the future. Prior to its construction Johnson offered to contribute five hundred dollars toward erecting the depot if the railroad would allow him to design it; the railroad accepted his offer, and Johnson set his architect to work designing and supervising the construction of the stone, stucco, and tile-roof building. The railroad executives were so pleased with the end result that they returned his five-hundred-dollar contribution.[16] Missouri Pacific then assigned Jerry S. Butterfield, a landscape engineer working out of their Lee's Summit office, to beautify the Hollister locale. W. P. Chapman, station master at the depot, became the first president of the Hollister Chamber of Commerce.

In 1911 W. H. Johnson replatted the town to face the depot and railroad track rather than Turkey Creek. This dramatic reorientation of the entire town symbolized the railroad's influence; the emerging town was literally rearranged to make the depot its focal point.

Because of the railroad's investment and its thoroughly modern vision of a suburban landscape, its officials insisted upon a stock law to prohibit open-range animals from wandering the village streets. Tourism's Arcadia certainly could not entertain swine in the streets! The controversy generated by this decision illustrated the latent tension that existed between local tradition and modernity. The Ozark frontier required the open range and the common use of all its resources while progressive agriculture mandated the confinement of stock in order to facilitate nonagricultural and nonstockman pursuits. Modernity prevailed in the end. After range animals had destroyed much of Butterfield's landscaping, the Hollister electorate complied with the railroad's wishes by implementing the first stock law in Taney County.[17] It would be another forty years, however, before Taney County finally closed the rural range.

With W. H. Johnson's dream of Hollister as a planned tourist community well on its way to becoming a reality, the stage was set to launch the resort industry that was to so profoundly shape the future of the White River valley. The Southwest Presbyterian Assembly was among the first institutions to grasp the vast potential of the region. The resounding success of the summer programs they conducted on their blufftop property

Looking upstream to Hollister
Postcard, Kalen and Morrow Collection

near Hollister gave a significant boost to the "tourist trade" throughout the Shepherd of the Hills country. The summer facilities of the Southwest Presbyterian Assembly and the nearby YMCA sent young people and adults back to their urban homes with a new-found appreciation for the Ozarks. The assembly, through its programs, aimed to shape attitudes and offer inspiration and spiritual regeneration to their guests; the White River hills provided the perfect Arcadian setting to pursue such lofty goals.

The Presbyterian Assembly of the Southwest purchased their 160-acre site atop the bluff east of Turkey Creek in 1910; they acquired the tract from W. H. Johnson in order to establish a White River Chautauqua Ground. The scenic location overlooked both Branson and Hollister. The assembly committee, representing Arkansas, Kansas, Missouri, Oklahoma, and Texas, chose Hollister out of nine possible locations because they sensed the potential of the new resort community to attract people who would "wish to get away from the dust and dirt of cities . . . for rest, refreshment, and recuperation," the very things that this Ozark Arcadia offered. To ensure harmonious surroundings the Missouri Pacific Railroad assigned landscape architect Butterfield to survey the grounds and lay out the streets.

Signpost, "Welcome, Hollister, Mo.," with camps listed at the White River
Railway depot

Postcard, Kalen and Morrow Collection

Workmen built a challenging 365-step stairway up the face of the bluff to
the grounds. Guests standing at the summit gazed into the spectacular
horizon of the Shepherd of the Hills country and its beckoning literary
sites.[18] The complex became known as Presbyterian Hill.

As the years passed, Presbyterian Hill expanded its activities. The first
program lasted only twenty-one days, but by the 1920s the assembly was
conducting numerous annual encampments, lecture programs, and conferences. In 1925 church leaders met there in February and during the next
seven months six conferences were held, concluding with a training school
for Presbyterian ministers. Presbyterians from the five-state Southwest
Assembly could use the grounds, but national conferences drew people
from other states as well.[19]

The assembly not only multiplied but also diversified the activities
on the hill as early as 1915. The hill hosted non-Presbyterian groups such
as the district convention of the Women's Christian Temperance Union.
Southwest Missouri Baptists from ten counties convened there, as did
Disciples of Christ. One of four national encampments of the DeMolay,

Pulpit Rock, Presbyterian Hill
Postcard, Kalen and Morrow Collection

a Masonic order for boys, was conducted at the hill—one thousand members from the south-central states attended the event. Groups of Campfire Girls met there, too.[20]

The widely publicized walks of Virginia Craig of Springfield brought attention to the hill. In 1906 Miss Craig had joined the original English faculty of the new Springfield Normal College and would become a legendary teacher and personality during an active career of nearly fifty years. An advocate of women's rights and healthy living, Craig decided in 1920 to walk from Springfield to Hollister and Presbyterian Hill. The next summer, Mary Woods, another female colleague in the English department, joined her. The pair did their highway walks five more times. They were part of an educated elite commonly seen at the hill during the twenties. A Webster Groves, Missouri, woman in 1929 confided to a friend, however, that not all activities on the hill revolved around rigorous exercise and intellectual fulfillment. She wrote that her mother was bored because of the social taboo on card playing "that innocent recreation, an indispensable pleasure to her. Sometimes conspirators gather for the crime in the cottages, where playing is tacitly optional."[21]

Bide-a-Wee Hotel, Presbyterian Hill
Postcard, Kalen and Morrow Collection

The leadership at Presbyterian Hill did not hesitate to voice its opinion on local government issues that threatened their perception of social morality. In 1915 their ministerial voice for temperance reminded readers of the *White River Leader* that they chose the White River site from nine others nationally, in part, because local option law banned open saloons. The authors of this article, Presbyterian pastors from urban Missouri, reminded local readers of the wholesome social environment for mothers, children, and decent citizens that had been created on the hill. It was a place where anyone could receive refreshment and recuperation from the fatigue and vices of the cities. They recounted their successful efforts to bring dozens of new property holders to Taney County—citizens without the local vote, but "not one among the entire number would favor saloons." They concluded their editorial by saying that sober thinking and voting would not jeopardize the continued development of the assembly. The March vote was three to one for the "drys," and Taney County remained dry, along with eighty other counties in Missouri.[22]

The appeal to city dwellers who wanted to get back to nature was evident in the expanding range of accommodations at Presbyterian Hill. In

1912 guests stayed in the rustic hotel Bide-a-Wee, a forty-room building set on posts and sided with board and batten; this was replaced a decade later by the more pretentious Grandview Hotel. In 1914, the first year that a car could be driven up the hill into the retreat, cottages were available for lease, or lots could be purchased if one wished to build a summer home.[23] To improve local roads Branson businessmen subscribed to a road-building fund. In 1916 workmen installed culverts and spread clay and gravel on the roadways.[24] In August 1910 the hill boasted the first electric lights in Taney County, and natives marveled at the lighted assembly pavilion and lodge for many years. A 1925 travelogue revealed that "A beautiful rustic dining hall" had been added to the grounds, as well as "scores of bungalows and, for those wishing to rough it, numerous tents." By 1926 there were close to one hundred cottages dotting the grounds. A Springfield Presbyterian donated money for a new administration building, and a 1927 article in Springfield described the "noble Mountain" in its "rustic loveliness" as possessing dormitories, too.[25]

One of the most popular events on the hill was the seasonal chautauqua of late summer. The midwesterners who camped on the hill were exactly the audience to whom chautauqua entertainments most appealed. From 1912 until it faded from prominence in the 1920s this seasonal celebration of democracy, education, patriotism, and religion charmed and uplifted visitors and locals alike. The great tents in the Missouri Ozarks temporarily housed a number of well-known personalities—such luminaries as William Jennings Bryan, Herbert Hadley, and Champ Clark. Douglas Mahnkey, a life-long resident of Taney County, encountered several new experiences as a youth at Presbyterian Hill. There, he heard his first orchestra and saw his second moving picture, accompanied by a lecture on India. He listened to instructive lectures on sex, disease, smoking, and drinking, and he consumed his first ice cream cone (which sold for a nickel).[26]

In the Ozarks the chautauqua also celebrated the region's best-known literary creation—Harold Bell Wright's *The Shepherd of the Hills*. Billed as a "masterpiece of literature" by 1922, the portable stage-play version of the novel had run for two years in New York before opening in southwest Missouri. Harold Bell Wright's morality tale shared the conservative family-oriented philosophy of chautauqua programs that were character-

ized by one author as "mother, home, and heaven lectures."[27] Mr. and
Mrs. J. K. Ross, already famed local characters, helped the assembly fix
its place in the White River hills. The Rosses presented their old dinner
bell to the assembly to awaken the conference delegates and herald important summer events.[28] J. K., who had been a rural correspondent to a
Branson newspaper since about 1900, became a popular attraction when
he started lecturing about works of fiction as an influence in personal lives
and on public opinion. Many came to hear his stories of local people who
provided background for character development in Wright's *The Shepherd
of the Hills.* This resident "native" had arrived only twenty years before,
but soon became well known in public arenas. He platted Garber in 1906
with hopes of selling town lots at a handsome profit, served as a justice
of the peace, and spent considerable time preaching at local country
schools. Ross became a consummate salesman of the Arcadian image in
the Shepherd of the Hills country.[29]

In 1919, the *Branson White River Leader* concluded that Presbyterian
Hill had "done more than any other institution to bring influential visitors
to this section," drawing thousands to the grounds. By the 1920s, thanks
in part to improved roads, the hill's dining hall drew people from the
Springfield area for its celebrated Sunday dinners. Presbyterian Hill became
so popular, that according to Springfieldian Marian Hoblit, who first stayed
there in 1912, "Everybody went to that area." And all visitors returned to
their homes with a new-found familiarity with the Lake Taneycomo district, with its recreational opportunities, and with the accommodating way
in which tourists were welcomed. The hill's most powerful promotional
tool was word of mouth. The success on the hill attracted the leadership of
the Branson Commercial Club. In 1913 the club had leased a tent on
Presbyterian Hill for its summer headquarters from which it issued promotional flyers. The foundational role of Presbyterian Hill as an anchor in
the Arcadian countryside of the 1920s was well established.[30]

The Young Men's Christian Association, like the Presbyterian Assembly,
established an early presence in the White River hills. Both institutions
shared a similar Arcadian strand insofar as they were antiurban and antimodernist in their view of the city's ill effects upon youth. This outlook
prompted the YMCA to expand its focus in the 1870s to include not only
young men but boys. Growing concern over urban immorality prompted

this change, and their view was reinforced at the turn of the century by new theories of child development, including those of pioneer psychologist G. Stanley Hall.[31] The YMCA formulated its own back-to-nature movement through a program of summer retreats. In the early twentieth century the institution expanded its camps into the Midwest. This summer camp program drew on the conviction that secluding young males in rural camps removed them from the evils and unhealthiness of modern city life, provided wholesome recreation in an atmosphere conducive to the cultivation of a good Christian character, and allowed boys to develop normal psyches through carefully regulated outdoor activities.

The Young Men's Christian Association first displayed an interest in Hollister in 1908 when an entourage of approximately forty people from the St. Louis YMCA came to inspect the area. It was one of the first groups to stay at the Camp Hollister resort on Turkey Creek that developer W. H. Johnson had just opened. The delegation was so impressed with what they saw that plans were made the following year for a permanent family YMCA campground, and in 1910 it opened. The campground was located on a sixty-acre site, donated by Johnson, on Turkey Creek downstream from Hollister and below the bluff of Presbyterian Hill.[32]

The camp was intended as a family retreat rather than as a facility restricted to youths; the first building to appear was a small cabin constructed in 1910 by the Banks family of Aurora, Missouri, for their personal use. The YMCA built several structures and more private cabins followed, including one owned by the Missouri Pacific Railway. Railroad landscape engineer Jerry Butterfield laid out a series of landscaped drives and paths that connected the YMCA camp, Presbyterian Hill, and the town of Hollister.[33]

The first two decades of the twentieth century were times of great building activity for the American YMCA. The Hollister YMCA camp participated in this movement. Between 1914 and 1917 an office building was erected to house a registration center, handicraft area, and, in time, a small library. By 1919 the camp had a gymnasium, and later a dining hall was built that, in its heyday, seated 283. In addition, there were about fifty individually owned cabins, and a number of tents were set up during the summer season.[34]

The Hollister YMCA Interstate Recreation Camp and Summer School, also called Camp Ozark, played a role in the promotion and development of the Shepherd of the Hills country similar to that of Presbyterian Hill. Both were affiliated with larger parent organizations, and both could effectively draw the attention and patronage of a larger group to the locale. The camp's official name testified to the fact that its visitors came from other states, under the auspices of the YMCA, to vacation on the White River. Many of these guests attended association-sponsored conferences. On one occasion 175 men from twenty colleges arrived in a group, and in 1919 the regional YMCA secretaries attended a training institute in Hollister.[35]

Use of the camp at Hollister was not restricted to YMCA members. There were families with cabins on the grounds who were not connected to the association, and there were vacationers who rented empty cabins. Otto Rayburn recalled that on a trip through the area about 1920, he and three companions, including women, "visited Rockaway Beach and spent a week at the YMCA Camp at Hollister, then open to tourists of both sexes." Groups such as the Boy Scouts utilized the camp and held regional meetings there in the early decades of the twentieth century. By the mid-1920s the camp sponsored physical education instructors from the ranks

Rockaway Beach Hotel and dance pavilion in distance
Postcard, Kalen and Morrow Collection

of well-known Missouri athletes and sporting instructors from Washington University, St. Louis.[36]

Hollister's growth blended tourism and marketing of regional products. Whether they were Ozarkers from Springfield or Fayetteville, or travelers from New York, Dallas, or San Francisco who journeyed by train to Hollister, all visitors stepped into a carefully crafted local "Arcadia" where the environment had become less pastoral and more commercial. In 1913 the Johnson family erected the English Inn, and in 1914 Jerry Butterfield and his Springfield associates opened the Taneycomo Club on former Bagnell Timber Company lands situated on the hillside west of the depot. This hillside resort club became so popular that trains made a special stop below it at the club's track-side waiting shelter. Butterfield's landscaping activities continued, and culminated in artistic plantings and the "Esplanade" on a slope west of the depot that was terraced with stone fences and a walkway that led to the Maine Club, a mile and a half away.[37] The rail company lavished special publicity on the Hollister area much as it did with the float trips. With the founding of the Taneycomo Club, the south side of the White River at Hollister now included the Maine Club, the YMCA Camp, Presbyterian Hill, the Log Cabin Hotel, and several smaller resorts.

The year 1913 was marked by a great event in local modernization, one that ensured the continuation of tourism into distant decades. The event was the construction of Powersite Dam, located just upstream from Forsyth. The dam created Lake Taneycomo—the area's greatest attraction—and miles of shoreline for resorts and recreation for vacationers from all over the Midwest.

Plans to build the dam had begun three years earlier when the Ambersen Hydraulic Construction Company examined possible sites for a power-generating dam planned by the Ozark Power and Water Company, headquartered in Joplin, Missouri. Construction started in 1911. The railroad delivered all machinery and materials to Branson and then floated them downriver on barges or hauled them overland by wagon. Camp Ozark, a construction boom town during 1911–13, and later a resort spot called Ozark Beach, sprang up overnight as the one thousand or more workers and their families arrived to set up temporary households.[38]

With the dam completed in August 1913, the lake completely filled in thirty-six hours. The railroad helped publicize the new lake with brochures having such enticing titles as "Play Places in the Ozarks: The White River Country." The company also offered special excursion rates to weekend and holiday visitors and summer tourists. Like earlier times when recreational elites came to the Shepherd of the Hills country to play and scout out investment opportunities, more and more middle-class businessmen were drawn to the region by the advent of the railroad and the new lake to seek relaxation and to consider the possibility of additional investments in the rapidly expanding tourist mecca.

Lake Taneycomo was a showcase where business and tourism promoters could parade their success. As the lake slowly formed between May 16 and August 1, 1913, six excursion boats were brought in—the *Minniehaha;* the McQuerter brothers' *Sammy Lane,* the largest passenger vessel on the lake and the one that carried the mail to Forsyth; R. W. Walden's *Golden Eagle,* which ran moonlight excursions to Camp Ozark; *Nightengale,* piloted by Harry Vanzandt; Capt. H. N. Paul's *Arkansas Traveler;* and the *Idyl Hour,* launched by E. S. Davis as Branson's first steamboat. Private craft also proliferated, including boats owned by people from distant cities such as St. Louis and Kansas City. The lure of the new lake can be illustrated by the fate of the local Fourth of July celebration at Flag, a hamlet southwest of Branson. As Lake Taneycomo filled in July 1913 locals abandoned the traditional Independence Day celebrations at Flag; instead, everyone planned a trip to Branson for a boat ride.[39]

Entrepreneurs recognized the potential demand for services and accommodations and envisioned a shoreline tourist-based economy. The power company advertised its intentions to lease lake-front property, touting "fine building and bungalow sites."

One of the largest of these development projects was Rockaway Beach. The *Branson White River Leader* reported on April 24, 1914, that "Merriam, Ellis and Benton of Kansas City [Kansas] have bought a large tract of land on the lake, near the mouth of Bull Creek, which is being platted as a pleasure resort to be known as Rockaway Beach." The general area was already known to tourists who had visited the former Springfield Club House at the mouth of Bull Creek. Losing no time in promoting its Rockaway Beach development, the company announced only six weeks after acquiring the site that it had fourteen men in Missouri, Kansas, and Oklahoma who were "strictly engaged in representing the advantages of Lake Taneycomo." Between September 1914 and January 1915 all lots were sold and twelve houses were already built.[40] A decade later, during the Roaring Twenties the resort village of Rockaway Beach boasted a dance pavilion, which was staffed all summer by an orchestra. New summer cottages had been built overlooking the lake, and the owner of Taneycomo Hotel added sixteen rooms to one of the lake's most popular attractions. Newly installed lake-side electric lights illuminated the warm water bathing beach and diving tower.[41]

R. W. Wilson's Cliff House Club, located just above Powersite Dam, enjoyed success similar to Rockaway Beach. Beginning as a tent camp in 1913–14, a decade later the club offered tennis courts, private dances, and an excellent dining room. In 1926, work started on a fifty-thousand-dollar clubhouse that was never completed. Wilson's clubhouse project was intended to blossom into a planned community of tree-lined boulevards and parkways, a golf course, city parks, and an electric railway. While never reaching its projected potential, Wilson's Cliff House Club brought lots of attention to the resort phenomenon on Lake Taneycomo as his was the first private resort. The Branson press in 1919 claimed that Wilson "had done more to popularize the Lake with resorters than any other man on the lake."[42]

In his promotion Wilson described the Cliff House Club in glowing terms. He advertised a retreat that was "1000 feet above the sea; fresh, pure embracing air and health so exhilarating; beautiful scenery, rich in landscape, swimming, boating, and tramping; abundant natural resources and raw materials; and excellent manufacturing facilities and cheap electric power." He built a boat dock and a road from the lake to the blufftop resort. His property was the first in the area to have a telephone. He also set up a Delco generating system and sold electric power to local residents. In 1915 he stocked the lake with one hundred thousand black bass that were provided by the federal fish commissioner. With these amenities and attractions and the promise of more to come, Cliff House Hotel attracted an upscale clientele.[43]

Wilson brought a constant flow of prominent guests from Kansas City. One of these guests, Burris Jenkins, a famous and controversial liberal pastor who was a celebrated World War I correspondent and journalist, became an officer in the Cliff House corporation and a successful promoter of the resort. Jenkins's doctors had prescribed outdoors exercise for the preacher-author, and like many others he chose the Shepherd of the Hills country as the setting to regain his health. Jenkins hosted numerous businessmen associated with his Community Church of Kansas City (later Linwood Christian Church), the largest in the city. Numbered among these guests who came to experience the Arcadian venue at the Cliff House were writers, architects, artists, merchants, naturalists, and politicians. Jenkins was a delegate to the 1920 National Democratic Convention and president of the Kansas City Izaak Walton League. He also sponsored several meetings for the Missouri Writers' Guild and hosted poet John Neihardt of Branson to address the writers at the resort. Jenkins was the first preacher to use radio in Kansas City, and audiences flocked to hear him debate his friend Clarence Darrow; Darrow became a director of the Cliff House Club in the mid-twenties. Wilson hosted float trips for various groups. The first issue of the *Ozarkian* in 1926 carried a photograph of Dr. Burris Jenkins and R. W. Wilson with the caption "True Sportsmen on a White River Float."[44]

The resorts along the shore line, like the Cliff House Club, required water transportation to accommodate the flow of tourists and overnight guests. Enterprising business people lost no time seeing that their resort connections were made. Among the first to provide water transportation was the Branson Boat Company, established in 1906 by St. Louisan and Maine Club member Vernon Todd. He expanded his fleet as resorts booked larger reservations. In July 1913, he enlarged his inventory of boats and fishing equipment to include tents, cots, and camp chairs. Downstream at the county seat, the Forsyth Outing Company opened in August 1913, similarly equipped and parallel in purpose.[45] Boat traffic from Branson originally headed for short-lived Camp Ozark, but soon most stopped at Rockaway Beach for overnight stays. Some of the long-distance floaters eventually stayed at Ozark Beach Resort, near old Camp Ozark, portaged around Powersite Dam, and journeyed on into Arkansas, as did those who set out from Forsyth.

Most entrepreneurs who took advantage of commercial opportunities were not natives but businessmen from the urban Midwest. St. Louis sportsmen, for example, founded the Maine Club, while another St. Louisan, Vernon Todd, started the Branson Boat Company and founded

Branson's first bank. The Branson Town Company, owned by a combination of St. Louis and Springfield timber company investors, directed it through their agent, Springfieldian Charles Fulbright. In 1907 the remaining property of the Town Company was sold to St. Louis men presided over by Vernon Todd. The resort town of Rockaway Beach was, likewise, developed by outsiders—the Merriam family from Kansas City, Kansas. W. H. Johnson, of Springfield, supported numerous enterprises in the Hollister area along Turkey Creek and the bluffs above the White River. Out-of-town investors owned the more upscale clubs at Taneycomo and the Cliff House on Lake Taneycomo, and the Aurora Club House, the Care Away, and Limberlost on the James River. Numerous realty companies outside the Shepherd of the Hills country speculated in local real estate.

These tourist business concerns modernized the local economy and transformed it from one based upon trading services and goods to a cash exchange. Individuals and families had traditionally provided themselves with necessities by using small amounts of cash and larger measures of barter. The railroad-related economies of tourism, timber, surplus agriculture, and land speculation stimulated the sale of both land and timber and commodified new services. Progressives in agriculture even coined such phrases as, "every farm a factory," and asserted that "no land should loaf." With statistics kept by the railroads, such modernizers increasingly quantified production and shipments. The stream of tourists with money to spend were considered another "cash crop," which meant that there was less barter in town and more cash exchange, and this transition rippled into the countryside as it did throughout America. Men who worked in the timber and the women and children employed in the canning factories enjoyed seasonal wages, but that return did not allow any surplus cash for business investments. It was outsiders with mobile capital who concentrated their resources in the expanding economy. The new investments and enterprises were driven by individual newcomers or the corporations that they represented.[46]

The national markets opened by the White River Division exploited and depleted the area's rich timber and wildlife in just a few years. By 1908 Stone County led Missouri in tie production; Taney was second in telegraph poles. Timber contractors moved quickly in harvesting the forest.

By 1909 Stone County was no longer a top county exporter of ties in Missouri, but Taney County had moved to third as the rapacious market economy in ties moved south.

Timber products were not the only regional commodities heading to the national marketplace. Hunters and trappers hauled hides and pelts to Springfield, helping to make Greene County the largest exporter, by far, of game and fish products. But it was local stockmen and their exports who created the largest category of cash flow for any industry in the Shepherd of the Hills country, as they always had—wealth for most folks was still mobile and still in the open-range forest.[47]

The potential profits to be had in rail export of dairy, poultry, fruits, and vegetables, moreover, inspired numerous small entrepreneurs to join the chorus of regional boosterism for the Shepherd of the Hills country. In 1903 thirty local fruit-growing organizations of southern Missouri and northern Arkansas formed themselves into one corporation known as the Ozark Fruit Growers Association. This organization provided speakers and agricultural advice to the White River fruit growers. By 1915 the affiliation grew to eighty-five local associations.

The railroad economies offered significant sources of income for the rural manufacturing concerns, and canneries opened in Galena and Branson as soon as rail export was available. The cheap labor of women and children was crucial to the success of the industry. This group found employment throughout the season handling the seed, planting, tending, and picking fruit. The canning industry, more than any other, symbolized the economic transformation in the lives of natives, especially women.[48]

By the first season of rail export in Stone County in 1906, sixty-two women (26 percent of the manufacturing labor force) worked seven-week jobs in late summer at three canneries. For ten hours a day, women and young girls peeled tomatoes, labeled, and filled cans, earning three to five dollars (while their fellow male workers earned five to eight dollars a day). It was probably the first cash income for most of these people. Hard work at some factories earned cash bonuses. Canners as a whole constituted one-half of the wage earners in Stone County. Three years later, women working in the canning industry made up one-third of the labor force in eight factories in Stone County; Taney County had three factories where three dozen women worked. By the time Lake Taneycomo was under construction in 1910, the comparative value of vegetable and fruit productions in both counties was over $121,000, while timber was near $600,000 and livestock almost $1,000,000. Nevertheless, the wages taken home by Ozark women were significant supplements to domestic incomes.[49] Moreover, the workplaces offered a new setting for socializing, communication among the working women of different neighborhoods, and a meeting place for young people. Some women boarded away from home to work in the canneries. Local society flourished at the canning factories much as it did at town literaries and school pie suppers.

By the twenties, southwest Missouri dominated the state in a concentration of dozens of small canning factories; Stone County had a greater number than any, with up to thirty-eight at one time. Taney County by contrast developed only an occasional factory.[50] Roy Nelson (1882–1929) of Marshfield began a canning factory in 1913 in Stone County. He eventually built eighteen canneries that employed twenty-seven hundred Ozarkers and was reputedly the largest canning manufacturer in the country. Nelson began his career in a Rogers, Arkansas, cannery. In 1902 he and his father opened the Marshfield Canning Company. The following year, Nelson was a cofounder of the Missouri Valley Canners' Association, that later became the Ozark Canners' Association. Two of Nelson's brands were "Taneycomo Tomatoes," and "Heart of the Ozarks" tomatoes. Local entrepreneur Frank Mease had a half-dozen factories near Reed's Spring. Canners usually placed notices in local papers offering seasonal tomato contracts to farmers willing to deliver their products to the nearest production site; later in the year want ads for peelers appeared. Farmers cultivated "ten to 140 acres" on rocky hillside tracts that earned them about one hundred dollars per acre.[51] In 1923 over four hundred women made up 65 percent of Stone County's wage-earning manufacturers; the county in that year shipped five hundred rail cars of canned tomatoes, the most of any county in the state. In summer, visitors might notice the seasonal tents that were set up to house many families who had spent a hot, monotonous day working in one of the many canneries. Springdale and northwest Arkansas was the center of canning in the Ozarks, but the small businessmen and farmers of Stone and other counties also reaped considerable profit from the regional canning industry. In 1926 the Missouri Pacific Railroad could announce through agent Dr. E. E. Corlis that 128 new canneries had

Reed's Spring Canning Company
Robert C. Emerson Collection

"Taneycomo Tomatoes"
Robert Wiley Collection

opened in southwest Missouri and northwest Arkansas.[52] The industry reached its peak production during the twenties and gradually had to downsize once the depression and drouth struck the region. New health regulations and competition from California did not help the Ozarks canning industry either. Finally, workers could acquire better-paying jobs for less-demanding work elsewhere.[53]

For local workers the canning industry was still part-time work and just one facet of multiple economic activities that families in the Ozarks continued to pursue. The experience of Clyde and Neva Davis was typical. Clyde Davis, born in 1900, married Neva Richardson at Galena in 1920. The newlyweds borrowed fifty dollars from Frank Mease and put in a four-acre crop of tomatoes. The young couple continued to grow tomatoes into the depression. In 1923, however, Clyde turned in the low bid for a mail route. Clyde and Neva then carried the mail for three years by horseback and buggy before purchasing a Model-T pickup in 1926. Meanwhile, they were running stock on the open range; this was a year-round undertaking, and Clyde also hauled ties to Reed's Spring from time to time. After their first house burned in 1927 and destroyed everything they owned, Clyde built a lean-to on the smokehouse and converted the building into temporary housing for his family, that now included three children, until they found another house, which took two years. For the Davis family and many other Ozarkers, the time-honored practices of "living off the land" by a variety of economic enterprises, and still making a living to support a family, by trading labor, services, and food during the depression accounts a great deal for the lingering "pioneer memory" of these "poor" but versatile people.[54]

When urban middle-class outsiders vacationed in the rural and, to them, backward Ozarks they brought with them the accouterments of their class—cars, money, nice clothes, the leisure to travel, and the cosmopolitan and condescending attitudes which were part of their social and cultural milieu. They were thoroughly accustomed to such modern amenities as electricity, running water, and comfortable transport. Travelers believed that even in the Ozarks money should be able to procure such creature comforts, and most expected them to be available. Local businesses made every effort to provide all the modern amenities their customers desired. To furnish electricity businessmen obtained gasoline-driven generators. By this means they powered electric lights and fans in the teens, nearly a decade before hydroelectrically generated energy was available in rural Stone or Taney Counties. A traveler who found any electricity available in the interior Ozarks in 1916 was indeed in a special place. However much electricity might appeal to tourists and progressive locals, not all were favorably impressed with the invasion of the new technology. One outdoorsman in 1919 criticized the arrival of electricity, saying that the "natives of the city love only frivolity and vice . . . they are the worshippers of the White Lights." Sportsmen who loved the primitive woods claimed that "hunters may be uneducated but at least they're men." These anomalous comments were fleeting in the local press and did not arrest progress. By 1920, however, the lure of the Shepherd of the Hills country for urban sportsmen who sought distant safaris had dimmed.[55]

The influx of tourists, attracted to Lake Taneycomo, mostly came in automobiles. As with the lack of electricity, it became evident that Taney and Stone Counties must provide better roads in order to keep visitors coming. An article in the *White River Leader* attributed people's growing awareness of the need for road improvement directly to the creation of Lake Taneycomo; the paper referred to "the education it has given the people in favor of good roads."[56] When traffic was local and consisted of horses, mules, and wagons the marginal and primitive road system sufficed. The number of automobile-driving people drawn to the playground of the Middle West was evidence enough to convince progressive residents of the pressing need for a better transportation system, one that could accommodate cars as well as horse-drawn wagons.

Despite pressures from the outside, significant change in internal improvements came slowly. Taney County resident Margaret Baker recounted moving to the area in 1911 when "few roads and no bridges" existed in the rural communities. Local businesswoman and author Pearl Spurlock arrived later, during the World War I years, but likewise remembered the roadways as "terribly rough and bad . . . there were no highways, and it would take two or more days to go to Springfield and back, only 60 miles."[57] Before cars became common tourists arrived by train then hiked or rode horses to local attractions. At some locations horse- or mule-drawn wagons could be hired, but even these rugged vehicles depended on the existence of roads. This is not to say that county officials gave no thought to road improvement prior to 1913, but the financing of new roads was not possible in poor Ozark counties with small tax bases. After the state's first highway commission was organized within the State Board of Agriculture in 1907, the town of Hollister voted seventy-five hundred dollars in bonds to construct a road to Kirbyville, expecting the state to match that amount. State funds, however, never materialized. Undeterred, Hollister moved ahead and also financed a road south to the Arkansas state line.[58]

The program to create an all-weather functional road system capable of handling automobile traffic occurred over an extended period of time and was ultimately dependent upon resources from state government. Local clamor for good roads began in earnest as an outgrowth of the lake's creation, but accelerated as a result of the state and national good-roads movement in the 1920s. For all the fabled independence of Ozarkians, modernization in transportation could not have happened without state and federal road-building programs. Local governments simply could not finance capital improvements on the scale required for massive road construction. But travelers wanted to drive their automobiles to the lake and to resorts. Between 1913, when the first wagon bridge spanned the White River in Missouri at Branson, and the 1920s automobiles became a common sight in the Shepherd of the Hills Country.

The growing numbers of visitors in automobiles no doubt spurred efforts of Ozark road-improvement organizations to increase citizen awareness of the need for a better road system. The press echoed the call for modern roads. The demands of what grew into a national grass-roots movement for good roads culminated in federal action. In 1916 President Woodrow Wilson signed into law the Federal Road Act. This act provided financial aid for rural road building and required state participation in administration and funding. This momentous step took road building out of the realm of sporadic volunteerism and county budgets and placed it under state government auspices. The impact of this act was still delayed in the White River country. Despite federal-state participation and the fact that automobiles were declared "no longer a novelty" in the Taneycomo region in 1915, a 1922 map showed no surfaced roads in Stone County. In Taney County only twelve miles of road was topped with gravel or chat.[59] Nevertheless, citizens witnessed widespread road improvement in Missouri during the 1920s. Locally, time-honored names like the Wilderness Road,

Wagon, later automobile, bridge at Branson; boatyards to the left
Postcard, Kalen and Morrow Collection

White River Trail, Ozark Trail, and others lingered, but the traveling public quickly adopted the official state road numbering system that was set
up during the 1920s.

The timely call for better roads was taken up by organizations devoted
to generating volunteer road improvement. The Ozark Trails Association,
founded in 1913 at Monte Ne, Arkansas, in the upper White River valley,
was one such association dedicated to achieving better roads in Arkansas,
Missouri, Kansas, and Oklahoma (and later Texas and New Mexico). The
Ozark Trails Association promoted good roads to foster tourism and
encouraged local commercial clubs and businessmen to raise money for
improving and marking the roads that served their communities.[60] Some
individuals involved in this landmark group later worked for the establishment of Route 66. A proposed new route from Springfield to Branson
was an important topic during 1914. As the ultimate direction this road
would take could mean economic life or death for affected communities,
the stakes were high. Jesse Tolerton chaired the Springfield Club promoters who decided that the first section should be from Springfield to

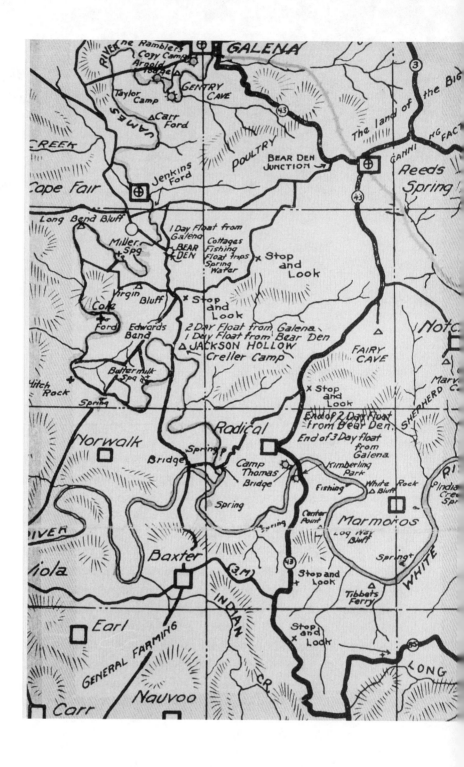

Ozark Playgrounds Association Master Maps, 1925

Powers Museum, Marion Powers Winchester Founding Collection, Carthage, Missouri

Spokane. South of Spokane there had to be a decision whether to proceed south on the Wilderness Road (to Reed's Spring, Notch, and Branson) or southeast on the Boston Road to Branson; the latter was the choice. The proposed road would transform what had been an overnight trip from the White River to Springfield to a two-and-one-half-hour automobile ride.[61]

In both Taney and Stone Counties the few improvements to local roads that were accomplished were woefully inadequate, or so it seemed to promoters. In Stone County the local leadership built a steel bridge across the James River at Galena and voted additional bonds to improve the Galena road district. But the construction and maintenance costs became far too much for the local tax base. The Stone County Court sought plans for four steel bridges across the James River and Flat Creek and for two more bridges across the White River. The resulting bids forced the court to reassess its goals, resulting in the elimination of all but two bridges. But rumors about additional dams across the James and White Rivers dampened the court's enthusiasm still more, with the result that they offered no contracts. Thus in 1913, despite the obvious benefits to the regional economy that roads capable of handling automobile traffic would bring, the only bridge across the White River in Missouri was at Branson.

Fortunately for the Taney County Court, the Ozark Water and Power Company that had built Powersite Dam was obligated to span local waterways impacted by the reservoir. Some months later Ozark Water and Power and county developers built bridges across Roark Creek, just north of Branson, and Coon Creek, adjacent to Presbyterian Hill. The following year, 1914, the county built a steel bridge over the mouth of Swan Creek at Forsyth, and at Branson spanned the White River connecting the railroad depot with easy access to Presbyterian Hill, utilizing the bridge previously constructed for wagon traffic only. Thanks to these improvements tourists traveled with increased ease in the Arcadian vacationland surrounding Lake Taneycomo. The increased economic benefits that had already come from the few road improvements were visible evidence that promoters used to forecast the greater future that would come from continued progress in road and bridge construction. Such a concentration of steel wagon and automobile bridges was rare in the interior Ozarks. When compared with the rest of the interior Ozarks, road improvement in the Shepherd of the Hills country was progressive indeed.[62]

Bothersome questions over county road bonds hampered Stone County's road improvement efforts in 1920. Although the county court judged the bonds valid, it sought an opinion on this question from a Chicago bond attorney. Two months later, the consultant deemed the bonds sound. Anticipating the first sale of Missouri state road bonds, the county then convened a special meeting to consider allocation of county money for a road which would be partially state financed. A large crowd attended the meeting, proof of the high public interest in transportation issues. The Stone County bond issue was one of the first to be passed in southwestern Missouri.[63]

Efforts were also initiated in Taney County to modernize local transportation. In 1916 the Taney County Court began construction of a bridge over Long Creek using county revenues. Unfortunately, the enterprise proved too expensive for the county budget. The uncompleted 340-foot three-span steel structure stood for ten years "without ever having borne the burden of a team of horses or a flivver car." Instead, travelers continued to use a low-water ford while staring up at the unfinished approaches to the bridge and its rotted-out decking. By 1925 the state highway department assumed direction of the project and completed the work. The new bridge connected southern Stone and Taney Counties into a sixty-mile circle drive promoted by the tourist industry.[64]

Missouri's Progressive Era governors from Hadley to Major to Gardner had lectured Missourians that taxes had to be significantly increased to finance the modernization of the state. The public must have sensed this need. By the mid-Twenties, if there were complaints about high taxes, their voices were mute in the local newspapers.[65]

Not all road improvements in the Shepherd of the Hills country were publicly financed. Due to their isolated locations, and because they had the money to do it, W. H. Lynch and R. W. Wilson took matters into their own hands. In 1913, Lynch, owner of Marvel Cave, built a road from Garber in Roark valley, the nearest White River Railway flag stop, to Marvel Cave. He ferried spelunkers between there and the cave in wagons. Later, when the need for automobile roads became obvious, Lynch underwrote improvements to the road that ran between Branson and the cave; the rough terrain, however, proved too difficult for much of an accomplishment. At the opposite end of the Shepherd of the Hills country Wilson completed a road in 1915 from his boat landing on Lake Taneycomo to his Cliff House resort and the fledgling village of Powersite. He also partially financed an automobile road. In 1926 he purchased a right of way for a road from Branson to Powersite and deeded it to Taney County, and encouraged the county to do the construction.[66] In both cases, Lynch and Wilson found that rugged topography combined with the distances from Branson and Hollister worked against success.

The good-roads movement, regardless of its episodic accomplishments, generated considerable promotional activity in a variety of campaigns. Tourist-supported enterprises such as the railway and boating companies extolled the Shepherd of the Hills country as an Arcadia that could be reached by automobile.

The Arcadian myth provided a common platform from which the various voices of promotion appealed to the public. Publicity for travelers presented the "Lake Taneycomo District" as a playground, a place where the weary could engage in recreation that would heal and rejuvenate their minds and bodies. As the lake rose before the resort town of Branson in 1913, the town newspaper, the *White River Leader,* adopted "The Playground of the Middle West" as its masthead motto and proclaimed that the area was destined to become "the great resort section of the middle west." The weekly paper went on to describe the local Arcadia as "God's great, natural park . . . easy of access to His tired children when playtime should come." Appealing to the middle-class notion of play as therapy, a chamber of commerce brochure described Lake Taneycomo and the Shepherd of the Hills country as a "favored playground." "Life is better after playtime," it affirmed, so "come play a while and catch the breath of a happier life."[67]

The image of southwest Missouri as a playground gained momentum while progressives called for better roads to get the tourists to this regional paradise. The Springfield press declared that the Ozarks "is coming to be recognized everywhere as . . . the play and recreation ground of the middle west," and this claim was borne out by the extensive geographical region from which tourists came. Tourists came from throughout Missouri, all the Great Lakes states, the lower Great Plains, and Arkansas and Louisiana. In eastern Missouri, a local paper celebrated the White River country as "America's Newest Playground," and Jewell Mayes, the secretary of the Missouri State Board of Agriculture, called the Ozarks "The new

Switzerland of health, beauty and happiness . . . the playground of the Southwest," an echo of the St. Louis commercial viewpoint.[68]

Rotarians in Joplin advanced the playground idea when they organized the Ozark Playgrounds Association in the fall of 1919 and brought thirteen counties in southwest Missouri and northwest Arkansas into the fold. Aimed at publicizing the Ozarks and encouraging tourism, the OPA started slowly, acquiring only one additional county member in the following four years. But by 1926, county membership swelled to thirty-three.[69] Individual businesses and towns within member counties could join the OPA, and many in Stone and Taney Counties did just that. The first OPA director, Eli Ashcraft, was a Jasper County businessman who moved to Stone County to become a prominent farmer and contractor. (In 1920 he built the new courthouse, now listed on the National Register of Historic Places.)[70]

The Ozark Playgrounds Association adopted "The Land of a Million Smiles" as its slogan, and it caught on like wildfire. The motto adorned picture postcards and became the title and subject matter of poems and songs. Even the Bank of Ponce de Leon, in Stone County, featured "The Land of a Million Smiles" on its stationery. The OPA annually chose a "girl with the million-dollar smile," who was featured in the following year's promotional programs. An emerging folklorist in Reed's Spring, Otto Rayburn, who became one of the most forceful proponents of an Ozarks Arcadia, penned a poem by the name in 1925.[71]

In 1925 the OPA launched two special publicity projects in addition to its illustrated annual guidebook.[72] The "Master Map of the Ozarks" identified float camps, clubhouses, agricultural areas, fishing spots, canning factories, and even scenic views which one should "stop and see." In May the OPA published the first of a series of forty advertisements that ran in the leading newspapers of ten southern and middle-western states. The organization reported amazing results—within a two-week period it received 730 inquiries by letter and phone. The OPA responded to these inquiries with a booklet about the region and a questionnaire designed to learn the respondent's travel desires. These efforts drew travelers from distant places; that summer visitors from as far away as South America, Mexico, and Nova Scotia registered at the OPA Ozark Tourist Bureau in Joplin.[73] The OPA maintained the largest compilation of statistics on Ozarks tourism. In 1927 officers announced that they had received more inquiries from St. Louis than any other area, including Kansas City, leading the OPA to designate Springfield as a local gateway. The OPA concluded in hindsight that "few tourists visited this district" prior to the creation of Lake Taneycomo. The creation of the lake was the master achievement that caused the region to blossom as a recreational destination.[74]

While the OPA concerned itself with the whole region of southwest Missouri and northwest Arkansas, smaller organizations promoted their own special places. They profited from the OPA example as growth in the tourist industry, and the improvement in roads caused the number of visitors to swell. In 1919 when the OPA formed, some fifty thousand "vacationists and health-seekers" had visited the greater region; in 1926 the number ballooned to a half-million, a ten-fold increase![75] The Lake Taneycomo Chamber of Commerce, a key member in the OPA, distributed tracts to resorts, hotels, and businesses, and donated one thousand dollars to the Ozark Playgrounds Association and five hundred dollars to the Springfield Chamber of Commerce. The latter contribution helped finance the publication of a Blue Book that apparently featured an illustrated page advertising the Taneycomo district. The Lake Taneycomo Chamber of Commerce later issued its own brochure entitled *Lake Taneycomo and the Shepherd of the Hills Country: In the Wonderland of the Ozarks*. This publication declared the area to be so fine that boating, bathing, fishing, and "mere living add new thrills to life each day."[76]

Two other groups, the Ozark Hills Tourist Association, organized in 1923 under the sponsorship of Marvel Cave owner W. H. Lynch, and the Springfield/Ozark Shepherd of the Hills Tourist Association, formed in 1926, promoted the famed vacationers' retreat. Despite their parallel purposes, relations between the two organizations were marked by strife. Shortly after the formation of the Springfield/Ozark group the Stone County newspaper carried an article entitled, "A Selfish Motive." The Stone and Taney Counties Ozark Hills group asserted that the Springfield/Ozark folks encroached upon its prerogatives. The local press, voicing the resentment of local resort owners, charged the Springfield promoters with unfair competition by appropriating the Shepherd of the Hills name for themselves.[77]

The Springfield group subsequently sent Lon Scott, its publicity director, to Galena to soothe local tempers by explaining that his organization intended to develop and improve the area, not to advertise and exploit it. This might have placated the Ozark hills business people had they not discovered that purported work on a new Table Rock Dam mentioned in a previous report, publicized in the Springfield press, was a hoax. Who was the culprit of this disinformation? The same Lon Scott who had released the bogus story for publicity purposes.[78]

This little tiff did not color all promotional alliances within Stone and Taney Counties; most relationships were cordial. For example, Galena merchants commissioned J. F. Lynley, a sign painter, to produce a large signboard. They placed it at the intersection of Highways 3 and 44 (now 160 and 176), on the old Wilderness Road, to direct tourists west to Galena. Following this model in highway advertising, businessmen from Galena and Crane hired Lynley to paint a sign that read "Short Cut to Lake Taneycomo by Way of Crane, Galena, and Shepherd of the Hills Country." Erected at the junction of Highways 43 and 16 (now 13 and 60) east of Aurora, this guidepost was intended to divert Springfield-bound traffic southward to Stone County.[79]

With the improved roads and increased auto traffic of the 1920s, a new automobile-related business opportunity arose. A local businesswoman, Pearl Spurlock, became an auto guide for tourists and gained as much celebrity as any of the river guides. Spurlock began her Shepherd of the Hills Taxi service about 1920. She entertained passengers with stories that illustrated the joy and fun of the Ozarks. Her clients came from as far away as Canada, London, Spain, Denmark, Australia, Persia, Egypt, China, Japan, Turkey, and the Sudan. They all shared the common experience of a Pearl Spurlock-guided tour through Harold Bell Wright's Shepherd of the Hills country.

Fortunately, Spurlock wrote down a portion of the presentation she had worked up for the tourists. Retold in her small book, *Over the Old Ozark Trails in the Shepherd of the Hills Country,* her tall tales enthusiastically emphasized the Arcadian healthiness of the climate. Believing that "a doctor could not prescribe a better tonic than plenty of this Ozark air," Spurlock wrote of an old Branson woman who became critically ill after going to California. Called to his mother's deathbed, her son from Branson revived her by letting the Branson air out of one of his automobile tires for her to breathe! In an antiurban vein Spurlock recounted the tale of some great-great-grandsons who wanted the family patriarch, aged 145, to die so they could finally receive their inheritance. They took him from the Ozarks to Chicago where he promptly expired. When the family brought him back home to be buried, however, the Ozark air resuscitated him. When he finally died of natural causes, the heirs interred him in Chicago to prevent another resurrection.[80]

By 1926, roads in Stone and Taney Counties were only somewhat improved. The best Stone County could boast of, in terms of an improved road system, was a twelve-mile stretch of State Highway 43 (later 13) with a graded earth surface; the rest of the highway remained unimproved. Automobiles bound for Marvel Cave usually came through Reed's Spring on that highway because it was the best route. The alternate way, from Branson around the southern foot of Dewey Bald Mountain, remained practically impassable, except for the most adventurous, until the creation of Highway 76 in 1933. Taney County had fared better in its road improvement program than Stone; the graveled portion of Highway 3 (later 65) extended southeast to Branson. Such improvements did shorten travel time considerably. By 1921 the trip from Springfield to Fairy Cave, west of Marvel Cave, a distance comparable to the mileage from Springfield to Branson, could be made in just over two and one-half hours. This was a far cry from Pearl Spurlock's two-day trip to Springfield of just a few years earlier.[81]

Middle-class Americans could now afford Ford flivvers, and they were not bashful about taking automobile tours on the new improved roads financed by Missouri state bonds. By the mid-1920s road maps produced by the Automobile Association of America, the Automobile Club of Missouri, the Ozark Playgrounds Association, and various petroleum companies became available to the traveling public. Such maps generated the desire to embark on "scenic tours" that could be enjoyed from the privacy of the family automobile. Urban journalists contributed travelogues for tourists in special Sunday features. In one, the Automobile Club of Kansas City provided a generalized map for a "Two-Day Motor Trip to the Ozarks and Return," accompanied with detailed milepost instructions. In the rough-and-tumble days of early motoring, such instructions could be invaluable. In detailing the return trip from Branson, when motoring into Galena, the travel guide warned of a "narrow, dangerous road with sharp drop to James River and to retaining wall. Approach to bridge here is very sharp. Use all possible care. Most dangerous point of trip, particularly so if approached at dawn or dusk."[82]

Of course, local officials were doing their best to eliminate such hazards to automobile travel. The solution to the dangerous James River crossing at Galena came when state road bonds financed one of Missouri's most distinctive concrete bridges. In December 1926 work began on the "Y-Bridge," an elegantly proportioned 760-foot span of concrete arches, the only such Y-bridge in Missouri. It is now enrolled on the National Register of Historic Places and currently used as a pedestrian bridge for viewing the James River. While still under construction the bridge weathered the disastrous effects of the 1927 flood and was finished in November of that year. A crowd of three thousand people celebrated the opening of the bridge and listened to Ozark orator Dewey Short dedicate the accomplishment. Short likened the improvement in transportation to "the cow, the fruit, and the hen" in importance to the Ozarks.[83]

Touring, whether floating on the rivers, boating on the lakes, or driving uncertain roads, was important to the expectations of tourists and to the economy of the Shepherd of the Hills country. By early 1926 continued improvement of state roads had created the opportunity for a new promotional concept of "circle drives." State government added its own promotional push to the circle drive concept. The 1922 *Official Manual* carried an article entitled, "The Spirit of Nature in Man," which encouraged enterprising citizens to sell "ozone and scenery to those who reside in other states." Such articles as this demonstrated the increased partnership of state government with conservation and tourism promoters. The author of the *Official Manual* article, E. T. Grether of St. Louis, was a leading conservationist in Missouri who called for the creation of "one grand state recreation park" along the public highways. His vision linked road improvement with communion with nature and the call of the wild.[84] Circle drives enhanced this opportunity. Grether hoped that anyone who studied the Missouri road map could see the unique circular transportation corridors that were now available in the White River hills to lift the spirit of the automobile traveling public. One of these circle drives looped Lake Taneycomo from Hollister to Forsyth and back to

Branson; another left Branson toward the northwest to Reed's Spring Junction then Reed's Spring, south on Highway 13 across the White River and back to Branson. Just north of Forsyth the highway department created a roadside stop, "Taney Vista," offering a sweeping view across Long Beach Bend. In the years between the two world wars, this vista became one of the most photographed scenic spots in all the Ozarks.[85]

Tourism was not the only commercial focus during this era. Throughout the 1920s, for example, the railway increased and varied its efforts to encourage and expand local agriculture. The line continued to run special exhibit cars that even utilized moving pictures, and worked to help local farmers diversify the production of such regional commercial cultivars as apples, wheat, tobacco, and cotton.[86] The Missouri Pacific

Y-Bridge dedication, November 1927
Robert Wiley Collection

encouraged commercial fruit growing by selling nursery stock at wholesale cost, which resulted in the area's first vineyard, and by showing growers the best planting and pruning methods. The headlines of a local paper
declared the effectiveness of railroad programs: "Missouri Pacific Fruit
Train a Success—Hundreds of Acres Will Be Set as Result of Expedition."
Farmers south of Hollister subsequently produced a variety of fruit.
Orchardists consequently shipped out a bountiful harvest of apples,
grapes, and peaches, while strawberries became a staple commercial crop
in Stone County. To help create high production, the Missouri Pacific
assigned a horticultural agent to Taney County in 1926.[87]

The railroad constructed fruit shipping and packing sheds at towns
along the line and took advantage of the 1925 Stone County Fair to

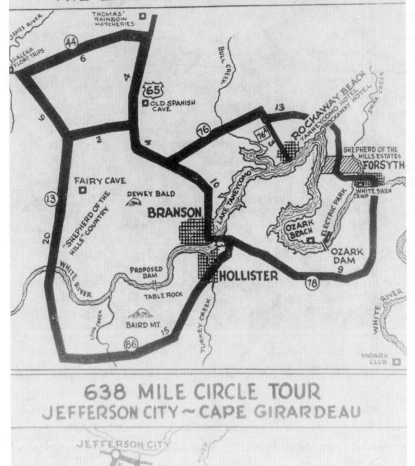

THREE CIRCLE TOURS
THE LAKE TANEYCOMO REGION

638 MILE CIRCLE TOUR
JEFFERSON CITY ~ CAPE GIRARDEAU

Circle drives around the Shepherd of the Hills country
Keith McCanse, Where To Go in the Ozarks, *1929*

demonstrate the latest methods for improving local cattle and poultry. It brought a dairy and poultry presentation to the fair and advertised a plan to give away a purebred bull calf for breeding to a group of five or more farmers. The only stipulation was that when the heifer of one group was bred the group must sell the bull to another club for similar purposes.[88]

Railroads also promoted immigration. Mindful of the long-range benefits of increased permanent population, new Missouri Pacific management established the White River Division Booster Club in 1924 and appointed a colonization (immigration) agent in August 1926. Reduced fares and low shipping rates for settlers were offered as inducements to tempt newcomers to the White River country. Dr. E. E. Corlis, Missouri Pacific's agricultural agent in Hollister, recorded that one new family per day relocated in the area between January and September 1927.[89]

The construction of the railroad, the dam, and better vehicular roads was foundational in the modernization of the Shepherd of the Hills country between 1905 to 1930. By the 1920s visitors could witness increased specialization of economic activities on both sides of the White River. Outside and local entrepreneurs shared an optimistic vision for future growth. Branson, on the north side of Lake Taneycomo, was the market town. It was the starting point for touring the legendary sites of Wright's great novel. It was the location for boatyards and float trips and the only city located right on the lake. Opposite Branson across the lake was Hollister, and the numerous southside resorts that attracted large groups and vacationers who wiled away days and weeks in riverside relaxation. W. H. Johnson had restrictions on manufacturing and commercial business in Hollister so most companies located in Branson. Nevertheless, town building in Branson and Hollister changed the White River hills forever from a place characterized by perpetuated socioeconomic frontier conditions to a tourist-commercialized playground. The real irony of this profound transition was that the modernization of this region brought waves of urban nature seekers who were on a quest for the mythic premodern Arcadia idealized by Harold Bell Wright. Promoters in Stone and Taney Counties evolved a commercial simulation of this rustic Arcadian simplicity while making sure to implement progressive communication, electric lights, transportation, recreation, and modern amenities for their urban clients. They well understood the desire of nature-seeking tourists for "naturalness" served up with a dose of modern convenience. From the beginning promoters possessed the key to understanding their clients' tastes and demands—a little primitivism went a long way.[90]

"Credulity Is Contagious"

Images of Arcadia and the Backwoods

THE PROMOTERS of modernity in the Shepherd of the Hills country needed a recognizable, marketable symbol for commercial tourism on the White River and in the railroad towns. Wright's novel in the early twentieth century and, by the early depression, the journalism of Vance Randolph and his peers provided a foundation to build on. The popular, sentimental cultures in which tourism thrived readily adopted the motifs of both *The Shepherd of the Hills* and the later journalistically created "hillbilly" without ever questioning the validity or credibility of those images. The Ozarks of the Southern Mountains, home to no large cities, became an arena for the flowering of rural romance, myth, and stereotypes. Conscious images created an expectation, and the twin forces of commercial tourism and local color have moved along together in creating a surreal Ozarks.

It is still common along the White River to hear someone refer to *The Shepherd of the Hills* as "the book." Literary tourists transformed the Shepherd of the Hills country and helped create a legacy still at work. The lives of the celebrated Lynch, Morrill, Powell, Ross, and other families were forever changed by the success of it. The cottage industries that arose from the triumph of Wright's famous novel have evolved into a vast complex of multi-million-dollar corporations that employ thousands. Local tour guides can be heard saying that "everything you read in the book is absolutely true." For them, and the salesmen of tourism, fiction is history.

This was exemplified by Kansas City honeymooners who made their epic journey to the Shepherd of the Hills country in July 1915.[1] Their Cadillac roadster could not negotiate the high flood waters in Bates County so, like other tourists, they stored their car and rode the train to Branson. Once there they rode the Sammy Lane tourist boat to Powersite, enjoyed fishing for a couple of hours, hiked to Forsyth, and took the ferry across the river and walked up the bluff to the Cliff House Club. At Powersite, locals introduced themselves as "hillbillies" and the young urban couple joined in dancing with them and "had no end of fun."

The Kansas Citians spent a week at the Cliff House and then moved to the Taneycomo Club above Hollister. They embarked on a three-day horseback tour of the Shepherd of the Hills country. Their stops included Rose O'Neill's home, Bonniebrook on Bear Creek, a dinner with Old Matt and Aunt Molly at Garber, after which the tourists "secured their pictures." Merchant J. K. Ross provided travel directions to Uncle Ike Morrill's post office and then Morrill sent them on to Marvel Cave and W. H. Lynch. Lynch pointed the newlyweds toward the Fall Creek mill site and to Old Matt's cabin, where they enjoyed repast and visiting with other tourists. The honeymooners saw Pete's Cave and the old mill engine and spring, and a boy who went by the name of Pete guided them to Dewey Bald. The couple stood on "Sammy's lookout" and cut their initials on the signal tree. Pete sent them through Mutton Hollow to Jim Lane's cabin where they registered their names. Then it was on to the Taneycomo Club over the trail "nobody knows how old" that cost very little and "worth nobody could say how much." There were no surprises on this trip. Locals and tourists knew exactly what to expect, and each must have felt satisfaction that the whole event went smoothly as planned. The cultural landscape was completely identified with the fiction created about it.

One Arcadian thinker who as a young man became attracted to the Ozarks finally came to see for himself and became quite a literary advocate of sentimentalized Arcadia. John Neihardt came to the Shepherd of the Hills country seeking a healthy environment for his sickly constitution and to raise a family. Ironically, he chose a house that had electricity, a convenience that his wife, Mona, finally had for the first time in their marriage.

Neihardt (1881–1973) was one of many health seekers who had come to the White River. Author Wright had come and returned many times over the decade 1896–1905, but Neihardt was already famous upon his arrival in 1920, seeking relief for his chronic bronchial condition. The poet was an avid outdoorsman and bought a house on a ridge above Roark Creek west of Branson. For almost three decades the family maintained a house there while the children went to school in Branson, Springfield,

John Neihardt
Missouri State Archives

and The School of the Ozarks. While Neihardt traveled extensively and lived much of the time in other towns, he wrote several of his books while a resident of Branson. His children grew up in the nearby outdoors where they and their father enjoyed hunting and recreation on the White River. Like a true Arcadian, who spent much of his time in the cities, the poet wrote to his mother, "The sweet, simple things are all that matter. Branson is the place to live . . . I want to eat plain, good meals, and I want to see the fog come up off Taney Como. . . . It is in the 'progressive' places people run themselves to death hunting happiness. We know how to stand still and be overtaken by it."[2]

Neihardt publicly voiced his Arcadian sentiments at the dedication of the J. K. Ross Memorial in 1925. The poet delivered the keynote address at a solemn assembly, saying that the virtues of kindness and love were typified in the Ross couple. Neihardt described the Rosses as "transfigured by the lens of larger truth into something more than our old neighbors. They have become symbolic of the sweet old fashioned goodness of so many of the people of these Hills." He called for recognition of Ross's virtue as a model for all to emulate. He echoed Wright's emphasis upon morality as the cement for society and opined that he who sought goodness need not look any further than Wright's characters or the Rosses.[3]

John Neihardt and his children enjoyed the outdoors for hiking, camping, swimming, and hunting. They spent nights on Dewey Bald and Cooley Ridge cooking on an open campfire, where the poet specialized in making his own stews. Turkey hunting in the fall became one of the family's favorite pursuits and cutting a cedar tree to bring home at Christmas was remembered fondly by the children. From St. Louis in January 1929 Neihardt wrote to his mother in Branson that, "I'd like better than anything else to live quietly in Branson and work."

But within two weeks, in February 1929, the poet was struck with the same spirit of anxious gain that most Americans have felt at one time or another. Again, he wrote his mother. "Now here is something important, Mamma. Please call up the best rental agent in Branson and the best in Hollister and list our places for rent. Do this as soon as you can. You may get advice from the agent as to what ought to be asked for the place. I want to hold the property until the boom is on down there. The work on the [Table Rock] dam is to begin in March . . . We both ought to be able to sell to a good advantage when things get going." Neihardt, like the real-estate promoters of the projected Arcadia Landing, a picturesque subdivision platted along a nearby nonexistent shoreline, was always interested in profit. The stock-market crash took care of the anticipated dam construction and boom, and Neihardt kept his property until 1947.[4]

Neihardt and tourists to the area were constantly reminded of Harold Bell Wright's wilderness novel by merchants who embraced the hillbilly term and capitalized upon the names in the book to maintain the sense of a literary Arcadia for the visitors. In doing so they demonstrated the renewable capacity of capitalism to market highly recognizable symbols. One of the most successful commercial advertisers was Hobart G. McQuerter. In 1913 he established the Sammy Lane Resort, a campground on the Branson lakefront south of the Main Street Bridge that extended over the lake. As a complement, he began the Sammy Lane Boat Line for sightseeing, excursions to other resorts, and summertime dance cruises complete with orchestras. McQuerter's fleet also had a contract to transport rural mail along the shoreline settlements and to deliver imported freight from Springfield merchants that arrived at the Branson depot. His bulk gasoline business supplied his fleet as well as other launches on the lake.

In 1923 McQuerter built a native-rock house-store, a building with living quarters above and commercial office below. The next year he expanded his campground into the Sammy Lane Tourist Park with twelve camp shelters, a response to the automobile traffic that wanted overnight space along the lake. In 1925 he constructed a large swimming pool, 60 x 150 feet and up to ten feet in depth, with a bathhouse on the side. Trees and landscaping were planted and a gate admission charged to the automobile campers. Another attraction was the screened-in kitchen and shower bath available for all guests.[5] The Tourist Park, nestled close to the Lake Taneycomo shore, was seen by all who visited Branson.

In 1926 McQuerter increased the shelters to thirty and purchased

Sammy Lane camping shelters and tourist camp, Branson
Photo by Domino Danzero (with permission of Leola Danzero Maschino)

shoreline formerly occupied by the Ozark Boat Line to continue his expansion. His Sammy Lane Boat Line ran four scheduled boats daily between Branson and the dam, while its *Virginia May,* the largest dance boat, with a capacity of two hundred, made moonlight excursions. Caretakers from Aurora managed this growing business while McQuerter erected eight new cottages on pilings over the lake's edge. By July 1926 the camping accommodations were filled throughout the season, and McQuerter had some eleven tourist boats plying the waters of the lake. He made the terminology of Wright's literary landscape central to the vision of visitors. Whether on land or water, tourists had a constant reminder of the Shepherd of the Hills in banks, inns, boats, postcards, and signage along the roads.[6]

The promotional success of the name Shepherd of the Hills also had local claimants for the book's characters. Famous fictional accounts commonly attract testimonials for model characters, and *The Shepherd of the Hills* was no different. During the depression Wright's distant cousins toured the area, stopping at Chula Vista gift shop and cabins on the "new Shepherd of the Hills road," Highway 65 north of Branson. The four sisters from Carthage, Missouri, signed the guest book using Wright in their name. As conversation proceeded the owner pressed the sisters for definitive information about the identities of Sammy Lane, Uncle Matt, Aunt Molly, and others. The cousins offered no explanation as they knew none, but Marion Wright Powers detailed the encounter by letter to cousin H. B. Wright. She even suggested to him that if he would return to the area incognito the author would "get a kick" out of what he saw and heard about his novel— Marion claimed that many were "cashing in" on ostensible connections with the book. Moreover, the cousins were amazed at the highway signs posted from Branson to Reed's Spring that included quotes from Wright's book.[7] The author wrote back from his California residence with direct answers. "Sammy Lane is not a portrait of any living person that I ever knew in the Ozarks or any place else. Several persons have claimed to be the original Sammy but I repeat there was no original Sammy. Uncle Ike, in the story, is a portrait. Uncle Matt and Aunt Molly are near portraits of Mr. and Mrs. Ross."[8]

Wright's answer made perfect sense. He lived with the Ross couple temporarily and visited with the local postmaster, Ike Morrill. Wright had returned to Branson briefly in 1918 and visited the countryside to view

Commercial stereotyping using the Arkansas Traveler story
Hobart Parnell Collection

locations for a motion picture. He stayed at the Branson Hotel, but no one in town even recognized him. While wandering about in his former Arcadian retreat he encountered at least three young women "each of whom claimed to be the book's heroine, Sammy Lane. Each Sammy offered to tell Wright her 'true life' story for a fee."[9] In an interview with Wright, as a local Bransonite pointed out a Sammy Lane character to the author, Gibbons Lacy quoted the author: "I am sometimes amused and often embarrassed by various people who persist in the mis-statement that I used my Ozark friends as models for the characters in my novel." The "Sammy Lane" lady had a pony and charged fifty cents for a ride.[10] Wright already knew that the locals had exploited his literary images long before his Missouri cousins revealed their observation to him.

Another view is that the book "is the Ozarkers' *Uncle Tom's Cabin,*" an insult thrown upon a proud and honest people. But Wright did not

An Ozark mountain orchestra on Roark Creek
Douglas Mahnkey Collection

condemn the Ozarks as Harriet Beecher Stowe denounced the South. Instead, in Wright's Ozarks, the traveler witnessed a bounteous nature, human virtue, and honest religion, and could experience a quiet repose. This atmosphere would bring one's body and soul to a vibrant health, suggesting that negative human traits like corruption and hypocrisy were unique to cities. Wright penned positive models in addition to simple caricatures, even though subsequent promotions successfully marketed a stereotype and composed a commercial landscape based on falsehood. A result is that the lore has become almost as fascinating as the Ozark Mountains, lakes, streams, and caves themselves. A tragedy in the image is that it has become self-perpetuating, one that has not attracted scholars to write analytical and interpretive works about the generations of Ozark settlement. Millions of travelers, however, still come to see the commodified regional folk life in the Shepherd of the Hills country for there is recreation and fun in the Ozarks and money to be made and spent. The editor of the *White River Leader* described the phenomenon in 1926 when commenting upon the success of taxi driver Pearl Spurlock and her

Shepherd of the Hills route. "What is in a name? The Shepherd of the Hills as introduced by Spurlock to many that live in a book land through her fine lectures . . . [is] a grip of romance [that] takes hold and the surrender to it is complete."[11] The detachment of Ozarks writings from the progressive elements of Ozarks society centered readers upon a cultural divergence from national trends. The results in 1930, as now, produced a literary tradition that the Ozarks had avoided modern progressivism.[12]

One facet of this literary tradition involved the use by journalists of the derisive term *hillbillies*. First imposed upon people in the Southern Appalachians by a Yankee culture from the northeast, the pejorative continued to appear in magazines and newspapers after 1900.[13] The use of *hillbilly* came from a market-based society impatient that rural people stood in the way of its exploitive economy. Suburbanites sneered at traditionalists who were not immersed in the accouterments of materialism so idolized by their own consumer society.[14] Native whites throughout America demonstrated a general proclivity to accept new inventions, fashion, tastes, and higher levels in their standard of living, but this did not prohibit the privileged classes from deprecating regions that lagged behind in these things. Derogatory labels for rural people filled the urban press and regardless of the country-life movement, rural America came to be seen as peculiar in the face of booming industrialism. The Ozarks, as rural America, moved from the country's "backbone to backwater."[15] And when Harold Bell Wright, a promising young turn-of-the-century author, needed an epithet for a wild Ozarker, possessed of character flaws that his urban audiences would understand, he used the term *hillbilly*.[16]

The 1904 World's Fair in St. Louis exhibited publicity photographs taken of rural folk in the Ozarks. They included scenes having a muzzle-loading rifle, rail fences, a blacksmith shop, a spinning wheel on the porch of a log house, a landscape of marginal buildings, a horse and buggy, homemade watercraft, and men and dogs around a spring. The display is so familiar to the modern viewer because the imagery of preindustrial, rural life marketed to tourists is still the same a century later.[17] Urban America expected to see these rustic, countryside scenes and not photographs of the new railroad towns or urban excursion trains that transported immigrants as new investors in the promises of American democracy. John Stilgoe concluded that "the once-honored agriculturalist became a hillbilly, the butt of jokes concerning traveling salesmen. He was, after all, a man without a lawn."[18]

Historians know that were it not for myth Americans would feel that they have no history at all. Whether that adage is applied to the Arcadian myth or to the hillbilly stereotype the conclusion is the same—midwestern Americans, whether from Chicago, St. Louis, Kansas City, or Springfield, enjoy myth more than history. Missouri journalist Walter Stevens celebrated a century of Missouri history in 1915 by publishing two volumes on the state. In his section on the Ozarks he wrote about fruit orchards and mining, but concentrated on the "strangeness of the Ozarks," its geologic freaks of nature, caves, tales of precious ore, legends, and outlaws. Stevens's approach was not far distant from that of Henry Rowe Schoolcraft a century earlier. Schoolcraft ignored progressive culture in the White River valley, too, as have most publications since. This pattern for writing about the Ozarks has allowed authors then and ever since to emphasize an Ozarkian Arcadia or an Ozarkian backwoods in keeping with selected themes that are designed to entertain an audience. Springfield journalist Fern Shumate, after considering Ozark storytelling, summed it up simply—"Credulity is contagious."[19] Whether engaging myth or stereotype, the forces of commercial tourism—consciously or not—have cultivated an image for the Ozarks, superimposed upon the blueprint of the fiction of Harold Bell Wright. Journalists, folklorists, and natives have supplied the commercial market for a century with genuine and fabricated lore that attempts to bolster this image of a rustic mountaineer, either startled or oblivious to the inroads of modernity.[20]

Twentieth-century Arcadians came to the White River expecting to see rustics whom the national press labeled as hillbillies, since journalists and tourists had used the term from the very beginning of commercial tourism. Ozarkers quickly learned to cash in on the demeaning hillbilly image. If the tourists wanted to see hillbillies, then hillbillies made their appearances. Float-fishing guides were model hillbillies at the gravel bar camps, telling tall tales and manipulating their Mid-South dialect for the enjoyment of sportsmen; locals at resorts and the legendary sites of Harold Bell Wright's novel took up the challenge of dramatizing the hillbilly stereotype for visitors. Within one year of the publication of Wright's novel, George Hall, recent immigrant from Illinois, advertised his 1908 series of Shepherd of the Hills postcards, documentary views of people and landscapes, but later added hillbilly stereotypes. Cost-effective post-cards proved to be great advertising. Over the years additional artists have continued the concept, but the exaggerated hillbilly stereotype postcard from the twenties has been widely marketed with contemporary views.

In 1908 the *Branson Echo* reprinted an article by B. W. Hale from the *Ruralist* that proclaimed "probably there is no scope of country under the sun that has been maligned so much as has the Ozark region of southern Missouri."[21] It carried the usual disparaging remarks about an unsettled country with "razor-back, hazel-splitter hog and tick-infested, long-horned, yellow-haired cattle" that reigned supreme. Natives were "shiftless and lazy," specialized in chewing tobacco, and were capable of amazing feats of spitting. The journalist dubbed such musings as lies based upon his recent tour via the railroad and visits to Ozark towns including those in the Shepherd of the Hills country. His impressions were that Ozarkers "have been so busy making money" that they have not communicated to others their good fortunes. The *Ruralist* admitted that the "shiftless humanity without energy or purpose" was a rapidly disappearing class. The writer said that "American energy has discovered this land" and that prosperous, progressive people abound. What's more, the symbol of success was evident—"everything is on a cash basis" at the mercantiles. Mr. Hale was witness to the remarkable change in town, but he did not tour the countryside. A dichotomy between town culture and rural tradition continued as Ozarks progress was viewed as a mixed blessing to those who preferred life on the open range and who chose not to move into town.

The following summer in 1909 the *Ruralist* continued to bring attention to the modernization of the Ozarks and satirize its detractors.[22] Emphasizing the markets brought by the railroad, the writer said, "Poor, suffering, uncivilized Ozarks! Her people do nothing but work and lay by wealth. They ship their lumber and hay and hogs and sheep and cattle and the opulent North and effete East send them money, more money. Wild desperate Ozarks! Her savage children tormenting the tenderfoot with the hospitality of their homes." The magazine brought special attention to the fact that the rapid advances in purebred stock and marketing should not be taken lightly. The *Ruralist* offered the prediction that the developing herds of cattle in the Ozarks would be the brood stock for her neighbors of the future.

By 1915 the term *hillbilly* had been in the American vernacular for many years, but it was not yet an everyday term in local White River newspapers until the release of a new film. *Billie—the Hill Billy* told the story of a city man who went to the Ozarks, fell in love with a mountaineer's daughter, and stole her away in marriage for his return to the city. By this time, movie makers had produced hundreds of films about moonshining and feuds. But not until the introduction of *Billie—the Hill Billy* did any of the commercial advertising associate hillbillies with the negative aspects common to feuding and moonshining films. In the Ozarks, as in Appalachia, the popularity of mass culture initiated an increased awareness of popular jargon.[23]

Increased trade and tourism by automobile in the new Lake Taneycomo district brought discussions of hillbillies more frequently into the local press. Progressive boosterism in Branson claimed in 1915 that "the poor hillbilly" was already gone. As editor E. J. Hoenshel knew, writers enjoyed "manufacturing hillbillies who wore horns, ran wild and ate acorns," a myth too many travelers believed, as they got no farther inland than a walk from the local railroad station. Instead, the *White River Leader* suggested that Ozarkers were like people in Kansas City who lived there for a lifetime and "did not know the Missouri River from the Kaw [Kansas]."[24] Ozark newspapermen knew that city folk could be just as provincial as rural dwellers.

J. K. Ross, living beside the railroad at Garber, was used to fielding questions about hillbillies. As Old Matt, Ross penned some of his thoughts for the Branson press.[25] "What is he? Where does he live? What are his habits? Is the hillbilly different from other people?" he wrote. The successful immigrant and noted local authority defined the hillbilly as a descendant from New England, the Middle West, or the more southern states —just about anyone who settled in the Ozarks. He lived with few privileges in material possessions or education, but was a master in the study of nature that lay all around him and knew about fishing or farming. The hillbilly was a competitive trader, not to be taken for a buffoon—his logic was masked by his slow manner of talking, said Ross, the merchant.

Ross pointed out that hillbillies served on the local judiciary and dealt out justice to bootleggers and settled disputes over boundary lines. He was the prosecuting attorney who warned tourists to obey the local laws or the defense attorney who would gladly take your money to keep you out of jail. The hillbilly was the schoolteacher who trained the local youth

Will T. Powell and J. K. Ross at Fall Creek Mill, c. 1905
Walker Powell Collection

for adulthood. In short, Ross said, the hillbilly was "a MAN capable of the position he holds." When asked how long it took to become a hill-billy, Ross said one need only remove store-bought clothes, don a pair of overalls, and with determination "go to work and do something" to become a full member in the brotherhood. Failing that calling, Uncle Matt advised the inquirer to "go back east to your wife's people, or north, or wherever you transported this disappointed bundle of 'know-it-all' for we have no room for loafers."

At the end of the year in December 1915 a state government report on the number of motor license registrations in Jefferson City was cause for celebration. The secretary of state announced that "almost every county in southwest Missouri has doubled its motor car population." Even though more than half the state registrations were in St. Louis, the trend was enough to proclaim that the purchase of cars in the Ozarks meant that the "remnants of provincialism" were being discarded and that "hillbillism that once made them fair game for humorists and cartoons" was disappearing. The press release lauded farmers in the forested interior counties who bought the machines to transport their sons and daughters to public schools in the county seat towns. A consumer society measured progress by numbers and the acquisition of material wealth.

The celebration of the Missouri centennial in 1921 gave occasion for the publication of a centennial history by Missouri journalist Walter Stevens. Stevens included almost a hundred pages on the Ozarks, but his main attraction was Marvel Cave. In addition to a detailed description of the great karst feature, the author wrote about Roark Mountain and its associations with guerrilla warriors and vigilantes. In a typical characterization, he wrote of warfare and violence, the romances of travelers looking for precious metals, traditions of Spanish treasure, and Truman Powell's claim that the "original Arkansas Traveler" had explored the cavern. The Ozark backwoods, according to Stevens, was the perfect place for these occurrences.[26]

By the twenties American journalism promoted an image of the Ozarks that rested upon polarized extremes: Wright's sentimentalized pastoralism, including a calm, rural, and romantic respite that sportsmen and feature writers enjoyed, was juxtaposed to yellow journalism that emphasized the historical anomalies of local vigilante violence in the 1880s, widespread commerce in moonshining, feuds, and the conclusion that the land was with-

BIN AT CHULA VISTA, BRANSON, MO.

Auto and cabin at Chula Vista on new Highway 65
Postcard, Kalen and Morrow Collection

out any modern people. Earlier pronouncements in the local press that "the poor hillbilly" had suffered a demise was premature.

"Hillbillism" became chic in Branson in the twenties. In fact, Ozarkers used the term among themselves as a point of debate or in poking fun at themselves. Town women formed the Hill Billies sorority and proudly announced their socials in the newspaper as any other club did. They had lunches together, talked of current affairs, and occasionally wrote poetry whose rhymes found their way into the local press.[27] The images of these genteel settings contrasted sharply with journalists who published in the national serials. Charles Morrow Wilson chose to emphasize the "high brush districts" of the White River country for their violence, ungodliness, immorality, and lest someone complain, he admired their "literature of speech," storytelling, music, and neighborliness with one another. Wilson boasted of one community in Taney County which had not had a social event in seventeen years without bloodshed. He stressed the oral traditions, saying that "there are yarns without limit either of length or number." But Wilson was not interested in town.[28]

But neither have most observers of the Ozarks been interested in the historic roles of town and shifting settlement histories that brought significant change to the region. In the first generation after the publication of Wright's novel, the environs of the Shepherd of the Hills country underwent the most dramatic change in its history, save the Civil War, with the founding of new towns, markets, and new immigration. While tourists came to the towns for their overnight stays and comfortable amenities, it was away from the railroad that journalists sought either an Arcadia or the backwoods. Travelers, in their subsequent writings, confirmed their perception of Arcadia or the backwoods while on float trips or on tours to the legendary literary sites. By 1930 vacationers motored into Branson along the newly constructed Highway 65 and visited the "twenty-eight summer resorts along Lake Taneycomo," but probably bypassed the "twenty-seven tomato and bean canning plants," the stock ranches, fruit orchards, sawmills, tie and timber camps, mineral diggings, new country schools, and churches. Instead, tourists and local-color journalists focused upon "natives," many of whom had recently arrived on the railroad, and were "down along the river telling big yarns to the popeyed summer guests, wearing out legends and tales speaking a jargon for the occasion they drop quickly when they get home."[29] Before long, the greatest practitioner of all, Jim Owen, would become legendary in the depression with his White River floats and his finely "trained hillbillies" who spoke a contrived dialect for visitors.

Dialect, however, had long standing as a principal attraction for outsiders who became interested in the Appalachians or the Ozarks; it represented a cultural diversity from that of the tourist. From the 1880s "dialect columns" could be read in dozens of newspapers throughout the southern uplands as local-color journalists tried to entertain their audiences. Vance Randolph (1892–1980), who began his Ozark writing career in the 1920s, became the region's expert on dialect. Randolph's research interests were "folksongs, dialect, superstitions, tall tales, etc." but not history. Randolph, moreover, communicated much of his observations in the format of journalism, including his two early books.[30] He concentrated upon families farthest removed from town and became the greatest exponent of a backwoods image for the Ozarks using a license of exaggeration to help make a name for himself and support his migratory style of living within the region.

Randolph, a midwest Kansan and adoptive Ozarker, after he had spent

Pleasure boat on Lake Taneycomo, with musicians at Rockaway Beach
Postcard, Kalen and Morrow Collection

a generation collecting and writing about the White River hills of Arkansas and Missouri, was fond of relating to his readers about his first experience in the Ozarks. In 1899 he was age seven when his parents took him on vacation to the O'Joe Fishing Club near the Elk River and the town of Noel in McDonald County, Missouri. The club was one of the earliest commercial resorts in the Ozarks, a respite for railroad men from Kansas City and Pittsburg, Kansas. Randolph remembered in the late depression, "I perceived at once that a guide named Price Payne was the greatest man in the world, and that the Ozark country was the garden spot of all creation."[31] As the region's foremost folklorist at the time, Randolph's memory of his first Ozark experience, as a tourist, was of an Arcadian discovery. In fact, he marketed several of his writings prior to the depression to tourists and sportsmen through the magazine serials of *Field and Stream, Forest and Stream, Outdoor Life, Sports Afield,* and others.[32]

But Randolph, unlike W. H. Lynch, Truman Powell, Ike Morrill, and

J. K. Ross, adopted a different emphasis for the Ozarks. While others rallied behind the boosterism of tourism, Randolph penned a lament about change, complaining about "the foreign invasion" of tourists that brought "nothing but trouble to the real hillbilly."[33] Randolph, sympathetic to leftist writings, echoed American antimodernism (as the 1888 founding of the discipline of folklore itself did), a compartmentalized mindset that considered modern change an anathema to traditional culture. Randolph and his contemporaries used antimodernism selectively. Randolph, the collector, for example, used phonographs and audio recorders to play "hillbilly music" to Ozarkers to stimulate their reactions and encourage musical performances so he could capture the singing of folk songs on modern recordings. Randolph's publishing career, though brilliant in its achievements, is demonstrative of one that was complex, evolving and maturing over time, and one that never analyzed historical process and change. Carl Sauer, the only scholar of the era who did write of changing Ozark lifeways that so interested collectors, identified strengths of the region and proposed significant governmental development.[34] The journalism of Randolph and contemporary observers who penned commentaries for their commercial audiences produced descriptive, impressionistic catalogs of what they saw in their own time and did not make comparisons through the generations; in doing so, they perpetuated popular stereotypes that all hillmen lived in the backwoods steeped in cultural tastes that never changed. But the wily Randolph continued this successful journalist's formula for writing about the Ozarks, and like a comedian at a country music show who needed sales to support himself, told his audiences what they wanted to hear—stories about the most anomalous Ozarkers of the day.[35]

Randolph's narratives, *The Ozarks: An American Survival of a Primitive Society,* 1931, and *Ozark Mountain Folks,* 1932 (with a strong emphasis on dialect), continued a popular journalistic genre of imagined dialogue and exaggerated generalizations, presenting a nostalgic Ozarks that was being eroded by the Industrial Age, immigration, and tourism—Randolph dreaded the new order of business in the Ozarks. At the same time, his writings in dialect and of tall tales complemented the culture of entertainment in tourism. He "never took any particular interest" in the established towns of Joplin, Springfield, Fayetteville, the new towns of Reed's

Blue Heaven cabin
at Sleepy Hollow
Camp, Hollister
*Postcard, Linda
Myers-Phinney
Collection*

Spring, Hollister, and Branson, or other towns in and on the Ozark bor-
ders and thought all of them "no different" than other cities. He was aware
of significant change, but wrote that "typical hillmen detest all city people,"
"ordinary hillmen read nothing at all," and that the Ozarker "despises all
uplifters."[36] He proclaimed that real Ozarkers "seldom come down to the
splendid new highways at all," but he apparently never kept track of family
histories like those of Truman Powell, Ike Morrill, J. K. Ross, Ben Stults,
Will Sharp, W. D. Sylvester, and others who encountered cultural options
in the Ozarks and made progressive choices. The Ingenthrons and

Mahnkeys, to name only a sample from whom Randolph received several traditional folktales, were quintessentially modern and progressive Ozark families. The large number of Ozark youths of the early twentieth century who migrated to cities, in and out of the Ozarks, to better their standards of living would think Randolph's monolithic view of Ozark families very strange. The famous folklorist, as journalist, asserted unqualified generalizations for dramatic effect. Many personalities that Randolph and other commentators admired manifested traditional traits of culture while embracing modernity at the same time. In fact, Randolph himself "liked a clean white shirt every day."[37] The "real hillbilly" of Randolph's mind was far distant from the Ozarks "first families" who migrated to the fertile Ozark river valleys to open farms, stock ranches, mills, ferries, orchards, and frontier institutions. The revered folklorist worked with a socioeconomic class bias to define a backwoods Ozarks for an audience saturated in myth and stereotype.

Randolph, however, in focusing upon the backwoods and using the term *hillbilly* widely, mirrored the popularity of this expression by the depression. In the mid-twenties American businessmen found a salable market for music with a "hillbilly image," a market that only grew with time. Ozarkers and others purchased records with hillbilly labels from Sears and Roebuck and Montgomery Ward catalogs.[38] Appalachia was the home of this musical flowering in America, but it should not seem too surprising, given the extraordinary success of Ozarks tourism, that decades later musical performances formed an important niche in the Shepherd of the Hills country, a historic centerplace for Ozarks folklore and fiction. Popular culture in film, tourism, and music shows has taken the once-sharp edge off the *hillbilly* term and made it palatable to many residents in the region.

Hillbillism in Wright's *The Shepherd of the Hills,* in Arcadian musings, or in Ozark folklore is a lingering symbol of the age-old tensions between rurality and the city, and Randolph's common use of the term *hillbilly* in his chapter titles and articles helped encourage a formal, even prideful, use of the term. During the depression regional newspapers included "Ozark Hillbilly" in titles of reports that referred to U.S. congressman Dewey Short, an influential Republican from Stone County; the caption opened contexts that suggested his practical, sensible vision of politics. After 1936, Branson entertainment was featured at the Jim Owen Hillbilly Theater, a landmark site in Ozarks image making. Folk singer May Kennedy McCord donned the title "The Queen of the Hillbillies" and became a much-loved public figure through her newspaper column and Springfield radio show, "Hillbilly Heartbeats." In turn, this encouraged the Springfield Chamber of Commerce to establish "Hillbilly Awards" for natives and business leaders throughout the country, and "commercial hillbillism" became just one more extractive industry in the Ozark southern uplands. Ironically, in 1954 the Ozark Playgrounds Association recognized Vance Randolph with an award for helping to bring attention to the Ozarks and boosting the tourist business.[39] In the end, Randolph worked at one cultural extreme, and progressive newspaper editors worked the other—the truth about an Ozarks Arcadia or backwoods was somewhere in between.

In 1927 journalist Charles Finger, an Arcadian Ozarker who loved the primitive backwoods, published a stream of consciousness that he entitled *Ozark Fantasia*. He told of his many travels throughout the region, his impressions of national and local figures, and international tales replete with dialogue. He romanticized the traditional Ozarks and thought that it would never be commercialized more than "high-way deep," never penetrating the quietude of the "happy poor" in the land. He took the famous Galena-to-Branson float trip and penned an Arcadian lament that must have made Vance Randolph nod in agreement.

> For at Branson commercialism yawns and the river is clean and pure no more. Golden youth has passed and there is left nothing but the seriousness of middle age. That abundant good humor and bubbling exhilaration vanishes and the river becomes a dull and sobered thing, stagnant and lusterless, bearing the burden of petty things and frivolous, of fussy motor boats, of noisy pleasure steamers and pursy and pompous houseboats ridiculous in their self-importance. The tall trees vanish and where they once stood are frankfurter stands, drinking stalls, ten-cent dancing halls, cheap shows, things tawdry and vulgar that invite to foolish wastefulness. So the romantic gives way to the common-place, natural beauty is no more, and the name of the river is on the lips of fools.[40]

Charles Finger, Vance Randolph, Charles Morrow Wilson, and others celebrated an Edenic, mythic Ozarks and promoted a nostalgic literature and community of interest among journalists who continue to market a similar genre to consumers. The writers, however, were well traveled and lived in town. They enjoyed visiting the hill men on the ridges, but they never took up permanent residence in the picturesque settings described in their work. Instead, they developed an organic relationship with tourism and its commercial market to produce an icon of hillbillism as an artifact to visit. A local schoolteacher who later assessed the lore of Shepherd of the Hills tourism blamed Randolph, and others, as principals in attributing characteristics to the Ozark hill man that made him "as some queer animal in the zoo."[41]

As tourism expanded, so did the audience for Ozarks journalism and folklore. The flowering of this symbiotic relationship did not come until the depression with the historically significant works in folklore of Randolph and Otto Rayburn, and a host of regional writers who produced a constant flow of Ozarks journalism. The success of their message was built upon the introduction of paved roads, radio, and government-owned recreational properties, especially state parks. Hillbilly music and literature became so much a part of vernacular speech that the federal government defended "hillbilly" as a regional term and potential name for a new "Hill Billy National Forest" during the depression.[42] Like opposition political parties, the antimodernist journalism glorifying a primitive Ozark society and mountain ways thrived in the presence of competition for the tourist dollar. The *Missouri Magazine* in 1929 observed the phenomenon and said that "our natives have already caught the tourist bunk idea and have been preparing themselves for the profession."[43] Native Ozarkers, once exposed to the conveniences of modernity and its capitalist ways did not shun them, they embraced them.

By the time of the Great Depression the cultural posturing by promoters, journalists, and local residents projected a gentle Arcadia and a thriving backwoods for immigrants, businessmen, tourists, retirees, and natives alike who sought a climate of romance, and all of them came under the influence of modernity. The "shiftless hillbilly" supported his family by hunting and fishing and raising a few open-range hogs as traditional American pioneers had always done in carving a subsistence lifestyle from one wilderness or another. At worst, the hillbilly of the early twentieth century was an anachronism to the advancing commercial culture and national markets; at best, he consciously chose "to live off the land" in an

Arcadian lifestyle venerated by nineteenth-century Americans, and later, in the 1960s and beyond by "back-to-the-landers" in the region.

For Ozarkers isolation and social integration could exist at the same time. Ozarkers, exposed to a market exchange, recognized the harshness of premodern life and welcomed new opportunities. One of those opportunities was to perpetuate the collective provincialism and hillbilly buffoonery into long-range commercial profits even at the expense of their own image. Outside the Ozarks, the anxieties accompanying modern urban life coalesced into nostalgic yearning for a romanticized, rural past which had in fact never existed. In reality, farm life consisted of hard physical labor, few creature comforts, and no vacations. But to a middle class which possessed growing wealth and leisure time the country represented a lost agrarian past which was less hectic, less artificial, and less complicated—the antithesis of their own lives. It seemed that if only they could get back to the country and all it symbolized, life's troubles would melt away. This was the modern myth of Arcadia.

Notes

"To the Heart of the Ozarks": An Introduction

1. Milton D. Rafferty, *The Ozarks: Land and Life* (Norman: University of Oklahoma Press, 1980), 3, 11, 16.

2. See the modern edition, "Delayed at the Beaver Creek Settlement," *Rude Pursuits and Rugged Peaks: Schoolcraft's Ozark Journal, 1818–1819,* ed. Milton D. Rafferty (Fayetteville: University of Arkansas Press, 1996).

3. See Lynn Morrow, "Trader William Gilliss and Delaware Migration in Southern Missouri," *Missouri Historical Review* 75 (January 1981): 147–67.

4. For steamboats on the White River, see *The White River Chronicles of S. C. Turnbo,* ed. James F. Keefe and Lynn Morrow (Fayetteville: University of Arkansas Press, 1994), 27–32, 277n.

5. See discussion by Robert Flanders, *Overview of Cultural Resources in the Mark Twain National Forest* (Springfield: Center for Archaeological Research, Southwest Missouri State University, 1979), 167–70.

6. Elmo Ingenthron, *The Land of Taney: A History of an Ozark Commonwealth* (Point Lookout, Mo.: School of the Ozarks Press, 1974), 191, and *Twenty-first Annual Report of the Bureau of Labor Statistics and Inspection for the Year Ending November 5, 1899* (Jefferson City, Mo.: Tribune Printing Company, 1899), 254–56.

7. See Don Payton, "Johnboat No Thing of Beauty but Performs Its Task Well," *Springfield News-Leader,* February 19, 1956, for an interview with johnboat builder Charley Barnes.

8. The scholarly literature on Turner and the frontier is vast. Readers can begin with *Rereading Frederick Jackson Turner* with commentary by John Mack Faragher (New York: Henry Holt and Company, 1994). The perceptions of the Midwest as a distinctive region are analyzed by James R. Shortridge, *The Middle West: Its Meaning in American Culture* (Lawrence: University Press of Kansas, 1989). Carl Sauer considered the Missouri Ozarks as part of the Middle West throughout his landmark study, *The Geography of the Ozark Highland of Missouri* (1920; reprint, New York: Greenwood Press, 1968).

9. For a longer discussion, see Lynn Morrow, "Ozark/Ozarks: Establishing a Regional Term," *White River Valley Historical Quarterly* (fall 1996): 4–11.

10. John R. Spears, "The Ozark Mountains," *Forest and Stream,* July 4, 1889.

11. See the classic essay by Alexander Wilson, "The View from the Road: Recreation and Tourism," reprinted in *Discovered Country: Tourism and Survival in*

the American West, ed. Scott Norris (Albuquerque, N.Mex.: Stone Ladder Press, 1994), 3–20.

Chapter 1
"Priests of Nature":
Arcadia Comes to the White River Country

1. *Seventeenth Annual Report of the State Board of Agriculture of the State of Missouri* (Jefferson City, Mo.: Tribune Printing Company, 1884), 31.

2. David I. MacLeod, *Building Character in the American Boy: The Boy Scouts, YMCA, and Their Forerunners, 1870–1920* (Madison: University of Wisconsin Press, 1983), 9–10, 114–16.

3. Bernard Weisberger, "The Forgotten Four Hundred: Chicago's First Millionaires," *American Heritage* (November 1987): 44; T. J. Jackson Lears, *No Place of Grace: Antimodernism and the Transformation of American Culture, 1880–1920* (New York: Pantheon Books, 1981), 69; William S. Kowinski, "There's Still Time to Hop a Trolley—Vintage or Modern," *Smithsonian* (February 1988): 131; and Liberty Hyde Bailey, *The Country-Life Movement in the U.S.* (New York: Macmillan, 1911), 55.

4. David Strauss, "Toward a Consumer Culture: 'Adirondack Murray' and the Wilderness Vacation," *American Quarterly 39* (summer 1987): 271, 277–78; and Charles Richmond Henderson, "Are Modern Industry and City Life Unfavorable to the Family?" *American Journal of Sociology 14* (March 1909): 668.

5. MacLeod, *Building Character,* 18.

6. Roderick Nash, *Wilderness and the American Mind* (New Haven: Yale University Press, 1967), 147, and Frederick Jackson Turner, "The Significance of the Frontier in American History," in *Rereading Frederick Jackson Turner,* with commentary by John Mack Faragher (New York: Henry Holt and Company, 1994), 31–60.

7. Lears wrote of the fear of growing technology which motivated the development of the arts-and-crafts movement at the turn of the century. Craft revivalists feared that urban life repressed spontaneity and led to neurasthenia, "the severest symptom of overcivilization." Some craftsmen believed that machinery, by taking away the burden of work, resulted in dulled mental capacity, which led to introspection, boredom, and nervous prostration. Mechanization bred another anxiety—the fear that "unprecedented comfort and convenience diminished the stature of the individual will." Labor-saving machines caused Oscar Lovell Triggs of the University of Chicago to predict "a perfect mechanical world and impotent humanity." See Lears, *No Place of Grace,* 67–70.

8. U.S. Congress, Senate, National Conference on Outdoor Recreation, S. Doc. 151, 68th Congress, 1st session, 1924: 2, 14, 204; and Bailey, *The Country-Life Movement,* 59.

9. Lears, *No Place of Grace,* 30–32.

10. Commenting on the back-to-nature trend, an anonymous author of the time wrote that "No sign of the times is more significant . . . than the number of volumes on flowers, trees, shrubs, [and] birds, which are constantly coming from the press." "Back to Nature," *Outlook 6* (June 1903): 305.

11. Hall founded the *American Journal of Psychology* in 1887 and the *American Journal of Religious Psychology and Education* in 1904. He also edited *Pedagogical Seminary* (now *Journal of Genetic Psychology*), a journal of child psychology. His writings included *The Contents of Children's Minds on Entering School* (1894), *The Story of a Sand Pile* (1897), *Adolescense* (1904), *Youth* (1907), and *Educational Problems* (1911). Hall supervised the master's thesis of Vance Randolph, and Randolph dedicated his book *Ozark Superstitions* (New York: Columbia University Press, 1947) to Hall.

12. Leonard Zusne, *Biographical Dictionary of Psychology* (Westport, Conn.: Greenwood Press, 1984), 168, and MacLeod, *Building Character,* 114–16.

13. John Jakle, *The Tourist: Travel in Twentieth-Century America* (Lincoln: University of Nebraska Press, 1985), 67.

14. Several magazines were begun in the early nineteenth century to exploit the growing interest in ruralism. Among them were *Country Life in America, Suburban Life,* and *Rural American.* See Frank Luther Mott, *American Magazines,* 5 vols. (Cambridge, Mass.: Belknap Press, 1930–68), vol. 4 (1957), 338.

15. Bailey edited the newly formed *Country Life in America* magazine beginning in 1901 and chaired Theodore Roosevelt's Country Life Commission in 1908. He also wrote *The Nature Study Idea* (1903), *The Outlook to Nature* (1905), *The Holy Earth* (1919), *Universal Service* (1923), and *The Seven Stars* (1923).

16. For a more thorough examination of Arcadian themes in American literature, see Leo Marx, *The Machine in the Garden* (New York: Oxford University Press, 1964); Henry Nash Smith, *Virgin Land: The American West as Symbol and Myth* (Cambridge: Harvard University Press, 1950); and Roderick Nash, *Wilderness and the American Mind* (New Haven: Yale University Press, 1967).

17. See Peter Schmitt's *Back to Nature: The Arcadian Myth in Urban America* (New York: Oxford University Press, 1969), 133–40, for a literary context of Wright's novels. H. B. Wright and his father stayed in the White Oak district of northeast Barry County among relatives. See Harold Bell Wright, *To My Sons* (New York: Harper and Brothers, 1934), 196–204.

18. Harold Bell Wright, *The Shepherd of the Hills* (Chicago: Book Supply, 1907; reprint, McCormick-Armstrong Company, 1987), 24–25.

19. Wright, *The Shepherd of the Hills,* 177.

20. Wright, *The Shepherd of the Hills,* 141–43.

21. Wright, *The Shepherd of the Hills,* 17, 45, 219, 224, 243, 250.

22. Lawrence V. Tagg, *Harold Bell Wright: Storyteller to America* (Tucson, Ariz.: Westernlore Press, 1986), 68; Roderick Nash, *The Nervous Generation: American Thought 1917–1930* (Chicago: Rand McNally and Company, 1970), 1, 139; and

"Harold Bell Wright Who Holds a World's Record," *American Magazine* (February 1918): 8.

23. "There's Gold in Those Ozark Hills," *St. Louis Post-Dispatch,* August 29, 1965, reprinted in the *Crane Chronicle, 1976,* Robert Wiley Collection, Western Historical Manuscript Collection, University of Missouri-Rolla (hereinafter WHMC-Rolla or -Columbia), and Otto E. Rayburn, *Forty Years in the Ozarks* (Eureka Springs, Ark.: Ozark Guide Press, 1957), 18, 54.

24. The legacy of place names drawn from the book is still evident, more than ninety years since its publication—Old Matt's cabin (now on the National Register of Historic Places), the Jim Lane cabin (moved and now razed), Inspiration Point, the Old Shepherd's Book Shop (recently razed), the Shepherd of the Hills Historical Cemetery (Evergreen), Uncle Ike's post office (now on the National Register of Historic Places), for many years the Wash Gibbs Museum stood along the highway until razed, and Mutton Hollow where Norman Wright built the Shepherd of the Hills Museum, devoted to his father. Today, practically all tourists drive the Shepherd of the Hills Expressway.

25. "Sammy Lane Boat Line Brochure," 1922, reprinted in *White River Valley Historical Quarterly* 6 (winter 1978): 13, and *Lake Taneycomo and the Shepherd of the Hills Country: In the Wonderland of the Ozarks* (Branson, Mo.: Lake Taneycomo Chamber of Commerce, 1926).

26. Harold Bell Wright, letter to Marian Wright Powers, January 6, 1936, M. P. Winchester Estate Founding Collection, Powers Museum, Carthage, Missouri.

27. The Rosses sold their homestead on the ridge to W. L. Driver in December 1910 and moved to Roark valley to develop Garber on the rail line.

28. "Old Matt's Homestead," *White River Leader,* October 23, 1914; "Old Matt's Cabin to Be Restored," *Stone County News Oracle,* April 14, 1926; and "Many Tourists Visit Old Matt's Cabin," *Stone County News Oracle,* June 9, 1926.

29. Morrill was born in 1837 and came from a prominent family—his brother Edmund N. Morrill governed Kansas, 1895–97, and an uncle served as President Grant's secretary of the treasury. He graduated from Bowdoin College at fifteen after studying law. Later, he set type for Horace Greeley, who reputedly uttered his famous advice to Morrill, "Go West." See "Uncle Ike Passes to His Reward," *Stone County News Oracle,* August 25, 1926; "The Postmaster at the Forks," reprinted from *Kansas City Star* in *Stone County News Oracle,* July 15, 1925; and "Stone County Is in the Movies—'Uncle Ike' and Shepherd of the Hills Country Filmed by Pathe News," *Stone County News Oracle,* December 16, 1925.

30. Marian Wright Powers, letter to Harold Bell Wright, January 1, 1936, M. P. Winchester Estate Founding Collection, Powers Museum, Carthage, Missouri, and Pearl Spurlock, *Over the Old Ozark Trails in the Shepherd of the Hills Country* (Branson, Mo.: By the author, 1942), 37.

Chapter 2
"The Bottomless Pit":
Marble Cave

1. For example, see the writings on Pemberton's Cave in Searcy County, Arkansas, in James J. Johnston, *Shootin's, Obituaries, Politics; Emigratin', Socializin', Commercializin'; and the Press* (Fayetteville, Ark.: James J. Johnston, 1991), 132–36. After the national centennial of 1876 commercial and state government publications claimed that caves in Stone County rivaled Mammoth Cave in Kentucky. For example, see Walter Davis and Daniel Durrie, *An Illustrated History of Missouri* (St. Louis, Mo.: A. J. Hall and Company, 1876), 451.

2. Tourism among Missouri's caves boasts the state's number-one national ranking in the number of recorded caves. Surveys by speleological societies all across the country since the 1960s have discovered thousands of caves in Missouri, Arkansas, and elsewhere. In Missouri the numbers have grown from 437 in 1956, 1,249 in 1963, to 2,952 in 1974, 3,400 in 1976, more than 4,200 in the 1990s, and 6,500 in the sixty thousand square miles of the Ozark region. See H. Dwight Weaver, *The Wilderness Underground: Caves of the Ozark Plateau* (Columbia: University of Missouri Press, 1992). In 1972 the federal government designated Marvel Cave a registered natural landmark for its exceptional value in natural history.

3. *Lamar Democrat,* June 7, 1883. Corporate consolidations of lines created a Kansas City, Springfield, and Memphis line in April 1888. See Kansas City, Fort Scott, and Memphis Railroad, Corporation files, Missouri State Archives, Jefferson City, Missouri (hereinafter MSA).

4. *Lamar Democrat,* August 9, 1883.

5. *Lamar Democrat,* November 22, 1883. Powell quotes are in the *Stone County Oracle,* June 23, 1904. See also Ronald L. Martin, *Official Guide to Marvel Cave* (Springfield, Mo.: Ozark Mountain Publishers, 1974). Small companies extracted bat guano from many caves around the Ozarks, one of the first being Ashley Cave on the Current River by 1818, mentioned in Henry R. Schoolcraft's journal. See the comments on several along the Gasconade River in 1894 in William J. Seever Diary, WHMC-Columbia.

6. Corporation Files, MSA; the town plat and property records may be reviewed in the Recorder of Deeds office, Stone County, Missouri. Jones actually purchased the property himself in March 1884 and sold it to the corporation in June. The official dissolution of the corporation took place in 1905. Capt. J. B. Emery authored perhaps the first professional description and promotion of the cave in "Description of Marble Cave, Missouri," *Kansas City Review of Science and Industry 8* (1885): 614–22. Emery, a native of Ohio, served the Union in the war as a captain and immigrated to Barton County in 1867 where he farmed, was postmaster 1881–85, a real-estate promoter, and in 1886 became a traveling salesman for

George McCann, owner of the Coon Tobacco Works in Springfield; McCann became a major investor with Moses Wetmore in the St. Louis Game Park in Taney County. F. D. W. Arnold was the proprietor of the Lamar House hotel where Emery lived. See *Lamar Democrat,* April 29, 1886. Clayton Abbott in *Historical Sketches of Cedar County, Missouri* (Greenfield, Mo.: Vedette Printing Company, 1988), 246–54, surveyed the boom resorts.

7. "Marvel Cave," *Rayburn's Ozark Guide* (summer 1948): 25. In 1872 Powell located in Carthage, Missouri, to take up merchandising, but soon became copublisher of the *Carthage Advocate.* Powell and other residents discovered and explored a large cave beneath the town and attempted to promote it commercially. See Marvin VanGilder, *Jasper County, the First 200 Years* (Carthage, Mo.: Jasper County Commission, 1995), 122, 127.

8. *Lamar Democrat,* June 24, 1886, March 10 and 31, and October 13, 1887. The *Advocate* was established in Lamar by Capt. R. J. Tucker and John B. Logan in the early 1870s. "Two young printers" took charge of the typesetting about 1874. These two were apparently Levi Morrill and Truman Powell. Powell later bought the paper. *Lamar Democrat,* March 31, 1887. In 1893 Morrill joined Powell in Stone County where he became justice of the peace and was immortalized by Harold Bell Wright as the postmaster at Notch.

9. Rackensack referred to a native of Arkansas, dating back as far as 1854. See the Oxford English Dictionary.

10. Quotes are from the *Lamar Democrat,* June 19, 1884. The Rackensack, an old name for Arkansas, became significant in Ozarks tourist history in 1963. Jimmy Driftwood and others formed the Rackensack Folklore Society in Mountain View, Arkansas, for the preservation of folk music and dance. Their success led to the establishment of the Ozark Folk Center, an Arkansas state park, set in the hills above the White River valley.

11. *Springfield Patriot-Advertiser,* August 5, 1880, December 1, 1881, and July 12, 1883. In 1886 the federal government awarded a post office, Marmaros (1886–1929), to the locale near Marble Cave. It stood among a handful of rough buildings and was later moved south and located near the timber traffic on the White River. Contrary to local tradition, there was never a town at Marmaros, but only a postal hamlet that resembled Notch.

12. The *Taney County News* reported Missouri Pacific's engineers in Roark Creek and south of Chadwick reviewing alternate routes. Extracts in "Names and Faces from the Past," *White River Valley Historical Quarterly* (summer 1962): 18–20.

13. E. O. Hovey, "The Marble Cave of Missouri," *Scientific American 68* (February 1893): 65, 70–71. DeGroff had made the acquaintance of Frank Arnold in Lamar, took photographs in Marble Cave in the late 1880s, homesteaded on Indian Creek, and then moved to Warrensburg. He was on the famous "Warrensburg Nimrods" float trip on the Current River and later returned to Stone County to found a large angora goat ranch in 1902 near Marble Cave and

became a national president of the Angora Goat Association. See D. X., *Warrensburg Nimrods,* 1891, and Celia Ray, "Nomadic Photographer Stays to Be Goat King," Lucile Morris Upton Papers, WHMC-Columbia.

Martin's *Official Guide to Marvel Cave* (1974) is a good historical overview, but includes fabricated folklore associated with the site. In 1933 midwesterners from Indiana and Iowa briefly revived the mining of bat guano at the cave site, reported in "Open New Industry in Ozarks Cavern," *White River Leader,* March 16, 1933, and Vance Randolph in *Tall Tales from the Ozarks* (Girard, Kans.: Haldeman-Julius, 1944), 16–19, interviewed a man who harvested bat guano from Gentry Cave and others in Stone County during the depression for thirty-five dollars a ton; he shipped it as fertilizer to Springfield and St. Louis on the train.

The specific data about the land records of Marble Cave are from the Recorder of Deeds office, Galena, Missouri, and listed in Linda Myers-Phinney, "Marble Cave Property, Chain of Title," fall 1997, hereinafter cited as Myers-Phinney, Chain of Title. Truman Powell acquired 320 acres from St. Louis businessman and mineral speculator Edwin Harrison in 1891; in 1896 Truman and son William each homesteaded another quarter section.

14. The original manuscript was never published and has remained in the possession of the cave's owners. Interview, Charles Stanley Prince by Linda Myers-Phinney at Branson, Missouri, March 25, 1988. Prince's collecting is noted in "Visitors from Many Points at Marvel Cave," *White River Leader,* September 7, 1933. Afterward, he compiled his manuscript, "The Cave Book, A true account of the Explorations, Surveys, and Studies of Marvel Cave, Missouri, With a brief account of the Ozarkian Uplift," S. Fred Prince, B.A., 1893–1929, By the author, 1935. His earlier draft in 1893 was "The Land You Live In, As the Mountains are Round About Southern Missouri, 1893," S. Fred Prince, 1893. See Suzanne Wilson, "S. Fred Prince," *Missouri Conservationist* 59 (December 1998): 9–13.

15. Newsclippings, photocopies, and manuscripts on Lynch, National Library of Canada, Ottawa, sent to Lynn Morrow, August 2, 1996, and "A Pioneer of the Ozark Awakening," *Arcadian Magazine* (July 1931): 9. The latter article claimed that Lynch's books, *Butter and Cheese* and *Scientific Dairy Practice,* sold in excess of seventy thousand and one hundred thousand, respectively.

16. See Jerry Vineyard, Introduction, in *Cave Regions of the Ozarks and Black Hills* (New York and London: Johnson Reprint Corporation, 1970), xxi–xxii, 37, 57. The Hovey article is E. O. Hovey, "The Marble Cave of Missouri," *Scientific American* (February 4, 1893).

17. Prof. A. C. Burrill, "Missouri Cave Remains—A Wonderland with Records of Ancient Life," *Official Manual* (Jefferson City, Mo.: Hugh Stephens Press, 1926), 962–67. See Luella Agnes Owen, *Cave Regions of the Ozarks and Black Hills* (1898; reprint, New York: Johnson Reprint Corporation, 1970) including Jerry Vineyard's introductory biography of Owen.

In 1911 Missouri congressman J. J. Russell proposed a bill to establish Marble

Cave as a national park, but it did not receive much attention. In 1919 the White River Boosters' League was incorporated, in part, "to secure a State wild game preserve or preserves in Taney County, Missouri, to promote and secure a National park in Taney and Stone Counties." In 1926 promoters pushed for Missouri to purchase some two thousand acres that would include Marvel Cave for the new park system, but negotiations failed.

In 1927, Keith McCanse, Missouri game and fish commissioner, met with the Lynch family about adding the property to the state park system, but the parties could not agree upon a price. Lizzie McDaniel, one of the boosters, went to Jefferson City to confer with McCanse to see if a plan could be made.

The following March 1928, Springfield congressman James F. Fulbright introduced H.R. 11477, "A Bill to Establish the Shepherd of the Hills National Park near Garber and Reed's Spring in Stone and Taney Counties, Missouri." The bill asked for an appropriation of $50,000 for a park "of undetermined location, but near Reed's Spring." By May representatives of the National Park Service joined those from the OPA to meet with Miriam Lynch and Waldo Powell. Lynch wanted $250,000 for the cave, and Powell priced Fairy Cave at $10,000. The bill failed in the face of Lynch's unrealistic price and the advent of the national depression as the Department of Interior dropped the proposal in 1932. See David Quick, "Old Matt's Cabin," National Register of Historic Places Nomination, Missouri Department of Natural Resources, Historic Preservation Program, October 1982, White River Boosters' League, Corporation Files, MSA; *White River Leader,* October 19, 1927, and April 25, May 9, and 16, 1928.

18. *Reminiscent History of the Ozark Region* (1894; reprint, Easley, S.C.: Southern Historical Press, 1978), 26–27.

19. See Emery, "Description of Marble Cave, Missouri," 614–22. The flamboyant Emery probably named them himself. In Missouri such caves as Mark Twain near Hannibal opened in 1886 and Crystal Cave north of Springfield in 1893. Early folklore about Marble Cave being a volcano is in *A Reminiscent History of the Ozark Region* (Chicago: Goodspeed Brothers, 1894), 26.

20. Recorder of Deeds, Galena, Stone County, Missouri, Book M, 236–37. How much cash Lynch received is unknown, but it would have been only a small percentage of the fifty thousand dollars.

21. Years later in 1911–12 the Quebec trustee's heirs in Canada pressed Lynch for cash settlements for their interests in the property. That conclusion is unknown.

22. William H. Lynch, letter to Wilfrid Laurier, May 19, 1898, Wilfrid Laurier Papers, National Library of Canada, Ottawa.

23. "Petition of May and September 1900," W. H. Lynch to Wilfrid Laurier, September 17, 1900; Clifford Sifton to Wilfrid Laurier, August 14, 1900; and W. H. Lynch to Wilfrid Laurier, September 10, 1900, all in Wilfrid Laurier Papers, National Library of Canada, Ottawa.

24. For example, see "Marvel Cave," *Stone County News Oracle,* January 11,

1906, where the local press suggested outside investors. The standard work on the railroad is Walter M. Adams, *The White River Railway* (Branson, Mo.: Ozarks Mountaineer, 1991).

25. Truman Powell, "Recent and Important Discoveries in Marble Cave," *Stone County News Oracle*, July 13, 1905. Meanwhile, Truman Powell and his sons William and Waldo had explored in 1896 what became in 1921 Fairy Cave, a family business. Truman managed a prominent real-estate business and was elected state representative in 1906 and again in 1918. Waldo homesteaded the adjacent property, but did not open the attraction until regular automobile traffic came to the region. See Don Meier, "Fairy Cave One of Nature's Marvels," *Springfield News and Leader,* September 17, 1950.

26. Margaret Gerten Hoten, "Life in the Ozarks—Then and Now," *White River Valley Historical Quarterly* (summer–fall 1967): 13–14.

27. *Branson Echo,* July 20 and August 3, 1906.

28. "One Pants Johnnie," *White River Valley Historical Quarterly* (winter 1971): 5, and Adams, *The White River Railway,* 108.

29. John Rullketter, "A Quick Sketch of Garber as It Was in My Time," *White River Valley Historical Quarterly* (winter 1971): 2. Professor Rullketter died in 1918, and the family moved back to Ohio.

30. "Vacationists" is the early twentieth-century term that evolved into the more common "vacationers" of today.

31. Martin, *Official Guide,* 19–21, 36; Velma Bass, interview by Linda Myers-Phinney, Notch, Missouri, November 18, 1987; *White River Leader,* June 6, 1913; and "Marvel Cave," *White River Leader,* September 10, 1915. Daughter Genevieve Lynch did not move to the cave property until she resigned her nursing career in Carthage, Missouri, in 1930. For roads, see Lynn Morrow and David Quick, "Transportation and Tourism in the Shepherd of the Hills Country: The Case of the Y-Bridge," parts I and II, *White River Valley Historical Quarterly* (fall 1989 and winter 1990): 4–10 and 4–10, respectively. Kansas City investors in 1915 considered purchasing Lynch's cave and building a hotel and access roads for a tourist bus line. *White River Leader,* April 2, 1915.

32. *White River Leader,* September 24, 1915; "Marvel Cave Celebration," *White River Leader,* September 17, 1915; "Marvel Cave," *Stone County News Oracle,* June 30, 1920; "Uncle Ike Passes to His Reward," *Stone County News Oracle,* August 25, 1926; and Otto Rayburn, *Forty Years in the Ozarks: An Autobiography* (Eureka Springs, Ark.: Ozark Guide Press, 1957), 55. "Ten Copyright Songs," by William Henry Lynch (Notch, Mo.: Marvel Cave Publishing House, n.d., Robert Wiley Papers, WHMC-Rolla). The songs were probably composed by Miriam Lynch, an operatic musician.

33. "Marvel Cave Contest," *White River Leader,* November 26, 1915; "Ozark Artists at Marvel Cave," *White River Leader,* September 10, 1925.

34. "Marvel Cave," *Stone County News Oracle,* April 13, 1921; "Marvel Cave," *White River Leader,* January 21 and February 14, 1916.

35. "An Ozark Painting at the Panama Exposition," *White River Leader,* February 26, 1915; "Ozark Paintings," *White River Leader,* May 7, 1915.

36. "Ozark School of Artists," *White River Leader,* October 29, 1915.

37. "Ozark Painters Organization Formed in Springfield," *White River Leader,* November 19, 1915; "Ozark Paintings Please St. Louis," *White River Leader,* December 10, 1915; and "Ozark Playgrounds News Flashes," *Stone County News Oracle,* May 6, 1925.

38. Flo Montgomery Tidgwell, "A Marvel of a Cave," *Ozarks Mountaineer* (March–April 1987): 26–27. "Graduating Class of S. of O. Visit Marvel Cave," *White River Leader,* May 22, 1919.

39. Frances Jones Munday, "Scenes from an Unforgettable Trip: Branson, 1924," *Ozarks Mountaineer* (April/May 1995): 40–41; Miles H. Scott, "The Marvelous Cave," *White River Valley Historical Quarterly* (winter 1985): 4–5.

40. Kenneth Ford, interview with Lynn Morrow and Linda Myers-Phinney, Hollister, Missouri, March 8, 1989. Kenneth Ford's father worked for Swift Packing Company in St. Joseph while Kenneth became an underwriter for fire insurance in Kansas City and purchased the old YMCA grounds in 1953. The Sycamore Club was the sporting club, Corporation Files, MSA.

41. By this time local boosters had incorrectly associated the Bald Knobber vigilante actions of the 1880s with Signal Tree and the Marvel Cave neighborhood. The signal tree was so designated by the Missouri Geological Survey due to its proximity to one of their markers as J. K. Ross pointed out in "Old Matt's View of It," *White River Valley Historical Quarterly* (reprint, spring 1975): 13–14. Twin Pines Inn, with several cottages, was located at the forks of the Dewey Bald and Compton Ridge Roads near Evergreen cemetery.

42. *White River Leader,* May 28, July 2, and September 10, 1925, and "6,020 Visited Old Matt's This Year," December 16, 1926.

43. "William H. Lynch of Cave Renown Dies in Hospital," *Springfield Daily News,* September 14, 1927.

44. Genevieve Lynch, "The Call," *Arcadian Magazine* (July 1931): 25.

Chapter 3

"As a Health Resort Taney Is Unequalled": The Game Park

1. See Lynn Morrow, "Estate Builders in the Missouri Ozarks: Establishing a St. Louis Tradition," *Gateway Heritage* (winter 1981–1982): 42–48.

2. In 1896 there were 122,000 acres of available government land in Taney County, and state government already proclaimed that "as a health resort Taney is unequalled; many have visited the county to build up a run down constitution." St. Louisans, especially, were resorting in the wilds of the White River. See

Eighteenth Annual Report of the Missouri Bureau of Labor Statistics (Jefferson City, Mo.: Tribune Printing Company, 1896), Part II, 350. From 1890 to 1895 county population increased 15 percent from 7,973 to 9,160. *Eighteenth Annual Report of the Missouri Bureau of Labor Statistics* , Part III, 414.

3. In early 1891 the incorporation was for the St. Louis Park and Improvement Company, but in November the officers changed it to the St. Louis Park and Agricultural Company. See Corporation Files, MSA. The stated reason for incorporation on the charter included "to maintain and conduct a pleasure and sporting park located in the county of Taney, State of Missouri, the main feature of which are to be a zoological collection, game and fish pleasure, shooting club and long distance range for rifle practice. Also in connection therewith the milling of lumber, grain, mineral paint, and other minerals, mining, the raising and sale of livestock, fruit and farm produce of every description and the buying and selling of minerals and for the purpose of the Corporation may buy, improve and sell real estate."

4. See Linda Myers-Phinney, "A Compilation of Land Acquisitions Listed from the Taney County Deed Records, Forsyth, Mo.," in possession of authors. It is worth noting that the acquisitions included land occupied by Alexander Majors during 1839–41, where he lived as a young bear hunter and which he later wrote about in his autobiography. See Alexander Majors, *Seventy Years on the Frontier* (Chicago and New York: Rand McNally and Company, 1893), 209–14, and Taney County Deed Book 11, 81–82, Taney County Courthouse, Forsyth, Missouri.

5. Carl Sauer wrote that within the interior Ozarks the hunter/frontiersmen ranked the White River country first in their particular desires for hunting and fishing. Sauer, *The Geography of the Ozark Highland,* 149.

6. J. P. Litton, "The St. Louis Park and Agricultural Company," *Forest and Stream* 47 (1896): 24. The leading authority was Judge John Dean Caton, whose individual work and writing in the general stocking of game parks were recognized nationally. See T. S. Palmer, "Private Game Preserves and Their Future in the United States," *Bureau of Biological Survey*, Circular No. 72 (Washington, D.C.: U.S. Department of Agriculture, 1910): 3. Fence statistics and Wisconsin elk source from Paul Dalke and David Spencer, "Development and Land Use on a Private Game Preserve in Southern Taney County, Missouri," *Journal of Wildlife Management* 8 (January 1944): 2–3. Game park owner M. B. Skaggs made company records available to Dalke and Spencer; current owners denied any cooperation to the authors and White River Valley Historical Society officers.

7. *Taney County Republican,* April 16 and 23, 1896, and for fence statistics, see Dalke and Spencer, "Development and Land Use on a Private Game Preserve in Southern Taney County, Missouri," 3. For background on Hunt, see Douglas Mahnkey, "The Game Park at Mincy," *Ozarks Mountaineer* (May–June 1983): 45–46.

8. *Taney County Republican,* October 22, 1896.

9. *Taney County Republican,* November 19, 1896. Wetmore, performing with

wit and humor, spoke to the audience and "advised his hearers to chew Star tobacco and raise their boys to do the same."

10. See *Appendix, Senate and House Journals,* 39th General Assembly (Jefferson City, Mo.: Tribune Printing Company, 1897), 107–12.

11. Prather, a Republican, wrote the poem in 1888. Later, during Governor Hadley's revision and passage of the Walmsley-Hadley game law in 1909, Prather served on the game and fish legislative committee.

12. The verse is on the back of sheet music, W. J. Bryan to M. C. Wetmore, November 1899, Missouri Historical Society, St. Louis. The Wyoming and black-tongue references are in Dalke and Spencer, "Development and Land Use on a Private Game Preserve," 3–4.

13. *St. Louis Republic,* November 19 and 21, 1899. With Colonel Wetmore and Major McCann were Maj. Harvey Salmon, Maj. James Hogan of Wisconsin, Capt. Fred Wishert of Joplin, Missouri, Col. W. J. Bryan, and more. Bryan traveled with state Democratic chairman Sam Cook. In Springfield, E. Y. Mitchell Jr., son of a Confederate general and brother-in-law of Richard P. Bland, introduced Bryan's speech. In December 1904 then-secretary-of-state Sam Cook and others accompanied Wetmore to the park, but without Bryan. *Galena News Oracle,* December 15, 1904.

14. Wetmore's obituary is in the Necrology files, November 10, 1910, Missouri Historical Society, St. Louis. Wetmore had extensive holdings in the Planter's Hotel, Commonwealth Realty Company, and several St. Louis financial institutions. However, his once-great personal fortune, apparently exceeding five million dollars, had been reduced to less than five hundred thousand dollars as a result of his trust-busting battle against the American Tobacco Company. See *St. Louis Globe-Democrat,* November 28, 1910.

15. See McCann's obituary in the *Springfield Leader,* March 3, 1920.

16. David Lantz, *Raising Deer and Other Large Game Animals in the United States,* USDA Biological Survey Bulletin No. 36 (Washington, D.C.: Government Printing Office, 1910): 45, 50. The T. S. Palmer survey, "Private Game Preserves and Their Future in the United States," USDA, Circular No. 72, May 4, 1910, missed the Wetmore game park. Had Palmer included it, the St. Louis Game Park would have ranked fourth in size among some five hundred in the United States.

17. St. Louisans resorted at the Maine Club for only a decade. It was sold at auction in 1913 to Harry Merritt of St. Louis, leased for a couple of seasons, and in 1915, it became the new school. See the *Branson White River Leader,* June 6 and 20, 1913, and descriptions of the Maine Club are in Helen and Townsend Godsey, *Flight of the Phoenix: A Biography of the School of the Ozarks* (Point Lookout, Mo.: School of the Ozarks Press, 1984): 638–39, and Kathleen Van Buskirk, "The Lodge That Traveled from Maine," *Ozarks Mountaineer* (March 1978): 20–21.

18. Hobart and Lee also founded the Branson Town Company for real-estate speculation along the new railroad town. In 1907, however, they sold out to St.

Louisans Vernon Todd and Willard Heath, who were prime movers in establishing the Maine Club in Taney County. Todd founded a boating company, a bank, and a lumberyard, and became a principal promoter of Branson. Branson Town Company, Corporation Files, MSA, and Kathleen Van Buskirk, "Branson and the Town Company," *Ozarks Mountaineer* (January–February 1988): 40–45.

19. *The Revised Statutes of the State of Missouri 1909,* vol. 2 (Jefferson City, Mo.: Hugh Stephens Printing Company, 1910), chap. 49, sect. 6591. The game market at the St. Louis World's Fair in 1904, interpreted by some as a display of unabandoned commercial plunder, signaled a public outcry that led, in part, to the first modern game law, the Walmsley bill in 1905. See Charles Callison, *Man and Wildlife in Missouri* (Harrisburg, Pa.: Stackpole Company, 1953), 7.

20. Maj. George McCann to Herbert Hadley, February 2, 1910, Hadley Papers, WHMC-Columbia. Model farms also attracted the attention of Hadley, and it was in Taney County that land was chosen as a prize for the best plan to cultivate five acres. See "Who Will Win This Farm in Taney Co.?" *Columbia University Missourian,* June 22, 1910, and "To Award Five-Acre Farm Prize Thursday," *Columbia University Missourian,* June 28, 1910. Hadley's log cabin still stands west of the country club in Jefferson City on private land.

21. The revised 1909 game law, embodied in the Walmsley-Hadley bill, was the foundation for regulations and collection of fees until the constitutional amendment of 1936 that established the Missouri Department of Conservation. Rep. Harry Walmsley, Kansas City, sponsored the 1905 bill that was written by St. Louisans. It was then repealed in 1907, but reintroduced and strengthened in Hadley's first legislative session, spring 1909. For extended discussion of the cultural alliance of early conservation and tourism, see Richard Sellars, "Early Promotion and Development of Missouri's Natural Resources" (Ph.D. diss., University of Missouri-Columbia, 1972), 120–41.

22. Francis Jones, postmaster, to Jesse Tolerton, November 15, 1912, Herbert Hadley Papers, f. 366, WHMC-Columbia.

23. Garry Yount to Jesse Tolerton, November 16, 1912, Hadley Papers, f. 366, WHMC-Columbia.

24. Herbert Hadley to Jesse Tolerton, November 16, 1912, Hadley Papers, vol. 8, p. 318, WHMC-Columbia.

25. Lantz, *Raising Deer and Other Large Game Animals in the United States,* 33. This is all the more impressive when a decade later, as the state imposed a five-year closed season on deer, Missouri newspapers reported that only some 140 deer remained in the Missouri wilds. See *Branson White River Leader,* November 12, 1925.

26. Jonathan Fairbanks and Clyde Edwin Tuck, *Past and Present of Greene County, Missouri* (Indianapolis: A. W. Bowen and Company, 1915), 516. Meetings at the game park may have influenced W. J. Bryan to visit Hadley in Jefferson City. See Jerena Giffen, *First Ladies of Missouri* (1970; reprint, Jefferson City, Mo.: Giffen Enterprises, 1996), 157.

27. "Brewers to Inspect Land for Ozark Game Preserve," *St. Louis Globe-Democrat,* November 29, 1910. Apparently, between 1906 and 1910 a number of St. Louis parties embarked from Branson by wagon for the park. The Busch family brought Harry B. Hawes and guests, black domestics, and wooden barrels packed with Budwieser beer. On one outing these sportsmen did not have any luck killing deer. Bill Hunt, the caretaker, and Floyd Jones, wagon driver, went to the woods and in a couple of hours brought back a wagonload of deer for eating and trophies. Floyd Jones memoirs, copy in possession of authors.

28. *White River Leader,* December 18, 1914.

29. Dalke and Spencer, "Development and Land Use on a Private Game Preserve," 4. The *Branson White River Leader* reported guests arriving for the park. See, for example, December 18, 1914, and December 10, 1915.

30. Taney County Deed Book 56, p. 9, Taney County Courthouse, Forsyth, Missouri. In 1910 Clemens, a manager for the Reserve Loan Life Insurance Company of Indianapolis, Indiana, moved to Springfield and located an office in the Woodruff Building. *Springfield Republican,* February 3, 1911.

31. Dalke and Spencer, "Development and Land Use," 4; Mahnkey, "Game Park at Mincy," 46; and E. Y. Mitchell Jr. to Gov. F. D. Gardner, October 11, 1919, E. Y. Mitchell Papers, WHMC-Columbia.

32. Other contenders who lost out to state acquisition because the price was too high included the large Ha Ha Tonka estate in Camden County, Roaring River in Barry County, Shepherd of the Hills properties in Taney County, the Shut-In Club at Lake Killarney in Iron County, and Onondaga Cave in Crawford County. The state, however, was convinced that the park system must be founded in the Ozarks. See, in part, "Report of Special Committee Appointed to Investigate Sites Offered for a Proposed State Park and Game Preserve," *Appendix to House and Senate Journals,* 48th General Assembly, State of Missouri, Vol. II, 1915.

33. Dr. T. M. Sayman to Gov. Arthur Hyde, July 30, 1924, Arthur Hyde Papers, f. 596, WHMC-Columbia. Sayman was encouraged by Springfield realtor W. N. Veirs, who represented the owner, W. J. Clemens.

34. Frank Wielandy to Dr. T. M. Sayman, August 5, 1924, and Wielandy to Gov. Arthur M. Hyde, September 9, 1924, Missouri Game and Fish Commission, State Parks Correspondence, 1924–29, Missouri Department of Natural Resources, Jefferson City.

35. Frank Wielandy to Arthur Hyde, September 11, 1924, Hyde Papers, f. 597, WHMC-Columbia. Sayman eventually purchased Roaring River and gave it to the state "without any strings tied to it." See "Dr. Sayman Gives Park," *Game and Fish News* (February 1929): 43, and an overview of Sayman (1853–1937) by Sen. Emory Melton, *The First 150 Years in Cassville, Missouri, 1845–1995* (Cassville, Mo.: Litho Printers, 1995), 97–101. Wielandy and the Game and Fish Department wanted to create game refuges on a Pennsylvania model. The idea of these large expanses of controlled open range reminded many of the game park. See *Branson White River Leader,* February 27, 1925.

36. *Branson White River Leader,* January 16, 1925, and "Donation of Fifteen Deer Made by Taney County Game Preserve," *Game and Fish News* (November 1925): 3.

37. In 1933 Skaggs's purchase of Frank Drury's fourteen-hundred-acre ranch on the north side of the game park increased his holdings to seventy-two hundred acres and gave him over six miles of White River frontage. *Branson White River Leader,* March 23, 1933. See also Dalke and Spencer, "Development and Land Use," 4–5; Mahnkey, "Game Park at Mincy," 47; and Michael Woodring, "Drury-Mincy Wildlife Area," *Missouri Conservationist* (January 1992): 10. The *Kansas City Star,* January 12, 1941, ran a photo feature of the "Deer Roundup in a Missouri Woodland" managed by L. W. Hornkohl and A. Starker Leopold. The concept of the game park or game farm ended in the depression. See discussion by Charles Callison, *Man and Wildlife in Missouri* (Harrisburg, Pa.: Stackpole Company, 1953), 89–91.

38. Mahnkey, "Game Park at Mincy," 47. The current owner of the game park land that includes the old lodge and center of social activity since 1987 is James Keeter of Royal Oak Enterprises, manufacturers of charcoal briquettes and activated carbon, headquartered in Atlanta, Georgia. Skaggs entered into a long-term lease with the Department of Conservation, which created the Drury Refuge in 1939 and the subsequent Mincy Public Hunting Area. In 1987, following the death of M. B. Skaggs in 1976, the Department of Conservation purchased several thousand acres from the Skaggs Trust, and the trust donated more land that currently surrounds the Keeter Ranch. See Woodring, "Drury-Mincy Wildlife Area," 9–11, and *Taney County Republican,* August 27, 1987. M. B. Skaggs is an enrollee of the Greater Ozarks Hall of Fame, College of the Ozarks, Point Lookout, Missouri.

39. For a description of the modern elk ranch, see the *Taney County Times,* December 18, 1996, and for growth of the elk economy in Missouri, *Taney County Times,* March 5, 1997.

Chapter 4
"Cows Rather than Plows": Newcomers Join the Natives

1. See the map in Ingenthron, *Land of Taney,* 16. Alphonso Wetmore used the term Taney District in the first substantial gazetteer of Missouri, *Gazetteer of the State of Missouri* (St. Louis, Mo.: C. Keemle, 1837), 77.

2. Homestead costs included a government fee, registration, commission, and a word cost. Lands close to railroads were much higher than the usually quoted $1.25 per acre. A man would have to save cash payments for his labor at fifty cents per day to meet the fourteen- or sixteen-dollar filing fees. The Springfield land office operated continuously from 1866 to 1922 and was the last office open in Missouri. Carl

Sauer in "The Economic Problem of the Ozark Highland," *Scientific Monthly* (September 1920): 215–27, discussed the agricultural issues of the Ozarks.

3. Whiskey production in the Ozarks was important for local or neighborhood trade and enjoyed some ascendance with the tourist trade, but whiskey was not exported out of the region in large volume. The largest illicit whiskey trade in Missouri, by far, was in south St. Louis, a regular destination for federal agents and their investigations.

4. Robert Prather, "The Big Road," c. 1935, in possession of the authors.

5. One of the more recent expository works is Edward Ayers, et al., *All Over the Map: Rethinking American Regions* (Baltimore: Johns Hopkins University Press, 1996). In a regional study of the southeast Missouri Ozarks by Donald L. Stevens Jr., *A Homeland and a Hinterland* (Omaha, Nebr.: National Park Service, 1991), 97, the newcomers after 1890 were from the lower Midwest, with Illinois ranking first in numbers, followed by Kentucky, Ohio, Indiana, and Tennessee. A similar study in the Gasconade/Big Piney watershed by Steven Smith, *Made It in the Timber: A Historic Overview of the Fort Leonard Wood Region, 1800–1940* (Normal, Ill.: Midwest Archaeological Research Center, Illinois State University, 1993), 54 ff., pointed to Illinois, Ohio, and Indiana as origins for the new Ozarks population.

6. "Early Gearhart Letters," *White River Valley Historical Quarterly* (summer 1981): 5.

7. See Isaac Workman, "The Good Old Times," in *Stories of the Pioneers,* comp. E. J. and L. S. Hoenshel (1915; reprint, Forsyth, Mo.: Little Photo Gallery, 1985), 11–17.

8. For example, in the *Seventeenth Annual Report of the State Board of Agriculture of the State of Missouri,* 183, the state reported average cattle in Stone County at $11.95, hogs at $1.80, and Taney County cattle at $9.22, hogs at $1.61.

9. John Solomon Otto, "The Migration of the Southern Plain Folk: An Interdisciplinary Synthesis," *Journal of Southern History* 51 (1985): 195.

10. See the discussion by James Ellis, *The Influence of Environment on the Settlement of Missouri* (St. Louis, Mo.: Webster Publishing Company, 1929), 142–65. The Missouri Bootheel was Missouri's last settlement frontier, a result of massive drainage projects in the early twentieth century, but corporations dominated the land ownership. See costs per acre in homesteading in the *Fifteenth Annual Report of the State Board of Agriculture of the State of Missouri* (Jefferson City, Mo.: Tribune Printing Company, 1881), 145, 258. The *Nineteenth Annual Report of the Bureau of Labor Statistics* (Jefferson City, Mo.: Tribune Printing Company, 1897), 225, reported 252,000 acres available in the White River counties of 309,000 total. Labor costs are in *Eighteenth Annual Report of the Missouri Bureau of Labor Statistics,* Part II, 345, 349. William Vogt, in his influential book for conservationists, *Road to Survival* (New York: William Sloan Associates, 1948), 33, claimed that "fire, the ax, the plow, and the firearm have been the four fundamental tools of our modern culture."

11. Laura Ingalls Wilder in *Laura Ingalls Wilder Country*, text by William Anderson (New York: Harper Perennial, 1990), 74. The Wilders settled in Wright County, Missouri, in 1894. For large trends in migration, see David B. Danbom, *Born in the Country: A History of Rural America* (Baltimore: Johns Hopkins University Press, 1995).

12. Missouri History Scrapbook, 1896, WHMC-Columbia. This immigration included the William Patrick O'Neill family to Bear Creek, Taney County, in 1894. The multitalented Rose O'Neill, creator of the Kewpie dolls, visited and lived there for a half century. See Rose O'Neill, *The Story of Rose O'Neill: An Autobiography*, ed. Miriam Formanek-Brunell (Columbia: University of Missouri Press, 1997).

13. *Eighteenth Annual Report of the Missouri Bureau of Labor Statistics,* Part II, 349–50. Rose O'Neill's parents were part of this immigration from Nebraska. She came from New York and visited the Taney County homestead in 1894 beginning a fifty-year relationship to the Ozarks where, according to her biographer, O'Neill attained emotional peace and gained inspiration for much of her work. See the superb biography by Shelley Armitage, *Kewpies and Beyond: The World of Rose O'Neill* (Jackson: University Press of Mississippi, 1994).

14. Walter B. Stevens, "The Ozark Uplift," *White River Valley Historical Quarterly* (1899; reprint, winter 1964–65): 9–15, 23.

15. For example, some depositions for ownership and transfer of title had to be taken for land along the White River as the work on Powersite Dam proceeded. The courthouse burned in December 1885, and corporate lawyers wanted to assure a good title. In 1912 James Oliver, age seventy-four, gave testimony about the Wheeler farm that Oliver's grandfather sold for a payment in gold prior to the Civil War. Oliver said, "No one ever questioned their title since as early as 1852, which I judge by my age. Ben McKinney and William E. Moore know about this. I do not know anyone that knows more than Ben and Billy." Noma Johnson, "History of James Oliver," *White River Valley Historical Quarterly* (spring 1988): 18. Hobart and Lee Tie Company spent considerable time in court clearing title to their lands for the Branson Town Company.

16. See the excellent work by Thad Sitton, *Backwoodsmen, Stockmen and Hunters along a Big Thicket Valley* (Norman: University of Oklahoma Press, 1995) for a comprehensive study in the evolution of open range. Missouri's range statutes are summarized by John H. Calvert, "Fencing Laws in Missouri—Restraining Animals," *Missouri Law Review* (fall 1967): 519–42.

17. See especially Wayne D. Rasmussen's essay, "Wood on the Farm," in *Material Culture in the Wooden Age,* ed. Brooke Hindle (Tarrytown, N.Y.: Sleepy Hollow Press, 1981), 15–34. Mail order deliveries were not taken for granted in the area until after 1900.

18. Carl Sauer, *Agricultural Origins and Dispersals* (New York: American Geographical Society, 1952), 103.

19. See a modern discussion on fire by Douglas Ladd, "Reexamination of the

Role of Fire in Missouri Oak Woodlands," in *Proceedings of the Oak Woods Management Workshop,* ed. George V. Burger et al. (Charleston: Eastern Illinois University, 1991), 67–80. See a general survey of man's relationship with the woods by Michael Williams, *Americans and Their Forests: A Historical Geography* (New York and Cambridge: Cambridge University Press, 1989), and a fire study by Richard Guyette and E. A. McGinnes Jr., "Fire History of an Ozark Glade," *Transactions of the Missouri Academy of Sciences* 16 (1982): 85–93.

20. John J. Mayer and I. Lehr Brisbin Jr., *Wild Pigs in the United States* (Athens: University of Georgia Press, 1991), 3. Government closed the open range in Arkansas in 1966 and in Missouri in 1969. These closings were late when compared to other southern states and offer some evidence for the persistence of traditional lifeways in the Ozarks. Natural erosion also impacted the Ozarks and contributed to the amount of gravel in the streams, but published studies are needed to address the specific variables in erosion. The increased population of people and stock led to the consumption of more water and a drop in the water table; this, too, requires a regional study to help answer the questions posed by gravel-choked streams.

21. *Jefferson City Daily Tribune,* June 14, 1892, and, for example, a travelogue through the county seat of Marshall, Arkansas, in 1898 complained of not seeing churches there. Johnston, *Shootin's, Obituaries, Politics,* 270.

22. See "United Brothern in Christ Church Book," copied by Avis Hawkins, *White River Valley Historical Quarterly* (fall 1972): 14–18.

23. The Mincy church story is summarized from "Minutes of the Mincy Valley Baptist Church of Christ, 1871 to 1885," *White River Valley Historical Quarterly* (summer and fall 1965, winter, spring, and summer 1966).

24. Lawrence O. Christensen and Gary R. Kremer, *A History of Missouri, Volume IV, 1875–1919* (Columbia: University of Missouri Press, 1997), 127.

25. *Eighteenth Annual Report of the Missouri Bureau of Labor Statistics,* Part II, 346, 349. The one Sunday school in Stone County is either a misprint or dramatically understated. Fraternal orders were universally popular throughout the nation during this period.

26. Claude A. Phillips, *A History of Education in Missouri* (Jefferson City, Mo.: Hugh Stephens Printing Company, 1911), 286–87. The institute law remained in effect until 1903 when the legislature replaced it with a statute for county teachers' associations. Readers may examine the emergence of Ozark society and popular culture at rural institutions in the excellent study by Robert K. Gilmore, *Ozark Baptizings, Hangings, and Other Diversions* (Norman: University of Oklahoma Press, 1984).

27. School District Records, Taney County, 1886–1918, MSA, and *Forty-first Report of the Public Schools of the State of Missouri* (Jefferson City, Mo.: Tribune Printing Company, 1891), 34–36. In 1891, average daily attendance in Stone and Taney Counties was about 10 percent less than Greene (57 percent) and almost 20

percent below populous Jackson (65 percent). McGuffey readers were mass produced for students in the grade classifications.

28. See Ruby Steele, "The Bolin Wilson Family," *White River Valley Historical Quarterly* (fall 1967): 1, for Stone County, and "Rules of Conduct," *White River Valley Historical Quarterly* (winter 1981): 6, for Christian County.

29. The Ridgedale story is summarized from Kathleen Van Buskirk, "When School Bells Rang in Ridgedale," *Ozarks Mountaineer* (July–August 1981): 40–43, 54. By the teens the area included a prominent orchard region tied to the economy of the White River Railway.

30. Phillips, *A History of Education in Missouri*, 33.

31. Robert K. Gilmore, "The Dogwood Canyon Area of Southern Stone County, Missouri," a report for Bass Pro Shops, June 1992, 14. Denver Hollars was born on the King's River in 1904.

32. The Welch story is summarized from Thomas Randolph Welch, "Autobiography of Thomas Randolph Welch," *White River Valley Historical Quarterly* (winter 1977): 9–13.

33. *Taney County Times,* March 21, 1889.

34. The Mahnkey story is summarized from Doug Mahnkey, "Freighters and the Free Jack Spring," *Ozarks Mountaineer* (March–April 1989): 38–39.

35. *Springfield Patriot-Advertiser,* February 3, 1881.

36. The wagonmaster was Robert Prather in his reminiscence, "The Big Road."

37. *Twenty-ninth Annual Report of the Bureau of Labor Statistics, the State of Missouri* (Jefferson City, Mo.: Hugh Stephens Printing Company, 1907), 111; *Thirty-second Annual Report of Labor Statistics, the State of Missouri* (Jefferson City, Mo.: Hugh Stephens Printing Company, 1910), 17; and see map of cotton gins in Ingenthron, *Land of Taney*, 321.

38. See *Statistics and Information Concerning the State of Missouri* (St. Louis, Mo.: Missouri Pacific Railway, 1900), and Christensen and Kremer, *A History of Missouri*, 79.

39. The Stults story is summarized from "A Sketch of the Many Ups and Downs in Life of Ben T. Stults, As a Boy to a Man as a Hunter," ed. Lynn Morrow and Linda Myers-Phinney, *White River Valley Historical Quarterly*, Parts I–VI (fall 1990 to winter 1992).

40. The Sharp story is summarized from the William E. Sharp Papers, typescripts in possession of the authors, and various news clippings from the *Springfield News and Leader* by Lucile Morris Upton and Sharp himself.

41. The Ingenthron story is summarized from the excellent book by Ella Ingenthron Dunn, *The Granny Woman of the Hills* (Branson, Mo.: Ozarks Mountaineer, 1978).

42. The Gerten story is summarized from Margaret Gerten Hoten, "Life in the Ozarks Then and Now," *White River Valley Historical Quarterly* (fall 1966 through summer–fall 1967).

43. The Sylvester story is summarized from "W. D. Sylvester: Journeyman Pioneer," *White River Valley Historical Quarterly*, ed. Lynn Morrow and Linda Myers-Phinney (spring 1992, and fall 1992 through summer 1993).

44. In 1920 the average number of cords of wood burned on farms in Stone and Taney Counties were eighteen and seventeen, respectively. *The Missouri Year Book of Agriculture, 1921* (Jefferson City, Mo.: State Board of Agriculture, 1921), 306.

45. See the superb reminiscence by H. Harold Shamel, *Seeds of Time: A Story of the Ozarks*, n.p., n.d. [c. 1950].

46. Preston Johnson later wrote the excellent book from his diary under the name John Preston, *Saucer Ears in the Ozarks* (Caldwell, Idaho: Caxton Printers, 1943).

47. The art of shooting fish with bow and arrow was common in the White River basin along the Missouri-Arkansas line well into the twentieth century. Local blacksmiths fabricated points for the arrow tips. For practitioners, see Ted Sare, *Some Recollections of an Ozarks Float Trip Guide* (Marshfield, Mo.: Webster County Printing, n.d. [1997]), 21.

48. Harold Bell Wright, *The Shepherd of the Hills* (New York: Grosset and Dunlap, 1976), 297. Wright stopped off in Galena in July 1905 on his way to Inspiration Point. *Stone County News Oracle,* July 13, 1905.

49. C. C. Blansit, "Taney County Missouri, The Homeseeker's Paradise," brochure, c. 1907.

50. J. W. Blankinship, "Southwest Taney County, Missouri with supplements in the White River Country," pamphlet, September 1, 1910.

Chapter 5
"Nature's Own Remedy":
Float Fishing and Ozark Tourism

1. Nathan Parker, *Missouri as It Is in 1867: An Illustrated Historical Gazetteer of Missouri* (Philadelphia: J. B. Lippincott and Company, 1867), 76.

2. Walter Davis and Daniel Durrie, *An Illustrated History of Missouri* (St. Louis, Mo.: A. J. Hall and Company, 1876), 370, 451; *The Commonwealth of Missouri,* ed. C. R. Barns (St. Louis, Mo.: Bryan, Brand and Company, 1877), 46–52, 550–53. In 1877, Barns and others began to write about the "Bottomless Pit" in Stone County, modern Marvel Cave, the deepest known cave in Missouri. Although Missouri has more than five thousand known caves, surveyors have recorded over forty-two hundred since the 1950s. Weaver, *The Wilderness Underground,* 7.

3. This railroad had many corporate names, but since 1876 until the merger with the Burlington in 1980 observers and residents have known it as the Frisco. See H. Craig Miner, *The St. Louis-San Francisco Transcontinental Railroad* (Lawrence: University Press of Kansas, 1972).

4. Charles Hallock, *The Sportsmen's Gazetteer and General Guide* (New York: "Forest and Stream" Publishing Company, 1877), 94; "Hunting and Fishing News," *St. Louis Globe-Democrat,* January 6, 1895. After 1873 sportsmen could ride a branch line to Salem and take a wagon for twenty miles to the Current River at modern Montauk State Park. See Lynn Morrow, "The Arlington Hearth: St. Louisans, Perry Andres, and Commercial Tourism," *Newsletter of the Phelps County Historical Society* 18 (October 1998): 3–18.

5. For example, *Report of the Fish Commissioners of the State of Missouri* (Jefferson City, Mo.: Tribune Printing Company, 1881), 39.

6. For example, Philip Kopplin, superintendent of the state hatcheries at Forest Park, organized a ten-day outing on the Gasconade for a float from the mouth of the Roubideaux to Arlington. *St. Louis Globe-Democrat,* August 18, 1895.

7. The St. Louis and Iron Mountain came from the north and the Cairo and Fulton from the east in 1872. The Frisco joined them in 1901–02. David Deem, *History of Butler County, Missouri* (Poplar Bluff Printing Company, 1940), 106–8.

8. Ozark Ripley, *Jist Huntin': Tales of the Forest, Field and Stream* (Cincinnati: Stewart Kidd Company, 1921). Ripley was John B. Thompson. He "adopted the Ozarks" and spent twenty years hunting and fishing, in canoes and johnboats, in the uplands of the Current and Eleven Point Rivers and the lowland swamps of the Little Black, Black, Castor, St. Francis, and Little Rivers. The johnboat references are on pages 142, 144, and 150. Ripley made at least one hunt to the St. Louis Game Park on the White River when Gov. Herbert Hadley was a guest. The evolution of the term *johnboat* is complex. See an exploratory essay by Lynn Morrow, "What's in a Name, Like *Johnboat?*" *White River Valley Historical Quarterly* (winter 1998): 9–24.

9. D. X., "Warrensburg Nimrods."

10. "Lumber Cut of the United States, 1870–1920," *Bulletin No. 1119,* comp. W. B. Greeley and Earle H. Clapp (Washington, D.C.: U.S. Department of Agriculture, April 23, 1923), 4.

11. It is a certain irony that the timber industry and its use of Ozark waters to float ties culminated in the 1954 Missouri Supreme Court decision, *Elder vs. Delcour,* that judged the streams to be navigable, ultimately allowing citizens "access to all Ozark streams for canoeing and fishing." See Jon L. Hawker, *Missouri Landscapes: A Tour through Time* (Rolla: Missouri Department of Natural Resources, 1992), 256. The economic viability of tie rafting, however, remains an open question in the understudied timber industry of the Ozarks.

12. *St. Louis Globe-Democrat,* September 26, 1897.

13. Thomas Hart Benton, *An Artist in America* (Columbia: University of Missouri Press, 1983), 144, and Benton, "The Ozarks," *Travel and Leisure* (June/July 1973): 32. Artist Benton spent many weeks on the Current and White rivers, and especially on the Buffalo River in Arkansas, from the 1940s through the 1960s. The Andres operation is described more fully in the St. Louis and San

Francisco, "Feathers and Fins on the Frisco" (St. Louis, Mo., 1898). During the 1890s, Booker H. Rucker, storekeeper at Arlington, tie contractor at Rolla, and Ozark immigration agent for the Frisco Railroad in St. Louis, helped sportsmen gain access to the Big Piney and Gasconade valleys for hunting and fishing.

14. R. S. Holcombe, *History of Greene County, Missouri* (St. Louis, Mo.: Western Historical Company, 1883), 568, 793–96.

15. Gov. Thomas Fletcher reputedly held an inaugural ball in 1868 in Fisher Cave in Franklin County.

16. "Fame Fleeting for Ponce," *Kansas City Star,* February 28, 1960, and Zoe Glossip, *Ponce de Leon, Mo. 1881–1981 Centennial Celebration* (n.p.: October 24, 1981).

17. See Lynn Morrow, "The St. Louis Game Park: Experiments in Conservation and Recreation," *White River Valley Historical Quarterly* (spring 1997): 7–19.

18. For example, *Eighteenth Annual Report of the Missouri Bureau of Labor Statistics,* Part II, 349–50, pointed out that the natives of Taney County were old Kentucky and Tennessee stock, but that "Newcomers are mostly from Iowa, Kansas, Nebraska, and North Missouri."

19. See H. Clay Neville, "Taney, Amid the Ozarks," *St. Louis Republic* in Missouri History Scrapbook, 1896, WHMC-Columbia. Charles Kinyon (1855–1900) came to Taney County from Clinton County, Missouri, in 1883 with his wife, Hattie; the family grew to fifteen children. His obituary is in the *Taney County Republican,* September 6, 1900.

20. W. H. Johnson, "With Fire-Jack and Gig," *St. Louis Globe-Democrat,* October 3, 1897. Johnson's illustrated article is a classic essay on gigging in the Ozarks. A half century later, Vance Randolph provided a good description in *A Reporter in the Ozarks* (Girard, Kans.: Haldeman-Julius Publications, 1944), 17–21.

21. Harold Bell Wright, *To My Sons* (New York: Harper and Brothers Company, 1934), 195–97. Pearl Spurlock reported a Wright fishing trip in her *Over the Old Ozark Trails,* 14. The White Oak district is in the northeast corner of Barry County.

22. Biography of Keith McCanse, typescript, c. 1950s, in author's possession. See Lynn Morrow, "Keith McCanse: Missouri's First Professional Conservationist," *White River Valley Historical Quarterly* (winter 1992): 3–12. McCanse was the first Missourian to publicly promote a commission form of conservation governance, later enacted by constitutional amendment in fall 1936.

23. See John Dunckel, *The Mollyjoggers: Tales of the Camp-Fire* (Springfield, Mo.: H. S. Jewell, c. 1906). The Mollyjoggers' lodge was restored into a residence by the Richard and Billie Stagner family. See "Former Club Now a Home," *Springfield News-Leader,* May 8, 1988.

24. Floyd Jones Memoir, 35, in possession of authors. Seining great catches of fish in the White River was a common event in the nineteenth century. Isaac Moore, home in fall 1865 right after serving the Confederacy, remembered wagon

after wagon coming from the north to the White River to seine fish. In one outing he saw seven thousand pounds gathered in one draw; the fish weighed from two to forty pounds. Charles A. Moore, *Moore Family History* (Blue Eye, Mo.: By the author, 1979), 32.

25. W. J. Burton, "History of the Missouri Pacific Railroad" (St. Louis, Mo.: Union Pacific Railroad, typescript, July 1, 1956), 781.

26. *Stone County News,* April 23 and May 1, 1903.

27. Burton, "History of the Missouri Pacific Railroad," 781.

28. The quote is in the *Stone County News,* July 16, 1903.

29. See "A Big Railroad Outfit," *Stone County News,* August 27, 1903. The major contractor company was William Kenefick and F. S. Hammond, who had done a lot of work for the Gould railroads. Lucia was a promotional real-estate name given by B. B. Price of Forsyth. The Lucia and Branson subdivision plats were both filed in October 1903, and on June 11, 1904, the Lucia post office was renamed Branson. There had been a Branson post office in a small country store since 1882. See Adams, *The White River Railway,* 28, 51–52.

30. *Stone County News,* September 17, 1903.

31. See "The Man from Notch," *Stone County News Oracle,* June 16, 1904.

32. See *Stone County News Oracle,* September 22, 1904, May 25, 1905, and March 28, 1906. McCord lost the state representative nomination to Truman S. Powell, who was elected in November. The Aurora Clubhouse was the first significant sportsmen's club on the James River.

33. *Stone County News Oracle,* June 15, 1905.

34. *Stone County News Oracle,* June 29, 1905.

35. *Stone County News Oracle,* September 28, 1905.

36. *Stone County News Oracle,* June 26, 1907. The local press does not mention the Barnes brothers floating on the river until late 1907, and then it is with each other.

37. *Stone County News Oracle,* May 29 and July 10, 1907.

38. *Report of the Board of Fish Commissioners of the State of Missouri for 1905–1906* (St. Joseph, Mo.: Lon Hardman Printer, 1906), 35. The James and the White were only two of almost four dozen rivers, creeks, ponds, lakes, and aquariums that received the bass.

39. *Report of the Board of Fish Commissioners covering the Biennial Period of 1911–1912* (Jefferson City: Missouri Fish Commission, December 31, 1912), 20. Four other rivers received more fish than the James and the White.

40. H.R. Bill 10550, 60th Congress, 10.

41. Prospectors traveled to Forsyth and Galena, the county seats, to obtain legal and mapping information to begin their explorations. What emerged, in part, during the 1890s was treasure hunts for silver ore in caves. See legends reported by Walter Stevens in *Missouri: The Center State, 1821–1915* (St. Louis, Mo.: S. J. Clarke Publishing Company, 1915), 625–43, 659–60.

42. Edith McCall, "When the Tales Grew Tall in the Ozarks," *Ozarks Mountaineer* (May–June 1987): 58. For historical contexts, see Lynn Morrow, "The Yocum Silver Dollar," *Missouri Folklore Society Journal* 5 (1983): 26–40; "Trader William Gilliss and Delaware Migration in Southern Missouri, *Missouri Historical Review* (January 1981): 147–67; and "Where Did All the Money Go? War and the Economics of Vigilantism in Southern Missouri," *White River Valley Historical Quarterly* (fall 1994): 3–16.

43. For example, Vernon Todd outfitted Secretary of State John Swanger and E. E. McJimsey, editor of the *Springfield Republican,* and wife for a float with expert rivermen Higdon Melton and Joe Kinyon, and the following year a Kansas City party of twenty-four businessmen, political appointments, and their wives traveled downriver in a flotilla to Cotter, Arkansas, hosted by several guides. See *Branson Echo,* July 26, 1907, and October 1, 1908.

44. The name was changed for the popularity of another Arcadian novel, Gene Stratton Porter's *A Girl of the Limberlost.* See the recent edition by Dell Publishing, New York, 1990.

45. An excellent overview of pearl fishing is Robert E. Coker, *Fresh-Water Mussels and Mussel Industries of the United States* (Washington, D.C.: Government Printing Office, 1919).

46. The diary is printed in the *White River Valley Historical Quarterly* (summer 1979): 6–8.

47. The form of the Ozark johnboat, a flat-bottom boat, was mature about 1915, but outfitters in southwest Missouri apparently did not use the term *johnboat,* but continued the use of flat-bottom or float boat until the depression or later. Meanwhile, the *johnboat* term was in use in southeast Missouri. Sheer is the fore-and-aft curvature from bow to stern, and rake is the inclination on the bow. Journalists began using the alternative spelling, *jonboat,* during the depression. See Morrow, "What's in a Name, Like *Johnboat?*"

48. *Branson White River Leader,* August 28, 1914.

49. *Branson White River Leader,* August 7, 1914.

50. Charley Barnes, interview by Townsend Godsey, Godsey Collection, College of the Ozarks, Point Lookout, Missouri.

51. Charley Barnes, interview by Townsend Godsey, Godsey Collection, College of the Ozarks, Point Lookout, Missouri.

52. Godsey and Godsey, *Flight of the Phoenix,* 76.

53. See "Picturesque Ozark School That Lives on Friendships," *Kansas City Journal-Post,* February 6, 1927, and *Kansas City Star,* "Empty Purse Necessary for Entrance to Ozarks School," September 2, 1945.

54. Harold C. Svanoe, "The Preaching and Speaking of Burris Jenkins" (Ph.D. diss., Northwestern University, August 1953), 62, and Neal Edgar and Lynn Morrow, "A Genteel Vacation," *Ozarks Mountaineer* (October 1982): 32–34. See a photograph of Jenkins and Wilson on a White River float trip in the first issue of the *Ozarkian* (April 1926).

55. Kathleen Van Buskirk, "Rockaway Is Reclaiming Its Beach," *Ozarks Mountaineer* (October/November 1995): 43.

56. Articles of Incorporation, Taney County Deed Book 30, 143–46. Hollister founder W. H. Johnson also organized his White River Club on Turkey Creek "to protect fish and game for sporting purposes." White River Club incorporation, 1908, Greene County Archives, Springfield, Missouri.

57. See especially *First Annual Report of the State Game and Fish Commissioner* (Jefferson City, Mo.: Hugh Stephens Printing Company, 1910). Tolerton brought significant attention to the James and White River sporting and recreation activities in text and photographs. Prior to his government service Tolerton launched the first gasoline boat on the White River at Branson. Kathleen Van Buskirk, "Branson and the Town Company," *Ozarks Mountaineer* (January–February 1988): 42.

58. *Thirty-fifth Annual Report, Bureau of Labor Statistics;* "Lure of the Land," Missouri Booster Pamphlet (Jefferson City, Mo., 1914), 488–90.

59. "Fishing Trips on the Beautiful Rivers in the Shepherd of the Hills Country," brochure, n.d., Nancy Barnhardt Papers, Galena. The large float-trip outfitter in Branson from 1911 to 1928 was the White River Boat Line operated by brothers Arthur and Judge Meredith Walker from Illinois.

60. Denver Hollars, interview by Robert Gilmore, January 15, 1992, typescript in possession of authors.

61. A sample map can be viewed in the *Joplin Globe* magazine, August 1921, or the *Kansas City Journal-Post,* May 31, 1925. Annual OPA booklets, "The Ozarks, The Land of a Million Smiles," can be reviewed at the Powers Museum, Carthage, Missouri.

62. *Missouri Game and Fish News* (April 1926): 8, 14–15. The oldest floating in the interior Ozarks by sportsmen looking for good fishing and recreation is the Gasconade and Big Piney Rivers due to the easy access from the Frisco Railroad from the 1870s onward. By the turn of the century sporting serials in St. Louis published specific directions and costs for float trips on several Ozarks rivers.

63. "The White River Country in the Ozarks," pamphlet, Missouri Pacific Railroad, c. 1923.

64. "James and White River Float Trips," brochure, Missouri Pacific Iron Mountain Railroad, c. 1925. Another one devoted to the float trip is "'Fishin's Fine' in the White River Country of the Ozarks," Missouri Pacific Lines, c. 1929.

65. "Arnold Lodge Is Being Rejuvenated," *Stone County News Oracle,* May 5, 1926, and Lawrence County Water, Light and Cold Storage Company, letter to Dewey Short, April 3, 1914, Robert Wiley Collection, Crane, Missouri.

66. "Publisher Pleased with Float Trip," *Chickasha* [Oklahoma] *Daily Express,* reprint, *Stone County News Oracle,* May 26, 1926.

67. W. W. Warren, "'Rattler' Guilliams' Own Story," *Ozarkian* (April 1926): 3–4, 28–29. Guilliams began guiding for the Galena Boating Company in 1921 at age thirty-four.

68. Floyd Sullivan, "Table Rock Lake to Change James River Floats," *Springfield Press,* October 4, 1930. Dr. J. H. Young and L. O. Stewart were the owners of the Galena Boating Company.

69. Sullivan, "Table Rock Lake to Change James River Floats."

Chapter 6
"God's Great Natural Park":
The Railroad Transforms Resorting and Commerce

1. Herbert Hadley, "The South's Most Northern State," *Missouri, Phelps County,* ed. B. H. Rucker (c. 1910; reprint, St. Louis, Mo.: Lumberman's Printing, c. 1919). Hadley's famous case against Standard Oil is best summarized by Bruce Bringhurst, *Antitrust and the Oil Monopoly: The Standard Oil Cases, 1890–1911* (Westport, Conn.: Greenwood Press, 1979), 89–97.

2. The powerful cultural and economic influence of railroads was recently outlined by Christensen and Kremer, *A History of Missouri, Volume IV, 1875–1919,* 28 ff.

3. Edith McCall, *English Village in the Ozarks: The Story of Hollister, Missouri* (Hollister, Mo.: By the author, 1985), 12–14.

4. One Stone County resident later told of some "Australian" (Austrian) railroad construction workers who shot, cooked, and ate a buzzard. The workers reportedly concluded that, "Big, black chick no good—she make you sick." R. C. Emerson, interview with Linda Myers-Phinney, November 2, 1988. This greatly amused locals as they assumed it was common knowledge that buzzards were not for eating. For an excellent description of the camps, see Eleanor Holbrook, "Diary of Horton Camp," *Boone County Historian* (April–June 1997): 28–35.

5. See *Official Manual of the State of Missouri for the Years 1913–1914* (Jefferson City, Mo.: Hugh Stephens Printing Company, 1914), 550–51. Taney, Ozark, and Shannon Counties had the lowest valuation in Missouri; *Thirty-fifth Annual Report, Bureau of Labor Statistics, State of Missouri,* 491, and *Fifteenth Census of the United States: 1930, Missouri* (Washington, D.C.: Government Printing Office, 1930), 24–25. Stone's population went from 9,892 in 1900 to 11,614 in 1930, and Taney's 10,127 in 1900 to 8,867 in 1930. Powell's quote is in "The Man from Notch," *Stone County News Oracle,* June 23, 1904.

6. *Branson Echo,* June 22, 1906.

7. Godsey and Godsey, *Flight of the Phoenix,* 638; Van Buskirk, "Branson and the Town Company," 42; and McCall, *English Village,* 32. A detailed description of Johnson's real-estate promotion named Hollister is in the *Stone County News Oracle,* May 24, 1906. While Johnson's office was in Springfield, his representative in Taney County was Prof. J. W. Blankinship. The latter was a distinguished promoter of the Ozarks. He was a Tennessean who claimed he came to the Ozarks for

his health. In 1889 he founded a monthly educational journal, *Mountain Educator,* in Marshall, Arkansas, where he was principal of the Marshall Seminary. In 1892 he established a Democrat paper, the *Mountain Wave,* and ran unsuccessfully for state representative in 1894. He moved to nearby Omaha, Arkansas, for a time and then to Pinetop in Taney County. He built his Forest Home Ranch, a large progressive agricultural development, and joined Johnson in the promotion of Hollister. Blankinship later went his own way as a real-estate promoter of agricultural lands and mineral deposits. See J. W. Blankinship, "Southwest Taney County, Missouri, with supplements, In the White River Country," 1910.

8. Cliff and Vi Edom, *Twice Told Tales and an Ozark Photo Album* (Republic, Mo.: Western Printing Company, 1983), 60, 120, 125; Godsey and Godsey, *Flight of the Phoenix,* 638–39.

9. "A Sketch of the Many Ups and Downs in Life of Ben T. Stults, As a Boy to a Man as a Hunter," ed. Lynn Morrow and Linda Myers-Phinney, *White River Valley Historical Quarterly* (fall 1991): 9, and (winter 1992): 15.

10. Quoted in Laurence C. Walker, *The Southern Forest* (Austin: University of Texas, 1991), 112.

11. "County Business Affairs," *Stone County News Oracle,* February 1, 1906.

12. The tie business heralded momentous economic changes inasmuch as it introduced significant and quick cash flow into what had been a cash-poor area. Ties were one of the first locally produced items for export outside the area. The tie economy whetted community appetites for relative prosperity, particularly in Stone County. The tie market continued into the 1920s. The 1907 figures are in H.R. Bill 10550, 60th Congress, Robert Wiley Collection, Crane, Missouri.

13. "Agricultural Development: Missouri Pacific Railroad," comp. Agricultural Development Department of the Missouri Pacific Railroad, 1948, 1.

14. "Agricultural Development: Missouri Pacific Railroad," 2–3.

15. McCall, *English Village,* 37, 40, 44. Springfieldians had commonly played major roles in the founding of Taney County towns including Forsyth, Kirbyville, Branson, and Hollister. For a good description of the Log Cabin Hotel, see Viola Hartman, "The Backward Trail," *Taney County Times,* October 9, 1996. The hotel and an associated mercantile were investments by George W. Outcalt of Oklahoma City.

16. "Hollister, Taney County," WPA Collection, Taney County, WHMC-Columbia.

17. McCall, *English Village,* 49–56. The stock law in Winslow, a northwest Arkansas tourist town, had a similar history to Hollister. See Mel H. Bolster, "The Mountain Mind," *Arkansas Historical Quarterly* (winter 1951): 320.

18. McCall, *English Village,* 53, and "To the Honorable County Court and All Other Good Citizens of Taney County, Missouri," *White River Leader,* February 5, 1915. The assembly was incorporated as a benevolent and religious body in April 1913, Corporation Files, MSA, and *Presbyterian Messenger* (December 1940).

19. McCall, *English Village,* 53; "Church Leaders Come to Presbyterian Hill," *White River Leader,* February 2, 1925; and "Ozark Area School for Training of Presbyterian Ministers," *White River Leader,* September 3, 1925.

20. "W.C.T.U. Convention," *White River Leader,* August 13, 1915; *White River Leader,* March 31, 1916; "DeMolay Encampment Plans Ozark Vacation," *White River Leader,* April 27, 1925; and *White River Leader,* November 19, 1925.

21. Letter, Lizzie T. A. to Marie Oliver Watkins, July 30, 1929, WHMC-Columbia. Years before, the Hollister town council in 1915 promulgated an ordinance that included, "Taking effect immediately, bathers are forbidden to go swimming without bathing suits on," a notice that Arcadian life along Turkey Creek included swimming in the nude. Ordinance sent to authors by Viola Hartman.

22. "To the Honorable County Court and All Other Good Citizens of Taney County, Missouri," *White River Leader,* February 5, 1915, and March 19, 1915, and Christensen and Kremer, *A History of Missouri,* 200.

23. In February 1915 over one hundred people had lots on Presbyterian Hill, many with completed cottages. Those who had cabins rented them to others when not using them. "To the Honorable County Court," *White River Leader,* February 5, 1915, and Marion Hoblit, interview with Lynn Morrow and Robert Flanders, February 12, 1988.

24. *White River Leader,* March 10 and 24, 1916.

25. "Grandview Hotel Has Early Season Business," *White River Leader,* April 24, 1925, "A Travelogue of Christian, Ozark, Taney, Stone, and Douglas Counties," *St. Louis Globe-Democrat,* October 25, 1925, and "Presbyterian Mecca Overlooks Hollister," *Springfield Leader,* September 25, 1927. Mrs. Madge Milligan Simmons was the donor for the administration building, dedicating it to her father, the Reverend Dr. Laird, former pastor of Calvary Presbyterian Church, Springfield. Madge and her husband, "Jude," joined St. Louis Frisco Railroad executive Harry Worman in 1927 to purchase lands for a private resort park called Devil's Pool, just east of Long Creek. Their estates, left "dry" in the depression without the construction of Table Rock Dam, later became the centerpiece in the development of Bass Pro's Big Cedar Resort. See *White River Leader,* July 29, 1926, Robert Flanders, "The Park at Devil's Pool, the History of a Private Resort," April 26, 1988, and Charlie Farmer, *Devil's Pool, A History of Big Cedar Lodge* (Springfield, Mo.: JLM Publishing Company, 1995).

26. Douglas Mahnkey, interview by Lynn Morrow and Linda Myers-Phinney, January 19, 1988.

27. Allen Albert, "The Tents of the Conservative," *Scribners* 72 (July 1922): 59, and Kay Hively, "When the Chautauqua Came to Town," *Ozarks Mountaineer* (March–April 1987): 41.

28. *Presbyterian Messenger* (June 1935).

29. *Branson White River Leader,* February 12, 1915. Ross became a justice of the peace in 1909. See *Branson Echo,* August 27, 1909.

30. *White River Leader,* August 8, 1913; "Presbyterian Hill Dates Fixed," *White River Leader,* April 17, 1919; and Marion Hoblit, interview by Lynn Morrow and Robert Flanders, February 12, 1988.

31. MacLeod, *Building Character,* xii.

32. McCall, *English Village,* 39; Taney County *Republican,* April 27, 1911; and Dwight Ford, interview by Lynn Morrow and Linda Myers-Phinney, at Hollister, Missouri, December 8, 1988. Ford owned and operated the YMCA site for many years.

33. Dwight Ford, interview by Lynn Morrow and Linda Myers-Phinney, and "YMCA Improvements at Hollister," *Taney County Republican,* April 13, 1911.

34. Howard Hopkins, *History of the YMCA* (New York: Association Press, 1951), 456, and *The Ozarks,* 18.

35. "YMCA Camp," *White River Leader,* June 12, 1919.

36. Rayburn, *Forty Years in the Ozarks,* 23; and Douglas Mahnkey, interview by Lynn Morrow and Linda Myers-Phinney, January 19, 1988; "Boys' Camp Affords Outing for Many," *Springfield Leader,* September 25, 1927; "Inspiration in Camp for Youth of Nation," *White River Leader,* July 29, 1926; and Hopkins, *YMCA,* 617.

37. Cliff and Vi Edom, *Ozark Photo Album,* 161; "Taney County in 1914," *White River Leader,* January 1, 1915; and McCall, *English Village,* 73, 79–80.

38. Van Buskirk, "Branson and the Town Company," 45.

39. "First Grand Excursion on Lake Taneycomo," *White River Leader,* May 16, 1913; "Finest Boat on Lake Taneycomo Is Launched at Branson," *White River Leader,* June 20, 1913; "Eight Young Ladies Have an Outing" and "Outing on Lake Taneycomo," *White River Leader,* July 4, 1913; and "Branson's First Steam Boat," *White River Leader,* July 25, 1913.

40. "Power Company Lands for Lease," *White River Leader,* October 2, 1914; *White River Leader,* April 24, 1914; "Second Open Letter to the People of Taney County," *White River Leader,* June 5, 1914; "Lake News," *White River Leader,* September 11, 1914; and "Taney County in 1914," *White River Leader,* January, 1, 1915.

41. "Land Boom," *White River Leader,* October 22, 1915; "Good Demand Now for Western Ozark Land," *White River Leader,* April 15, 1926; Stephen Burton, "The Origin and Growth of Rockaway Beach, Missouri," *White River Valley Historical Quarterly* (spring 1963): 17; "Vacation Rush Slackens," *White River Leader,* September 3, 1925; "Rockaway Beach," *White River Leader,* February 13 and August 13, 1925; *White River Leader,* March 6, 1925, and April 24, 1914.

42. "Cliff House Country Club," *The Ozarks: The Land of a Million Smiles* (Joplin, Mo.: Ozark Playgrounds Association, 1926), 19; "New Club House," *Stone County News Oracle,* September 15, 1926; and *White River Leader,* February 20, 1919.

43. Edgar and Morrow, "A Genteel Vacation," 32–34.

44. For Jenkins's biography, see Harold C. Svanoe, "The Preaching and Speaking of Burris Jenkins" (Ph.D. diss., Northwestern University, 1953). Local articles about the Cliff House include those in the *White River Leader,* February 27,

July 16, and October 1, 1925, April 22, May 13, July 29, August 12, and November 11, 1926. The photograph is in Warren, "'Rattler' Guilliam's Own Story."

45. Van Buskirk, "Branson and the Town Company," 42, *White River Leader,* July 11, 1913, and Ingenthron, *The Land of Taney,* 302.

46. The growth in farm cooperatives or exchanges, promoted at Farmers' Week conferences, contributed to the "factory idea." See "Every Farm a Factory," in *The Missouri Yearbook of Agriculture, Forty-seventh Annual Report* (Columbia, Mo.: 112–124 Agricultural Building, 1915), 244–45. Walter Kline remarked that "the Lake Taneycomo Region, under the advisory of the Missouri Pacific Railway, is a fine example to other communities which might also coordinate specialized farming activities with their scenic wonders," in "Ozark Observations and Impressions," *Year Book, Public Museum of the City of Milwaukee, 1928* (Milwaukee: Board of Trustees, 1929), 119.

47. *Surplus Products of Missouri Counties for the Year Ending December 31, 1907,* supplement to annual report (Jefferson City, Mo.: State Labor Bureau, 1908), 19–20, and 1909 supplement, 108. H. M. Dixon and J. M. Purdom published a federal report of a detailed county-level study, including Taney County, "Farm Management in the Ozark Region of Missouri," *Bulletin No. 941* (Washington, D.C.: U.S. Department of Agriculture, 1921) that demonstrated that farm families earned two-thirds of all receipts from livestock. Although stock were central to the Ozarks economy, the actual numbers lagged far behind those in north Missouri counties.

48. G. K. Renner, "Strawberry Culture in Southwest Missouri," *Missouri Historical Review* (October 1969): 28–29, for a summary of the associations. In Stone County the Powell family at Fall Creek, Frank Mease near Reed's Spring, and a factory at Hurley had already begun canning prior to the completion of the railroad. Small businessmen followed in building canneries at Galena, Garber, Gretna, and Branson as the rail lines were complete. The poultry economy was more important to women and the family on an annual basis than was canning, but it did not have the social aspects that canning did.

49. See *Twenty-ninth Annual Report of the Bureau of Labor Statistics, State of Missouri,* 664–67; *Thirty-first Annual Report of the Bureau of Labor Statistics of the State of Missouri* (Jefferson City, Mo.: Hugh Stephens Printing Company, 1909), 398; and *Surplus Products of Missouri Counties for the Year Ending Jan. 1, 1910* (Jefferson City, Mo.: Hugh Stephens Printing Company, 1910), 184–88.

50. *History of Stone County, Missouri* (Cassville, Mo.: Litho Printers, 1989), 204, and *The Missouri Year Book of Agriculture, Fifty-third Annual Report* (Jefferson City, Mo.: State Board of Agriculture, 1921), 259–62, published the first statewide roster. Investors in canning could purchase from a number of model factories as close as Springfield, Missouri. See *Catalog, Thos. M. Brown Canning Factories* (Springfield, Mo., 1918). Brown began manufacturing in 1905.

51. *Forty-fourth Annual Report, Bureau of Labor Statistics, State of Missouri*

(Jefferson City, Mo.: Missouri Bureau of Labor Statistics, 1924), 290–91, 298; "The Stone County Booklet," prepared by A. L. McQuary, Fair Commission of Stone County, 1927, 24–25; and Martha McGrath, "Tomato Canning in the Ozarks," *Webster County Historical Society Journal* (December 1976): 7–8. Nelson's brother-in-law B. Frank Julian was a partner in the large Nelson business.

52. *White River Leader,* July 15, 1926.

53. Milton D. Rafferty, "Agricultural Change in the Western Ozarks," *Missouri Historical Review* 69 (April 1975): 311.

54. Clyde Davis, "The Early Years of My Life," *White River Valley Historical Quarterly* (winter 1985): 18–19. Two good articles about the canneries are Kathleen Van Buskirk, "When the Tomatoe Was Queen," *Ozarks Mountaineer* (April 1978): 16–17, 24; Brenda Hendrix, "Tomatoes on the Hillsides," *Ozarks Mountaineer* (September–October 1985): 43, 48–49.

55. Presbyterian Hill generated electricity for years on top of its majestic view of the White River valley. Utilities illuminated Branson in 1916, and in the 1920s Galena installed a streetlight system powered by its own water-driven generator. In 1925 lines were strung from Powersite Dam upriver to Rockaway Beach. Telephone service was available surprisingly early. According to Elmo Ingenthron, three companies built lines as early as 1898; these connected Forsyth with Walnut Shade, Protem, and Chadwick. In March 1904 lines linked Forsyth, Kirbyville, and Branson, and in 1909 three phone systems centered at Hollister. McCall, *English Village,* 42, 75; "Local News," *Stone County News Oracle,* February 16, 1921; "Rockaway Beach," *White River Leader,* February 13, 1925; Ingenthron, *The Land of Taney,* 291; and Van Buskirk, "Branson and the Town Company," 41. The "white lights" comment is from the *White River Leader,* February 6, 1919.

56. "Fortune Smiles on the White River Country," *White River Leader,* January 16, 1914.

57. "It Happened In?" *Southwest Missourian,* August 11, 1988; Spurlock, *Over the Old Ozark Trails in the Shepherd of the Hills Country,* 11–12.

58. *Fortieth Annual Report of the Missouri State Board of Agriculture* (Jefferson City, Mo.: Hugh Stephens Printing Company, 1908), 56–58. The new state highway engineer planned to issue a bulletin of instructions to county engineers and develop a "road laboratory" with the University of Missouri Engineering College. The idea was that coalitions in road building would develop at the local level, while the state could utilize prison labor to quarry and operate rock crusher plants.

59. The extant road work did, however, encourage visitors. Springfield merchant families, such as the Bissets, usually drove to Rockaway Beach in 1922 and beyond because of the improvements in local roads. Marion Hoblit, interview by Lynn Morrow and Robert Flanders, Springfield, Missouri, February 12, 1988. Elmo G. Harris published a comprehensive view of the roads in "Road Problems in the Ozarks," *Bulletin of the School of Mines and Metallurgy* (Rolla: University of Missouri, 1919) that presented the statutory, engineering, construction, and financial aspects of

the great undertaking. There were many regions in America whose road conditions were similar to those in the Ozarks.

60. Clara B. Kennan, "The Ozark Trails and Arkansas's Pathfinder, Coin Harvey," *Arkansas Historical Quarterly* (winter 1948): 299, 301, 308.

61. *White River Leader,* October 16 and 23, and November 20, 1914. By 1919 Missouri officials told Ozark promoters that work would proceed on a White River Trails National Highway from Springfield to Tulsa, Oklahoma, and that a link from Lake Taneycomo to Stone County was crucial in the overall planning. "State to Build the White River Trail," *White River Leader,* May 8, 1919.

62. *White River Leader,* August 1 and October 13, 1913; "Branson Has the Only Wagon Bridge Crossing White River in Missouri," *White River Leader,* July 11, 1913; "Commercial Club of Branson Held Special Meeting," *White River Leader,* August 8, 1913; and "Roark Bridge Near Completion," *White River Leader,* September 12, 1913; "The First Auto Road," July 13, 1914; "Taney County in 1914," January 1, 1915, in *White River Leader,* and *Bureau of Labor Statistics, State of Missouri,* Missouri "Booster" Edition (Jefferson City, Mo.: Hugh Stephens Printing Company, 1914), 488–90, 497–99.

63. "The Road Bonds," January 7, 1920, "Local News," January 21, 1920, "Bonds Valid," March 31, 1920, and "Road Building in Missouri," October 21, 1920, all in *Stone County News Oracle,* and *Stone County News Oracle,* April 7, 1920.

64. "Long Creek Bridge Will Be Put to Use," *White River Leader,* May 28, 1925.

65. See a summary of the progressive governors in Christensen and Kremer, *A History of Missouri, Volume IV, 1875 to 1919,* 186–98.

66. *White River Leader,* June 27, 1913, and May 15, 1915, "Marvel Cave Adds Bus Service for Summer," *White River Leader,* July 2, 1925, and "Good Road Will Be Built to Powersite," *White River Leader,* April 29, 1926.

67. "The White River Country as a Pleasure Resort," *White River Leader,* November 21, 1913, and *Lake Taneycomo and the Shepherd of the Hills Country,* 1926.

68. "The Ozarks Coming Fast," reprinted from *Springfield Republican* in the *White River Leader,* January 29, 1915; "A New Playground—Missouri Ozarks," *Eminence* [Missouri] *Current Wave,* October 6, 1921; and "Mayes Calls Area New Switzerland," *Springfield Leader,* September 25, 1927. Bill McCurdy and his father from Springfield, Missouri, traveled to Powersite Dam to fish in 1913, driving down to Chadwick and following the Swan Creek road to the White River. Before the trip he bought a new set of tires for his Overland auto. Nonetheless, they suffered thirty-two flat tires and threw them away after the trip. Bill McCurdy, interview by Linda Myers-Phinney, Springfield, Missouri, November 14, 1995. See map by Myers-Phinney, "The Land of a Million Smiles," 60.

69. Missouri's member counties in 1926 were Dade, Polk, Dallas, Laclede, Texas, Wright, Webster, Greene, Lawrence, Jasper, Newton, McDonald, Barry, Stone, Christian, Taney, Douglas, Ozark, and Howell. Arkansas counted Benton, Carroll, Boone, Marion, Searcy, Newton, Madison, Washington, Crawford,

Sebastian, Franklin, Logan, Johnson, and Pope Counties as members. See *1926 Ozarks Playgrounds Map,* Ozark Playgrounds Association, 1926. The name spins off the Playground Association of America founded for similar reasons in 1906. The Ozark association continued until 1979.

70. *Come to the Ozarks: The Land of a Million Smiles* (Joplin, Mo.: Ozark Playgrounds Association, 1924), 2, and *The Ozarks,* 4. Eli Ashcraft's father, Granville P. Ashcraft (1842–1911), was a principal developer of the Webb City mines in the late nineteenth century. See Joel T. Livingston, *A History of Jasper County, Missouri, and Its People,* vol. II (Chicago: Lewis Publishing Company, 1912), 857–59.

71. James Braswell, "In the Land of a Million Smiles," The Stephen A. Douglas Music Normal Association, Aldrich, Missouri, 1925; "Smile Girls," *Stone County News Oracle,* March 18, 1925. Joe Manlove, a successful Republican attorney from Joplin, and a long-time secretary of the OPA coined the "Land of a Million Smiles" term. Manlove was elected to Congress in 1922, 1924, 1926, and 1928. See *Kansas City Journal,* December 20, 1926. Rayburn's poem is in the *White River Leader,* April 24, 1925. He edited the *Arcadian* magazine in Eminence, Missouri, 1931–32, and the *Arcadian Life* magazine at Caddo Gap, Arkansas, 1933–42.

72. Designed for prospective residents as well as tourists, OPA guidebooks described both recreational and economic opportunities in the Ozarks. The 1926 edition listed apples, grapes, tomatoes, dairy and poultry, livestock, tobacco, and lead and zinc as profitable. It also pointed out the industrial possibilities afforded by inexpensive hydroelectric power and good rail transportation. *The Ozarks,* 93.

73. *The Ozarks,* 4, and "Ozark Playgrounds News Flashes," *Stone County News Oracle,* May 27 and August 26, 1925.

74. "Expect Million to Visit Ozarks in 1927," *White River Leader,* May 4, 1927.

75. *The Ozarks,* 4.

76. "Bulletin Tells Work of Taneycomo Chamber of Commerce," *White River Leader,* August 6, 1925; *Roads, Rivers, Recreation around Springfield, Missouri* (Springfield: Missouri Chamber of Commerce, August 1, 1929); and *Lake Taneycomo and the Shepherd of the Hills Country.*

77. "Ozark Hills Tourist Association to Hold Meeting at Crane," *Stone County News Oracle,* March 10, 1926; "Woodruff Speaks on Ozark Improvement," *White River Leader,* March 11, 1926; and "A Selfish Motive," *Stone County News Oracle,* March 10, 1926.

78. "Lon Scott Speaks at Galena," *Stone County News Oracle,* March 31, 1926; "The Story of Twenty-five Trucks," *Stone County News Oracle,* April 7, 1926.

79. "Local News," *Stone County News Oracle,* September 23, 1925; "Sign Board Is Erected," *Stone County News Oracle,* April 7, 1926.

80. Spurlock, *Over the Old Ozark Trails,* 11–12, 36–37, 44–45.

81. Quinta Scott and Susan Croce Kelly, *Route 66: The Highway and Its People* (Norman: University of Oklahoma Press, 1988), 8; "Marvel Cave," *White River*

Leader, September 10, 1915; "Missouri Shows Road Progress," *White River Leader,* January 5, 1933; "Wilderness Ridge," *Stone County News Oracle,* November 16, 1921; "Missouri State Road Progress Map," *Stone County News Oracle,* May 5, 1926; and "Famed Book Led to Tourist Surge," *Kansas City Star,* April 9, 1967.

82. *Kansas City Star,* June 13, 1926. The Kansas City Automobile Club served as a clearinghouse for tourist information as did the Ozark Playgrounds Association.

83. Morrow and Quick, "Transportation and Tourism in the Shepherd of the Hills Country," part II, 9–10; and Lynn Morrow and David Quick, "Y-Bridge," National Register of Historic Places Nomination, Historic Preservation Program, Missouri Department of Natural Resources, Jefferson City, Missouri, 1989. The highway department closed vehicular traffic on the bridge in December 1985 and opened a new bridge upstream.

84. *Official Manual* (Jefferson City, Mo.: Hugh Stephens Printing Company, 1922), 838. The proposed map of the state highway network of July 30, 1921, is on p. 846; the loop around Lake Taneycomo is unique.

85. Morrow and Quick, "Transportation and Tourism in the Shepherd of the Hills Country," part II, 6–8.

86. *Twenty-first Annual Report of the Bureau of Labor Statistics,* 254–56. St. Louis businessmen still participated in the promotion of the rail economies. For example, W. P. Heath was president of the Tobacco Growers' Investment Company and its successor Homeland Farms real-estate development, while his brother-in-law V. C. Todd in Branson was vice-president. Tobacco Growers' Investment Company, Corporation Files, MSA.

87. "Marketing Train in Successful Tour," *White River Leader,* February 20, 1925; "Fruit Train to Bring Good Nursery Stock," *White River Leader,* November 5, 1925; Douglas Mahnkey interview by Lynn Morrow and Linda Myers-Phinney, January 19, 1988; "Agricultural Development: Missouri Pacific Railroad," 7, "Missouri Pacific Fruit Train Success—Hundreds of Acres Will Be Set as Result of Expedition," *Stone County News Oracle,* November 25, 1925; and "Introducing the Missouri Pacific Horticultural Agent," *Stone County News Oracle,* January 27, 1926.

88. "Orchards Redeemed by Springfield Men," *White River Leader,* February 27, 1925; "Strawberry Shed Is Now Complete," *Stone County News Oracle,* April 21, 1926; "State Exhibition and County Fair," *Stone County News Oracle,* July 22, 1925; and "Attention Farmers," *Stone County News Oracle,* August 12, 1925.

89. See Laura J. Gallagher, "Hollister Chamber of Commerce to Renovate Historic American House," *Taney County Republican,* June 27, 1985; Van Buskirk, "Branson and the Town Company," 41; "Ozarks Playgrounds News Flashes," *Galena Stone County News Oracle,* July 1, 1925; "Plan Ozark Excursion," *Stone County News Oracle,* March 31, 1916; "Town Has Its Face to Road," *Springfield Leader,* September 25, 1927; "Agricultural Development: Missouri Pacific Railroad," 11–12; and "New Settlers Arrive Daily: Missouri Pacific Averages Locating Family Per Day in Valley Region," *Springfield Leader,* September 25, 1927. Dr. Corlis was a

physician who came to the Ozarks for his health in 1924 under the new management of the Missouri Pacific extension division. In 1938 the railroad discontinued the agricultural department, and Corlis returned to medical practice in Branson. See discussion by Adams, *The White River Railway,* 103–4 and 138.

90. A listing of businesses and resorts for Branson and Hollister may be reviewed in *Lake Taneycomo and the Shepherd of the Hills Country* and "Hollister and Taney County," WPA Collection, WHMC-Columbia. A 1926 state highway department survey of out-of-state tourists in Missouri concluded that the average traveler stayed 10.7 days in the state. *Citizen's Road Bulletin,* June 1928.

Chapter 7
"Credulity Is Contagious":
Images in Arcadia and the Backwoods

1. The story is summarized from "Honeymooners Romantic Experience in the Ozarks," *White River Leader,* July 16, 1915.

2. Neihardt quoted in Townsend Godsey, "Branson Honors John Neihardt," *Ozarks Mountaineer* (March–April 1989): 33.

3. "John G. Neihardt's Address at Dedication of Ross Memorial," *White River Leader,* October 8, 1925.

4. John Neihardt, letters to Mamma, January 24 and February 9, 1929, and Alice Neihardt, letter to Elmer Holm, April 7, 1939, John Neihardt Papers, WHMC-Columbia.

5. "Swimming Pool Will Be Opened Next Week," *White River Leader,* June 25, 1925.

6. "McQuerter Buys More Lake Front," *White River Leader,* July 29, 1926. McQuerter operated the business for twenty years, selling out to Drury McMillan in 1933, *White River Leader,* February 16, 1933. In early 1926 Atchison, Kansas, investors platted almost three hundred acres into fifteen hundred lots above the county seat of Forsyth into the Shepherd of the Hills Estates, including a golf course. The construction of Bull Shoals Lake caused Forsyth to be relocated in the middle of the development in 1950. See a series of articles in the *White River Leader* in March–April 1926. The Shepherd of the Hills Bank and Inn were in Reed's Spring.

7. Marion Wright Powers, letter to H. B. Wright, January 1, 1936, Powers Museum, Carthage, Missouri.

8. Harold Bell Wright, letter to Marion Wright Powers, January 6, 1936, Powers Museum, Carthage, Missouri.

9. Chris Whitley, "White River: Current for a Culture," *Springfield News-Leader,* September 25, 1990.

10. Locals have also mistakenly ascribed Wright's 1918 visit to one in 1906

where he supposedly wrote some of the novel in the hotel—nothing could be farther from the truth. Regarding Dad Howitt, the shepherd, Sammy Lane, Wash Gibbs, Jim Lane, Ollie Stewart, and all other characters, "not one was even suggested by a living person." See Gibbons Lacy, "Characters of 'Shepherd of the Hills' Not Drawn from Life," *Ozarks Mountaineer* (February 1956): 9. The best and most detailed explanation of local characters is Eva Eakin Grizzard, *Characters and Community of the Shepherd of the Hills* (Point Lookout, Mo.: Textor Printery, 1934).

11. *White River Leader,* May 13, 1926.

12. The context for publications in this chapter does not extend past the depression. However, it would still be another fifty years before scholars produced any significant body of professional work that began to have a positive influence in the popular mind about Ozarks history or that acknowledged that the Ozarks even had a history. Ironically, no historian has published a regional history. Geographer Milton D. Rafferty's, *The Ozarks: Land and Life,* 1980, remains as the only professional survey. Other works, published and unpublished, have addressed selected themes.

13. The first recorded usage found by Archie Green was in the *New York Journal* of April 23, 1900, reported in his "Hillbilly Music: Source and Symbol," *Journal of American Folklore* (July–September 1965). Journalists and other commentators have wrongly assumed for a century that the hillbilly, cracker, redneck, and similar pejorative terms are synonymous with "poor white" or poverty. For example, see William Atherton DuPuy, "Remaking the Poor Whites," in *Uncle Sam's Modern Miracles* (New York: Frederick A. Stockes Company, 1914), 118–27. In similar fashion, St. Louisans still use the term *hoosier* as a synonym for poor whites.

14. Interpretations for the creation of hillbillies and mountaineers in the popular mind include Henry D. Shapiro, *Appalachia on Our Mind: The Southern Mountains in the American Consciousness, 1870–1920* (Chapel Hill: University of North Carolina Press, 1978) and David E. Whisnant, *All That Is Native and Fine: The Politics of Culture in an American Region* (Chapel Hill: University of North Carolina Press, 1983).

15. See David B. Danbom's *Born in the Country: A History of Rural America* (Baltimore: Johns Hopkins University Press, 1995), 132–84.

16. Wright, *The Shepherd of the Hills,* 154.

17. See the photographs in "The Ozarks in 1900," Missouri Historical Society *Bulletin* 8 (April 1952): 270 ff.

18. John Stilgoe, *Metropolitan Corridor: Railroads and the American Scene* (New Haven, Conn.: Yale University Press, 1983), 280.

19. Fern Nance Shumate, "Broken Dreams and Scattered Schemes," *Ozarks Mountaineer* (September/October 1992): 29. Shumate, using her pen name, Nancy Clemens, was coauthor and collaborator on several projects with Vance Randolph. See George Lankford, "'Beyond the Pale': Frontier Folk in the Southern Ozarks," in *The Folk: Identity, Landscapes and Lores* (Lawrence: University of Kansas, 1989),

53–70; and Walter Stevens, *Missouri, The Center State, 1821–1915,* vol. II (Chicago: S. J. Clarke Publishing Company, 1915).

20. Edgar McKinney in his "Images, Realities, and Cultural Transformation in the Missouri Ozarks, 1920–1960" (Ph.D., diss., University of Missouri-Columbia, 1990), states similar conclusions throughout his work; for example, see pp. 71–74. Wright's images were strong enough for promoters in the Queen City of the Ozarks (Springfield) to propose the unfulfilled commission of a statue of the Shepherd to become the centerpiece for a city park in the middle of the town square. See "Plan for Springfield of 150,000," *Springfield Press,* November 6, 1930. The growth of folklore around famous places is a common phenomenon, not unlike the proliferation of tales at the battle sites of the Alamo and Gettysburg.

21. Comments are summarized from "The Ozark Region," *Branson Echo,* September 18, 1908.

22. The following is summarized from "The Poor Old Ozarks," *Branson Echo,* June 25, 1909.

23. See J. W. Williamson, *Hillbillyland* (Chapel Hill: University of North Carolina Press, 1995), 37–38.

24. "Gone the Poor Hillbilly," *White River Leader,* August 20, 1915.

25. Ross's comments are summarized from his "The Hill Billy," *White River Leader,* September 10, 1915.

26. Walter Stevens, *Centennial History of Missouri,* Vol. I (St. Louis: S. J. Clarke Publishing Company, 1921), 573 ff.

27. See, for example, *White River Leader,* December 10, 1925.

28. Charles Morrow Wilson, "Backhill Culture," *Nation,* July 17, 1929.

29. William R. Draper, "The Ozarks Go Native," *Outlook and Independent* (vol. 156, September 10, 1930): 62.

30. Vance Randolph, letter to Mary Louise Clifton, February 23, 1940, in Special Collections, Southwest Missouri State University, Springfield, Missouri. Randolph's refusal to provide scholarly documentation was a major reason why academics of his day often ignored and refused to acknowledge his work in professional reviews. Journalism without a disciplinary structure of widespread research, documentation, analysis, and peer review does not produce informed historical conclusions. This journalistic legacy of Ozark writing is central to the overall weakness of it.

31. See Vance Randolph, *Vance Randolph in the Ozarks* (Branson, Mo.: Ozarks Mountaineer, 1981), 5, and *Noel Centennial, 1887–1987* (Shawnee Mission, Kans.: Kes-Print, 1987), 21. Randolph remembered Price Payne in his "Lure of the Ozarks," *Arcadian Life* (May 1936): 13.

32. Randolph produced more in the Haldeman-Julius booklets and dabbled in the areas of "religion, philosophy, natural science, social science, and foreign language; none dealt with folklore or Americana." See Cochran and Luster, *For Love and for Money: The Writings of Vance Randolph,* 2.

33. Randolph, *Vance Randolph in the Ozarks,* 81. Randolph first wrote of the "foreign invasion" in his *The Ozarks: An American Survival of Primitive Society,* 1931.

34. Carl Sauer's *The Geography of the Ozark Highland of Missouri* was and still is a classic in Ozarks scholarly literature. Its enormous breadth outlined generational and social change in the region and proposed conservation and development of resources for widespread benefits in the twentieth century; occasionally journalists of the 1920s made reference to Sauer's work. Randolph ignored Sauer's much larger conceptual work while writing about his own interests.

35. This view was shared by historian Janet Allured in "Letter to the Editor," *White River Valley Historical Quarterly* (fall 1987): 4–5.

36. Randolph, *Vance Randolph in the Ozarks,* 82–85.

37. Quote from Robert Cochran, interview with Lynn Morrow, March 9, 1998.

38. See Archie Green's classic "Hillbilly Music: Source and Symbol," *Journal of American Folklore* (July–September 1965).

39. Cochran, *Vance Randolph,* 222.

40. Charles Finger, *Ozark Fantasia* (Fayetteville, Ark.: Golden Horseman Press, 1927), 76–77. Randolph acknowledged Finger's help, among others, in the publication of his *The Ozarks: An American Survival of Primitive Society.*

41. Grizzard, *Characters and Community of the Shepherd of the Hills,* 105.

42. Kay Hively, "The Naming of a Forest," *Ozarks Mountaineer* (January–February 1985): 48.

43. "Filling the Tourist with Bunk Stories," *Missouri Magazine* (May 1929): 27. The commercial success of the hillbilly stereotype in the Ozarks must account for little-to-no opposition of the term in the late twentieth century; we find that few people under the age of forty give it a second thought.

Works Cited

Books

Abbott, Clayton. *Historical Sketches of Cedar County, Missouri.* Greenfield, Mo.: Vedette Printing Company, 1988.

Adams, Walter M. *The White River Railway.* Branson, Mo.: Ozarks Mountaineer, 1991.

Anderson, William. *Laura Ingalls Wilder Country.* New York: Harper Perennial, 1990.

Armitage, Shelley. *Kewpies and Beyond: The World of Rose O'Neill.* Jackson: University Press of Mississippi, 1994.

Ayers, Edward, et al. *All over the Map: Rethinking American Regions.* Baltimore: Johns Hopkins University Press, 1996.

Bailey, Liberty Hyde. *The Country-Life Movement in the U.S.* New York: Macmillan, 1911.

Bailey, Liberty Hyde. *The Holy Earth.* Ithaca, N.Y.: L. H. Bailey, 1919.

Benton, Thomas Hart. *An Artist in America.* Columbia: University of Missouri Press, 1983.

Bringhurst, Bruce. *Antitrust and the Oil Monopoly: The Standard Oil Cases, 1890–1911.* Westport, Conn.: Greenwood Press, 1979.

Callison, Charles. *Man and Wildlife in Missouri.* Harrisburg, Pa.: Stackpole Company, 1953.

Christensen, Lawrence O., and Gary R. Kremer. *A History of Missouri, Volume IV, 1875–1919.* Columbia: University of Missouri Press, 1997.

Cochran, Robert, and Michael Luster. *For Love and for Money: The Writings of Vance Randolph.* An annotated bibliography. Batesville, Ark.: Riverside Graphics, 1979.

The Commonwealth of Missouri. Ed. C. R. Burns. St. Louis, Mo.: Bryan, Brand and Company, 1877.

Danbom, David B. *Born in the Country: A History of Rural America.* Baltimore: Johns Hopkins University Press, 1995.

Davis, Walter, and Daniel Durrie. *An Illustrated History of Missouri.* St. Louis, Mo.: A. J. Hall and Company, 1876.

Deem, David. *History of Butler County, Missouri.* Popular Bluff, Mo.: Poplar Bluff Printing Company, 1940.

Dunckel, John. *The Mollyjoggers: Tales of the Camp-Fire.* Springfield, Mo.: H. S. Jewell, c. 1906.

Dunn, Ella Ingenthron. *The Granny Woman of the Hills.* Branson, Mo.: Ozarks Mountaineer, 1978.

Edom, Cliff, and Vi Edom. *Twice Told Tales and an Ozark Photo Album.* Republic, Mo.: Western Printing Company, 1983.

Ellis, James. *The Influence of Environment on the Settlement of Missouri.* St. Louis, Mo.: Webster Publishing Company, 1929.

Fairbanks, Jonathan, and Clyde Edwin Tuck. *Past and Present of Greene County, Missouri.* Indianapolis, Ind.: A. W. Bowen and Company, 1915.

Finger, Charles. *Ozark Fantasia.* Fayetteville, Ark.: Golden Horsemen Press, 1927.

Gerlach, Russell. *Settlement Patterns in Missouri.* Columbia: University of Missouri Press, 1986.

Giffen, Jerena. *First Ladies of Missouri.* 1970. Reprint, Jefferson City, Mo.: Giffen Enterprises, 1996.

Gilmore, Robert K. *Ozark Baptizings, Hangings, and Other Diversions.* Norman: University of Oklahoma Press, 1984.

Glossip, Zoe. *Ponce de Leon, Mo., 1881–1981, Centennial Celebration.* n.p., October 24, 1981.

Godsey, Townsend, and Helen Godsey. *Flight of the Phoenix: The Biography of The School of the Ozarks.* Point Lookout, Mo.: School of the Ozarks Press, 1984.

Grizzard, Eva Eakin. *Characters and Community of the Shepherd of the Hills.* Point Lookout, Mo.: Textor Printery, 1934.

Hallock, Charles. *The Sportsmen's Gazetteer and General Guide.* New York: Forest and Stream Publishing Company, 1877.

History of Stone County, Missouri. Cassville, Mo.: Litho Printers, 1989.

Holcombe, R. S. *History of Greene County, Missouri.* St. Louis, Mo.: Western Historical Company, 1883.

Hopkins, Howard. *History of the YMCA.* New York: Association Press, 1951.

Ingenthron, Elmo. *The Land of Taney: A History of an Ozark Commonwealth.* Point Lookout, Mo.: School of the Ozarks Press, 1974.

Jakle, John A. *The Tourist: Travel in Twentieth-Century America.* Lincoln: University of Nebraska Press, 1985.

Johnston, James J. *Shootin', Obituaries, Politics; Emigratin', Socializin', Commercializin'; and the Press.* Fayetteville, Ark.: James J. Johnston, 1991.

Lears, T. J. Jackson. *No Place of Grace: Antimodernism and the Transformation of American Culture, 1880–1920.* New York: Pantheon Books, 1981.

Livingston, Joel T. *A History of Jasper County, Missouri, and Its People.* Chicago: Lewis Publishing Company, 1912.

McCall, Edith. *English Village in the Ozarks: The Story of Hollister, Missouri.* Rev. ed. Hollister, Mo.: By the author, 1985.

MacLeod, David I. *Building Character in the American Boy: The Boy Scouts, YMCA and Their Forerunners, 1870–1920.* Madison: University of Wisconsin Press, 1983.

Madsen, Jerry S. *The History: Those Who Walked With Wright.* Branson, Mo.: By the author, 1985.

Majors, Alexander. *Seventy Years on the Frontier.* Chicago: Rand McNally and Company, 1893.

Martin, Ronald L. *Official Guide to Marvel Cave.* Springfield, Mo.: Ozark Mountain Publishers, 1974.

Material Culture of the Wooden Age. Ed. Brooke Hindle. Tarrytown, N.Y.: Sleepy Hollow Press, 1981.

Marx, Leo. *The Machine in the Garden.* New York: Oxford University Press, 1964.

Mayer, John J., and I. Lehr Brisbin Jr. *Wild Pigs in the United States.* Athens: University of Georgia Press, 1991.

Melton, Emory. *The First 150 Years in Cassville, Missouri, 1845–1995.* Cassville: Litho Printers, 1995.

Miner, H. Craig. *The St. Louis-San Francisco Transcontinental Railroad.* Lawrence: University Press of Kansas, 1972.

Moore, Charles A. *Moore Family History.* Blue Eye, Mo.: By the author, 1979.

Mott, Frank Luther. *A History of American Magazines.* 5 vols. Cambridge, Mass.: Belknap Press, 1930–68.

Nash, Roderick. *Wilderness and the American Mind.* New Haven: Yale University Press, 1967.

Nash, Roderick. *The Nervous Generation: American Thought, 1917–1930.* Chicago: Rand McNally and Company, 1970.

O'Neill, Rose. *The Story of Rose O'Neill: An Autobiography.* Ed. Miriam Formanek-Brunell. Columbia: University of Missouri Press, 1997.

Noel Centennial, 1887–1987. Shawnee Mission, Kans.: Kes-Print, 1987.

Owen, Luella Agnes. *Cave Regions of the Ozarks and Black Hills.* 1898. Reprint, New York: Johnson Reprint Corporation, 1970.

Oxford English Dictionary.

Parker, Nathan. *Missouri as It Is in 1867: An Illustrated Historical Gazetteer of Missouri.* Philadelphia: J. B. Lippincott and Company, 1867.

Phillips, Claude A. *A History of Education in Missouri.* Jefferson City, Mo.: Hugh Stephens Printing Company, 1911.

Porter, Gene Stratton. *A Girl of the Limberlost.* 1909. Reprint, New York: Dell Publishing Company, 1990.

Preston, John. *Saucer Ears in the Ozarks.* Caldwell, Idaho: Caxton Printers, 1943.

Rafferty, Milton D. *The Ozarks: Land and Life.* Norman: University of Oklahoma Press, 1980.

Randolph, Vance. *The Ozarks: An American Survival of Primitive Society.* New York: Vanguard Press, 1931.

Randolph, Vance. *Ozark Mountain Folks.* New York: Vanguard Press, 1932.

Randolph, Vance. *Ozark Superstitions.* New York: Columbia University Press, 1947.

Randolph, Vance. *Vance Randolph in the Ozarks.* Branson, Mo.: Ozarks Mountaineer, 1981.

Rayburn, Otto Ernest. *Ozark Country.* American Folkways Series. New York: Duell, Sloan, and Pearce, 1941.

Rayburn, Otto Ernest. *Forty Years in the Ozarks.* Eureka Springs, Ark.: Ozark Guide Press, 1957.

Reminiscent History of the Ozark Region. 1894. Reprint, Easley, S.C.: Southern Historical Press, 1978.

Ripley, Ozark. *Jist Huntin', Tales of the Forest, Field and Stream.* Cincinnati, Ohio: Stewart Kidd Company, 1921.

Sare, Ted. *Some Recollections of an Ozarks Float Trip Guide.* Marshfield, Mo.: Webster County Printing, n.d. [1997].

Sauer, Carl. *Agricultural Origins and Dispersals.* New York: American Geographical Society, 1952.

Sauer, Carl. *The Geography of the Ozark Highland of Missouri.* 1920. Reprint, New York: Greenwood Press, 1968.

Schmitt, Peter J. *Back to Nature: The Arcadian Myth in Urban America.* New York: Oxford University Press, 1969.

Schoolcraft, Henry Rowe. *Rude Pursuits and Rugged Peaks: Schoolcraft's Ozark Journal, 1818–1819.* Ed. Milton D. Rafferty. Fayetteville: University of Arkansas Press, 1996.

Schultz, Gerard. *Early History of the Northern Ozarks.* Jefferson City, Mo.: Midland Printing Company, 1937.

Scott, Quinta, and Susan Croce Kelly. *Route 66: The Highway and Its People.* Norman: University of Oklahoma Press, 1988.

Shamel, H. Harold. *Seeds of Time: A Story of the Ozarks.* n.p, n.d. [c. 1950].

Shapiro, Henry D. *Appalachia on Our Mind: The Southern Mountains in the American Consciousness, 1870–1920.* Chapel Hill: University of North Carolina Press, 1978.

Shortridge, James R. *The Middle West: Its Meaning in American Culture.* Lawrence: University Press of Kansas, 1989.

Sitton, Thad. *Backwoodsman: Stockmen and Hunters along a Big Thicket River Valley.* Norman: University of Oklahoma Press, 1995.

Smith, Henry Nash. *Virgin Land: The American West as Symbol and Myth.* Cambridge: Harvard University Press, 1950.

Spurlock, Pearl. *Over the Old Ozark Trails in the Shepherd of the Hills Country.* 1936. Reprint, Branson, Mo.: *White River Leader,* 1942.

Stevens, Walter. *Missouri, The Center State, 1821–1915.* Two volumes. Chicago: S. J. Clarke Publishing Company, 1915.

Stilgoe, John. *Metropolitan Corridor: Railroads and the American Scene.* New Haven: Yale University Press, 1983.

Tagg, Lawrence V. *Harold Bell Wright: Storyteller to America.* Tucson, Ariz.: Westernlore Press, 1986.

Turnbo, Silas. *The White River Chronicles of S. C. Turnbo.* Ed. James F. Keefe and Lynn Morrow. Fayetteville: University of Arkansas Press, 1994.

Ulster and North America, Transatlantic Perspectives on the Scotch-Irish. Ed. H. Tyler Blethen and Curtis W. Wood Jr. Tuscaloosa: University of Alabama Press, 1997.

VanGilder, Marvin. *Jasper County, the First 200 Years.* Carthage, Mo.: Jasper County Commission, 1995.

Vogt, William. *Road to Survival.* New York: William Sloan Associates, 1948.

Walker, Laurence C. *The Southern Forest.* Austin: University of Texas Press, 1991.

Weaver, H. Dwight. *The Wilderness Underground: Caves of the Ozark Plateau.* Columbia: University of Missouri Press, 1992.

Wetmore, Alphonso. *Gazetteer of the State of Missouri.* St. Louis, Mo.: C. Keemle, 1837.

Whisnant, David E. *All That Is Native and Fine: The Politics of Culture in an American Region.* Chapel Hill: University of North Carolina Press, 1983.

Williams, Michael. *Americans and Their Forests: A Historical Geography.* New York: Cambridge University Press, 1989.

Williamson, J. W. *Hillbillyland.* Chapel Hill: University of North Carolina Press, 1995.

Wright, Harold Bell. *The Shepherd of the Hills.* 1907. Reprint, New York: Grosset and Dunlap, 1976. Reprint, McCormick-Armstrong Company, 1987.

Wright, Harold Bell. *To My Sons.* New York: Harper and Brothers, 1934.
Year Book, Public Museum of the City of Milwaukee, 1928. Milwaukee: Board of Trustees, 1929.
Zusne, Leonard. *Biographical Dictionary of Psychology.* Westport, Conn: Greenwood Press, 1984.

Articles

"A Pioneer of the Ozark Awakening." *Arcadian Magazine* 1 (July 1931): 9.
Albert, Allen. "The Tents of the Conservative." *Scribners* 72 (July 1922): 54–59.
"Back to Nature." *Outlook* 6 (June 1903): 305–7.
Benton, Thomas Hart. "The Ozarks." *Travel and Leisure* 3 (June–July 1973): 31–33.
Bolster, Mel H. "The Mountain Mind." *Arkansas Historical Quarterly* 10 (winter 1951): 307–27.
Burton, Stephen. "The Origin and Growth of Rockaway Beach, Missouri." *White River Valley Historical Society Quarterly* 1 (spring 1963): 16–21.
Calvert, John H. "Fencing Laws in Missouri—Restraining Animals." *Missouri Law Review* 32 (fall 1967): 519–42.
Dalke, Paul, and David Spencer. "Development and Land Use on a Private Game Preserve in Southern Taney County, Missouri." *Journal of Wildlife Management* 8 (January 1944): 1–6.
Davis, Clyde. "The Early Years of My Life." *White River Valley Historical Quarterly* 8 (winter 1985): 18–20.
"Dr. Sayman Gives Park." *Game and Fish News* 5 (February 1929): 43.
"Donation of Fifteen Deer Made by Taney County Game Preserve." *Game and Fish News* 1 (November 1925): 3.
Draper, William R. "The Ozarks Go Native." *Outlook and Independent* 156 (September 10, 1930): 60–62, 77–78.
DuPuy, William Atherton. "Remaking the Poor Whites." In *Uncle Sam's Modern Miracles* (New York: Frederick A. Stockes Company, 1914): 118–27.
"Early Gearhart Letters." *White River Valley Historical Quarterly* 7 (summer 1981): 4–6.
Edgar, Neal, and Lynn Morrow. "A Genteel Vacation." *Ozarks Mountaineer* 30 (October 1982): 8–9.
Emery, J. B. "Descriptions of Marble Cave, Missouri." *Kansas City Review of Science and Industry* 8 (1885): 614–22.
"Filling the Tourist with Bunk Stories." *Missouri Magazine* (May 1929): 27.
Godsey, Townsend. "Branson Honors John Neihardt." *Ozarks Mountaineer* 37 (March–April 1989): 32–33.
Green, Archie. "Hillbilly Music: Source and Symbol." *Journal of American Folklore* 78 (July–September 1965): 204–28.
Guyette, Richard, and E. A. McGinnes Jr. "Fire History of an Ozark Glade." *Transactions of the Missouri Academy of Sciences* 16 (1982): 85–93.
"Harold Bell Wright Who Holds a World's Record." *American Magazine* (February 1918): 8.

Henderson, Charles Richmond. "Are Modern Industry and City Life Unfavorable to the Family?" *American Journal of Sociology* 14 (March 1909): 668–80.

Hendrix, Brenda. "Tomatoes on the Hillsides." *Ozarks Mountaineer* 33 (September–October 1985): 43, 48–49.

Hively, Kay. "The Naming of a Forest." *Ozarks Mountaineer* 33 (January–February 1985): 48–51.

Hively, Kay. "When the Chautauqua Came to Town." *Ozarks Mountaineer* 35 (March–April 1987): 40–41.

Holbrook, Eleanor. "Diary of Horton Camp." *Boone County Historian* 20 (April–June 1997): 28–35.

Hoten, Margaret Gerten. "Life in the Ozarks—Then and Now." *White River Valley Historical Quarterly* 2 (fall 1966; spring, summer, fall 1967): 13–19, 18–23, 11–19, 10–13, 23 respectively.

Hovey, E. O. "The Marble Cave of Missouri." *Scientific American* 68 (February 1893): 65, 70–71.

Jarman, Rufus. "Idyll in the Ozarks." *Saturday Evening Post* 25 (June 1925): 36–37, 88–89, 92, 94.

Johnson, Noma. "History of James Oliver." *White River Valley Historical Quarterly* 9 (spring 1988): 16–19.

"Journal of Charles Heinrich, 1849–1856." Ed. John Quincy Wolf. *The Independence County Chronicle* 18 (April 1977): 2–40.

Kennan, Clara B. "The Ozark Trails and Arkansas's Pathfinder, Coin Harvey." *Arkansas Historical Quarterly* 7 (winter 1948): 299–316.

Kowinski, William S. "There's Still Time to Hop a Trolley—Vintage or Modern." *Smithsonian* (February 1988): 128–38.

Lacy, Gibbons. "Characters of 'Shepherd of the Hills' Not Drawn from Life." *Ozarks Mountaineer* 4 (February 1956): 9.

Ladd, Douglas. "Reexamination of the Role of Fire in Missouri Oak Woodlands." *Proceedings of the Oak Woods Management Workshop.* Ed. George V. Burger et al. (Charleston: Eastern Illinois University, 1991): 67–80.

Lankford, George. "'Beyond the Pale': Frontier Folk in the Southern Ozarks." In *The Folk: Identity, Landscapes and Lores* (Lawrence: University Press of Kansas, 1989): 53–70.

Litton, J. P. "The St. Louis Park and Agricultural Company." *Forest and Stream* 47 (1896): 24.

Lynch, Genevieve. "The Call." *Arcadian Magazine* 1 (July 1931): 25.

McCall, Edith. "When the Tales Grew Tall in the Ozarks." *Ozarks Mountaineer* 35 (May–June 1987): 58–59.

McGrath, Martha. "Tomato Canning in the Ozarks." *Webster County Historical Society Journal* 4 (December 1976): 7–11.

Mahnkey, Douglas. "Freighters and the Free Jack Spring." *Ozarks Mountaineer* 37 (March–April 1989): 38–39.

Mahnkey, Douglas. "The Game Park at Mincy." *Ozarks Mountaineer* 31 (June 1983): 44–47.

"Marvel Cave." *Rayburn's Ozark Guide* 6 (summer 1948): 25.

"Minutes of the Mincy Valley Baptist Church of Christ, 1871 to 1885." *White River Valley Historical Quarterly* 2 (summer and fall 1965, winter, spring, and summer 1966): 14–16, 24,28, 21–28, 25–28, and 24–27, respectively.

Morrow, Lynn. "The Arlington Hearth: St. Louisans, Perry Andres, and Commercial Tourism." *Newsletter of the Phelps County Historical Society* 18 (October 1998): 3–18.

Morrow, Lynn. "Estate Builders in the Missouri Ozarks: Establishing a St. Louis Tradition." *Gateway Heritage* 2 (winter 1981–82): 42–48.

Morrow, Lynn. "Keith McCanse: Missouri's First Professional Conservationist." *White River Valley Historical Quarterly* 31 (winter 1992): 3–12.

Morrow, Lynn. "Ozark/Ozarks: Establishing a Regional Term." *White River Valley Historical Quarterly* 36 (fall 1996): 4–11.

Morrow, Lynn. "The St. Louis Game Park: Experiments in Conservation and Recreation." *White River Valley Historical Quarterly* 36 (spring 1997): 7–19, and *Gateway Heritage* 18 (spring 1998): 16–25.

Morrow, Lynn. "Trader William Gilliss and Delaware Migration in Southern Missouri." *Missouri Historical Review* 75 (January 1981): 147–67.

Morrow, Lynn. "What's in a Name, like *Johnboat?*" *White River Valley Historical Quarterly* 37 (winter 1998): 9–24.

Morrow, Lynn. "Where Did All the Money Go? War and the Economics of Vigilantism in Southern Missouri." *White River Valley Historical Quarterly* 34 (fall 1994): 3–16.

Morrow, Lynn. "The Yocum Silver Dollar." *Missouri Folklore Society Journal* 5 (1983): 26–40.

Morrow, Lynn, and David Quick. "Transportation and Tourism in the Shepherd of the Hills Country: The Case of the Y-Bridge." *White River Valley Historical Quarterly* 10 (fall 1989 and winter 1990): 4–10, respectively.

Munday, Frances Jones. "Scenes from an Unforgettable Trip: Branson, 1924." *Ozarks Mountaineer* 43 (April–May 1995): 40–41.

"Names and Faces from the Past." *White River Valley Historical Quarterly* 1 (summer 1962): 18–20.

"One Pants Johnnie." *White River Valley Historical Quarterly* 4 (winter 1971): 5–6.

Otto, John Solomon. "The Migration of the Southern Plain Folk: An Interdisciplinary Synthesis." *Journal of Southern History* 51 (1985): 183–200.

"The Ozarks in 1900." Missouri Historical Society *Bulletin* 8 (April 1952): 270–78.

"Paramount News Films James and White River Float." *Missouri Game and Fish News* 3 (November 1927): 1.

Presbyterian Hill Messenger. June 1935.

Presbyterian Messenger. December 1940.

Rafferty, Milton D. "Agricultural Change in the Western Ozarks." *Missouri Historical Review* 69 (April 1975): 299–322.

Randolph, Vance. "Lure of the Ozarks." *Arcadian Life* (May 1936): 13–14.

Renner, G. K. "Strawberry Culture in Southwest Missouri." *Missouri Historical Review* 64 (October 1969): 18–40.

Ross, J. K. "Old Matt's View of It." 1915. Reprint, *White River Valley Historical Quarterly* 5 (spring 1975): 9–18.

"Rules of Conduct." *White River Valley Historical Quarterly* 7 (winter 1981): 6.

Rullketter, John. "A Quick Sketch of Garber as It Was in My Time." *White River Valley Historical Quarterly* 4 (winter 1971): 1–4.

Sauer, Carl. "The Economic Problem of the Ozark Highland." *Scientific Monthly* (September 1920): 215–27.

Scott, Miles H. "The Marvelous Cave." *White River Valley Historical Quarterly* 8 (winter 1985): 4–5.

Shumate, Fern Nance. "Broken Dreams and Scattered Schemes." *Ozarks Mountaineer* 40 (September/October 1992): 28–29.

Spears, John R. "The Ozark Mountains." *Forest and Stream* 32 (July 4, 1889).

Steele, Ruby. "The Bolin Wilson Family." *White River Valley Historical Quarterly* 2 (fall 1967): 1–4.

Stevens, Walter. "The Ozark Uplift." 1899. Reprint, *White River Valley Historical Quarterly* 2 (winter 1964–65): 9–15, 23.

Strauss, David. "Toward a Consumer Culture: 'Adirondack Murray' and the Wilderness Vacation." *American Quarterly* 39 (summer 1987): 270–86.

Stults, Ben T. "A Sketch of the Many Ups and Downs in the Life of Ben T. Stults, as a Boy to a Man as a Hunter." Ed. Lynn Morrow and Linda Myers-Phinney. *White River Valley Historical Quarterly* 10 & 31 (Parts I–VI, fall 1990–winter 1992).

Sylvester, W. D. "W. D. Sylvester: Journeyman Pioneer." Ed. Lynn Morrow and Linda Myers-Phinney. *White River Valley Historical Quarterly* 31 & 32 (spring 1992; fall 1992–summer 1993).

"That Ozark Shack." *Missouri Game and Fish News* 2 (November 1926): inside cover.

Tidgwell, Flo Montgomery. "A Marvel of a Cave." *Ozarks Mountaineer* 35 (March–April 1987): 26–27.

Turner, Frederick Jackson. "The Significance of the Frontier in American History." In *Rereading Frederick Jackson Turner* with commentary by John Mack Faragher (New York: Henry Holt and Company, 1994): 31–60.

"United Brethren in Christ Church Book." Comp. Avis Hawkins. *White River Valley Historical Quarterly* 4 (fall 1972): 14–18.

Van Buskirk, Kathleen. "Branson and the Town Company." *Ozarks Mountaineer* 36 (February 1988): 40–45.

Van Buskirk, Kathleen. "The Lodge That Traveled from Maine." *Ozarks Mountaineer* 26 (March 1978): 20–21.

Van Buskirk, Kathleen. "Rockaway Is Reclaiming Its Beach." *Ozarks Mountaineer* 43 (October–November 1995): 42–45.

Van Buskirk, Kathleen. "When School Bells Rang in Ridgedale." *Ozarks Mountaineer* 29 (July–August 1981): 40–43, 54.

Van Buskirk, Kathleen. "When the Tomatoe Was Queen." *Ozarks Mountaineer* 26 (April 1978): 16–17, 24.

Warren, W. W. "'Rattler' Guilliams' Own Story." *Ozarkian* 1 (April 1926): 3–4, 28–29.

Weisberger, Bernard. "The Forgotten Four Hundred: Chicago's First Millionaires." *American Heritage* 38 (November 1987): 34–45.

Welch, Thomas Randolph. "Autobiography of Thomas Randolph Welch." *White River Valley Historical Quarterly* 6 (winter 1977): 9–13.

Wilson, Alexander. "The View from the Road: Recreation and Tourism." In *Discovered Country: Tourism and Survival in the American West.* Ed. Scott Norris. Albuquerque, N.Mex.: Stone Ladder Press, 1994.

Wilson, Charles Morrow. "Backhill Culture." *Nation* (July 17, 1929).

Wilson, Susan. "S. Fred Prince." *Missouri Conservationist* (December 1998): 9–13.

Woodbury, Charles. "The White River, 1907." *White River Valley Historical Society Quarterly* 6 (summer 1979): 6–8.

Woodring, Michael. "Drury-Mincy Wildlife Area." *Missouri Conservationist* (January 1992): 9–11.

Newspapers and Broadcasts

Branson, Missouri, *Echo,* November 17, 1905–October 29, 1909.

Branson, Missouri, *Southwest Missourian,* August 11, 1988.

Branson, Missouri, *Taney County Republican,* June 27, 1985, and August 27, 1987.

Branson, Missouri, *White River Leader,* May 9, 1913–May 3, 1916; January 9, 1919– June 12, 1919; January 9, 1925–December 23, 1926; October 19, 1927; April 25, May 9 and 16, 1928; January 5, February 16, March 16 and 23, and September 7, 1933.

Columbia, Missouri, *University Missourian.* June 22 and 28, 1910.

Eminence, Missouri, *Current Wave,* October 6, 1921.

Forsyth, Missouri, *Taney County Republican,* November 7–December 26, 1895; April 16 and 23, and October 1–November 25, 1896; November 4–December 30, 1897; September 6, 1900; May 9–July 4, 1901; September 29–December 31, 1904; October 1–December 30, 1909; October 6–December 31, 1910; April 6– October 26, 1911; and June 27, 1985.

Forsyth, Missouri, *Taney County Times,* March 21, 1889, October 9, 1996, and March 5, 1997.

Galena, Missouri, *Recorder-Advertiser,* April 30–November 3, 1908.

Galena, Missouri, *Stone County News,* April 9–October 8, 1903.

Galena, Missouri, *Stone County News Oracle,* January 7, 1904–December 31, 1907; January 7, 1920–December 28, 1921; and November 19, 1924–December 29, 1926.

Jefferson City, Missouri, *Daily Tribune,* June 14, 1892.

Kansas City, Missouri, *Journal,* December 20, 1926.

Kansas City, Missouri, *Journal-Post,* February 6, 1927.

Kansas City, Missouri, *Kansas City Star,* June 13, 1926, January 12, 1941, September 2, 1945, February 28, 1960, April 9, 1967.

KYTV. Springfield, Missouri. "Action News at 10:00." October 6, 1988.

Lamar, Missouri, *Democrat,* September 1, 1882–December 31, 1887.

St. Louis, Missouri, *Citizen's Road Bulletin,* June 1928.

St. Louis, Missouri, *Globe-Democrat,* January 6, and August 18, 1895; September 26, and October 3, 1897; November 28 and 29, 1910; and October 25, 1925.

St. Louis, Missouri, *Republic,* November 19 and 21, 1899.

Springfield, Missouri, *Daily News,* September 14, 1927.

Springfield, Missouri, *Leader,* March 3, 1920, September 25, 1927.

Springfield, Missouri, *News-Leader,* September 25, 1927, September 17, 1950, February 19, 1956, May 8, 1988, and September 25, 1990.

Springfield, Missouri, *Patriot-Advertiser,* August 5, 1880, February 3 and December 1, 1881, and July 12, 1883.

Springfield, Missouri, *Press,* July 20, 1929, October 4 and November 6, 1930.

Springfield, Missouri, *Republican,* February 3, 1911.

Pamphlets, Booklets, Brochures, and Maps

Agricultural Development: Missouri Pacific Railroad. Agricultural Development Department of the Missouri Pacific Railroad, 1948.

Agricultural Resources in the White River Country of the Ozarks. Missouri Pacific Railroad, c. 1926.

Blankinship, J. W. *Southwest Taney County, Missouri: With Supplements, In the White River Country.* September 1, 1910.

Blansit, C. C. *Taney County, Missouri: The Homeseeker's Paradise.* c. 1907.

Braswell, James. *In the Land of a Million Smiles.* Aldrich, Mo.: Stephen A. Douglas Music Normal Association, 1925.

Come to the Ozarks: The Land of a Million Smiles. Joplin, Mo.: Ozark Playgrounds Association, 1924.

D. X. *Warrensburg Nimrods.* 1891.

Farmer, Charlie. *Devil's Pool, A History of Big Cedar Lodge.* Springfield, Mo.: JLM Publishing Company, 1995.

Fairy Cave. c. 1930.

Feathers and Fins on the Frisco. St. Louis, 1898.

Fishin' Fine in the White River Country of the Ozarks. Missouri Pacific Lines, c. 1929.

Hoenshel, E. J., and L. S. Hoenshel. *Stories of the Pioneers.* 1915. Reprint, Forsyth, Mo.: Little Photo Gallery, 1985.

James and White River Float Trips. Missouri Pacific Iron Mountain Railroad, c. 1925.

Lake Taneycomo and the Shepherd of the Hills Country: In the Wonderland of the Ozarks. Branson, Mo.: Lake Taneycomo Chamber of Commerce, 1926.

Master Map of the Ozarks. Joplin, Mo.: Ozark Playgrounds Association, 1925.

McQuary, A. L. *The Stone County Booklet.* Fair Commission of Stone County, 1927.

1926 Ozark Playgrounds Map. Joplin, Mo.: Ozark Playgrounds Association, 1926.

The Ozarks: The Land of a Million Smiles. Joplin: Ozark Playgrounds Association, 1926.

Randolph, Vance. *A Reporter in the Ozarks.* Girard, Kans.: Haldeman-Julius, 1944.

Randolph, Vance. *Tall Tales from the Ozarks.* Girard, Kans.: Haldeman-Julius, 1944.

Roads, Rivers, Recreation Around Springfield, Missouri. Springfield: Chamber of Commerce, 1929.

Rucker, B. H. *Missouri, Phelps County.* St. Louis, Mo.: Lumberman's Printing, c. 1919.

"Sammy Lane Boat Line Brochure." Reprinted in *White River Valley Historical Society Quarterly* 6 (winter 1978): 13–15.

Statistics and Information Concerning the State of Missouri. St. Louis: Missouri Pacific Railway, 1900.

The White River Country in the Ozarks. Missouri Pacific Railroad, c. 1923.

Collections, Papers, and Reports

Bryan, William J., Papers. Missouri Historical Society, St. Louis.

Flanders, Robert. *Overview of Cultural Resources in the Mark Twain National Forest.* Springfield: Center for Archaeological Research, Southwest Missouri State University, 1979.

Gilmore, Robert K. "The Dogwood Canyon Area of Southern Stone County, Missouri." Springfield, Mo.: Bass Pro Shops, June 1992.

Godsey, Townsend, Papers. Lyon Memorial Library, College of the Ozarks, Point Lookout, Missouri.

Hadley, Herbert, Papers. Western Historical Manuscripts Collection, University of Missouri-Columbia.

Hyde, Arthur, Papers. Western Historical Manuscripts Collection, University of Missouri-Columbia.

Laurier, Wilfrid, Papers. National Library of Canada, Ottawa.

McCanse, Keith, Papers. In author's possession, Jefferson City, Missouri.

Missouri Game and Fish Commission Correspondence, 1924–29. Missouri State Parks Archives. Department of Natural Resources, Jefferson City, Missouri.

Missouri History Scrapbook. Western Historical Manuscripts Collection-Columbia.

Mitchell, E. Y., Papers. Western Historical Manuscripts Collection, University of Missouri-Columbia.

Neihardt, John, Papers. Western Historical Manuscripts Collection, University of Missouri-Columbia.

Prince, S. Fred. "The Cave Book, A true account of the Explorations, Surveys, and Studies of Marvel Cave, Missouri, With a brief account of the Ozarkian Uplift." By the author, 1935.

Prince, S. Fred. "The Land You Live In, As the Mountains are Round About Southern Missouri, 1893." By the author, 1933.

Seever, William J., Papers. Western Historical Manuscript Collection, University of Missouri-Columbia.

Sharp, William E., Papers. In possession of the authors.

Short, Dewey, Papers. Western Historical Manuscript Collection, University of Missouri-Columbia.

Upton, Lucile Morris, Papers. Western Historical Manuscript Collection, University of Missouri-Columbia.

Wiley, Robert, Papers. Western Historical Manuscript Collection, University of Missouri-Rolla and Crane, Missouri.

Winchester, M. P., Estate Founding Collection. Powers Museum, Carthage, Missouri.

Works Progress Administration. Taney County. Western Historical Manuscripts Collection, University of Missouri-Columbia.

Government Records

Coker, Robert. E. *Fresh-Water Mussels and Mussel Industries of the United States.* Washington, D.C.: Government Printing Office, 1919.

Corporation Files. Missouri State Archives. Jefferson City, Missouri.

Dixon, H. M., and J. M. Purdom. "Farm Management in the Ozark Region of Missouri." *Bulletin No. 941.* Washington, D.C.: U.S. Department of Agriculture, 1921.

Harris, Elmo G. "Road Problems in the Ozarks." *Bulletin of the School of Mines and Metallurgy.* Rolla: University of Missouri, 1919.

Hawker, Jon L. *Missouri Landscapes: A Tour through Time.* Rolla: Missouri Department of Natural Resources, 1992.

House and Senate Journals: Appendix. 39th General Assembly. Jefferson City, Mo.: Tribune Printing Company, 1897.

House and Senate Journals: Appendix. 48th General Assembly. Jefferson City, Mo.: Tribune Printing Company, 1915.

H.R. Bill 10550, 60th Congress.

Lantz, David. *Raising Deer and Other Large Game Animals in the United States.* USDA Biological Survey, *Bulletin No. 36.* Washington, D.C.: Government Printing Office, 1910.

"Lumber Cut of the United States, 1870–1920." Ed. W. B. Greeley and Earle H. Clapp. *Bulletin No. 1119.* Washington, D.C.: U.S. Department of Agriculture, April 23, 1923.

Missouri. *Eighteenth Annual Report of the Missouri Bureau of Labor Statistics.* Jefferson City, Mo.: Tribune Printing Company, 1896.

Missouri. *Fifteenth Annual Report of the State Board of Agriculture of the State of Missouri.* Jefferson City, Mo.: Tribune Printing Company, 1881.

Missouri. *First Annual Report of the State Game and Fish Commissioner.* Jefferson City, Mo.: Hugh Stephens Printing Company, 1910.

Missouri. *Fortieth Annual Report of the Missouri State Board of Agriculture.* Jefferson City, Mo.: Hugh Stephens Printing Company, 1908.

Missouri. *Forty-first Report of the Public Schools of the State of Missouri.* Jefferson City, Mo.: Tribune Printing Company, 1891.

Missouri. *Forty-fourth Annual Report, Bureau of Labor Statistics, State of Missouri.* Jefferson City, Mo.: Missouri Bureau of Labor Statistics, 1924.

Missouri. *The Missouri Yearbook of Agriculture: Forty-seventh Annual Report.* Columbia, Mo.: 112–124 Agriculture Building, 1915.

Missouri. *The Missouri Year Book of Agriculture, 1921.* Jefferson City, Mo.: State Board of Agriculture, 1921.

Missouri. *Nineteenth Annual Report of the Bureau of Labor Statistics.* Jefferson City, Mo.: Tribune Printing Company, 1897.

Missouri. *Official Manual.* Jefferson City, Mo.: Hugh Stephens Printing Company, 1914, 1922, and 1926.

Missouri. *Report of the Fish Commissioners of the State of Missouri.* Jefferson City, Mo.: Tribune Printing Company, 1881.

Missouri. *Report of the Board of Fish Commissioners of the State of Missouri for 1905–1906.* St. Joseph, Mo.: Lon Hardman Printer, 1906.

Missouri. *Report of the Board of Fish Commissioners Covering Biennial Period of 1911–1912.* Jefferson City: Missouri Fish Commission, December 31, 1912.

Missouri. *The Revised Statutes of the State of Missouri 1909.* vol. 2. Jefferson City, Mo.: Hugh Stephens Printing Company, 1910.

Missouri. *Seventeenth Annual Report of the State Board of Agriculture of the State of Missouri.* Jefferson City, Mo.: Tribune Printing Company, 1884.

Missouri. *Surplus Products of Missouri Counties for the Year Ending December 31, 1907.* Supplement to the annual report. Jefferson City, Mo.: State Labor Bureau, 1908.

Missouri. *Surplus Products of Missouri Counties for the Year Ending Jan. 1, 1910.* Jefferson City, Mo.: Hugh Stephens Printing Company, 1910.

Missouri. *Thirty-fifth Annual Report, Bureau of Labor Statistics, State of Missouri.* Jefferson City, Mo.: Hugh Stephens Printing Company, 1914.

Missouri. *Thirty-first Annual Report of the Bureau of Labor Statistics of the State of Missouri.* Jefferson City, Mo.: Hugh Stephens Printing Company, 1909.

Missouri. *Thirty-second Annual Report of Labor Statistics, the State of Missouri.* Jefferson City, Mo.: Hugh Stephens Printing Company, 1910.

Missouri. *Twenty-first Annual Report of the Bureau of Labor Statistics and Inspection For the Year Ending November 5, 1899.* Jefferson City, Mo.: Tribune Printing Company, 1899.

Missouri. *Twenty-sixth Annual Report of the Missouri State Board of Agriculture.* Jefferson City, Mo.: Tribune Printing Company, 1894.

Missouri. *Twenty-ninth Annual Report of the Bureau of Labor Statistics, the State of Missouri.* Jefferson City, Mo.: Hugh Stephens Printing Company, 1907.

Morrow, Lynn, and David Quick. *Y-Bridge.* National Register of Historic Places Nomination, Missouri Department of Natural Resources, 1989.

Quick, David. *Old Matt's Cabin.* National Register of Historic Places Nomination, Missouri Department of Natural Resources, 1982.

Palmer, T. S. "Private Game Preserves and Their Future in the United States." *Bureau of Biological Survey.* Circular No. 72. Washington, D.C.: U.S. Department of Agriculture, 1910.

Recorder of Deeds. Forsyth, Taney County, Missouri.

Recorder of Deeds. Galena, Stone County, Missouri.

School District Records, Taney County, 1886–1918. Missouri State Archives.

Smith, Steven D. *Made It in the Timber: A Historic Overview of the Fort Leonard Wood Region, 1800–1940.* Normal: Midwest Archaelogical Research Center, Illinois State University, for the U.S. Army Corps of Engineers, 1993.

Stevens, Donald L., Jr. *A Homeland and a Hinterland.* Omaha, Nebr.: National Park Service, 1991.

U.S. Bureau of the Census. *Fifteenth Census of the United States: 1930, Missouri.* Washington, D.C.: Government Printing Office, 1930.

U.S. Congress. Senate. *National Conference on Outdoor Recreation.* S. Doc. 151, 68th Cong., 1st sess., 1924.

U.S. Congress. Senate. *Report of the Country Life Commission.* S. Doc. 705, 60th Cong., 2nd sess., 1909.

White River Club incorporation. Greene County Archives, Office of County Clerk, Springfield, Missouri.

Theses and Dissertations

McKinney, Edgar. "Images, Realities, and Cultural Transformation in the Missouri Ozarks, 1920–1960." Ph.D. diss., University of Missouri, 1990.

Myers-Phinney, Linda. "The Land of a Million Smiles: Tourism and Modernization in Taney and Stone County, Missouri, 1900–1930." Master's thesis, Southwest Missouri State University, 1989.

Sellars, Richard. "Early Promotion and Development of Missouri's Natural Resources." Ph.D. diss., University of Missouri, 1972.

Svanoe, Harold C. "The Preaching and Speaking of Burris Jenkins," Ph.D. diss., Northwestern University, August 1953.

Interviews

Bass, Velma. Interview with Linda Myers-Phinney, November 18, 1987.

Cochran, Robert. Interview with Lynn Morrow, March 9, 1998.

Emerson, R. C. Interview with Linda Myers-Phinney, December 13, 1987, and November 2, 1988.

Ford, Dwight. Interview with Lynn Morrow and Linda Myers-Phinney, December 8, 1988.

Hembree, Alden. Interview with Linda Myers-Phinney, November 10, 1987.

Hoblit, Marian. Interview with Lynn Morrow and Robert Flanders, February 12, 1988.

McCurdy, Bill. Interview with Linda Myers-Phinney, November 14, 1995.

Mahnkey, Douglas. Interview with Lynn Morrow and Linda Myers-Phinney, January 19, 1988.

Maxwell, Clint. Interview with Lynn Morrow and Linda Myers-Phinney, February 4, 1989.

Prince, Charles Stanley. Interview with Linda Myers-Phinney, March 25, 1988.

Other Materials

Allured, Janet. "Letter to the Editor." *White River Valley Historical Quarterly* (fall 1987): 4–5.

Burton, W. J. "History of the Missouri Pacific Railroad." St. Louis, Mo.: typescript, July 1, 1956.

Catalog, Thos. M. Brown Canning Factories. Springfield, Mo., 1918.

Flanders, Robert. "The Park at Devil's Pool, the History of a Private Resort." Typescript, April 26, 1988.

Jones, Floyd, Memoirs. Typescript, in possession of the authors.

Lizzie T. A. Letter to Marie Oliver Watkins, July 30, 1929. Western Historical Manuscripts Collection-Columbia.

Lynch, William H. "Ten Copyright Songs." Notch, Mo.: Marvel Cave Publishing House, n.d. In Robert Wiley Papers, Western Historical Manuscript Collection-Rolla.

Myers-Phinney, Linda. "A Compilation of Land Acquisitions from the Taney County Deed Records, Forsyth, Mo." summer 1997.

Myers-Phinney, Linda. "Marvel Cave Property, Chain of Title." fall 1997.

Necrology Files. Missouri Historical Society, St. Louis, Missouri.

Prather, Robert. "The Big Road." Typescript, in possession of the authors.

Randolph, Vance. Letter to Mary Louise Clifton, February 23, 1940, in Special Collections, Southwest Missouri State University, Springfield.

Index

gigging, 122, 124, 136; objections to, 123, 141, 145

ginseng, 100

Goetz, Jacob, *14*

goldenseal, 100

Goltra, Edward, 72

good-roads movement, 16

Goodspeed, 47

government land: offices, 78, at Springfield, 81, 83, 229; price of homestead, 78; for sale, 62, 224; squatters, 77, 83. *See also* homesteads

grain: for market, 2

Granby Mining and Smelting Company, 61

Grandview Hotel, 160

Greasy Creek, 108

Greeley, Horace, 218

Green, Archie, 250

Greene County, Mo., 1, 8, 42, 45, 72, 120, 122

Grether, E. T., 185

Grey, Zane, 31

Guilliams, Walt (Rattler), 144, 145

Gulf of Doom, 47

Ha Ha Tonka, 228

Haberman, Marie and Bertha, 57

Hadley, Herbert, 64, 69, 70, *71*, 126, 140, 160, 235; float trips, 147; log cabin, 227; state game farm, 70

Hale, B. W., 201

Hall, Ethel, *45*

Hall, George, 200

Hall, Granville Stanley, 24, 162

Hallock, Charles, 116

Hammond, F. S., 237

handle factory, 3

Hawes, Harry B., 228

Hawthorne, Nathaniel, 26

Heart of the Ozark Mountains, 8, 112

Heath, W. P. (Willard), 227, 248

Helman, Will, 137

Hemingway, Earnest, 31

Henderson, Charles Richmond, 22

Hercules, Mo., *87*

highways: No. 3 (65, 160), 183, 196, *205*, 206; No. 44 (176), 183; No. 43 (13), 183, 184, 186; No. 16 (60), 183

Hill Billies Sorority, 205

hillbilly, 17, 41, 138, 191, 192, 202, 204, 205, 208, 212; commercial use of, 200, 206, 210–11, 213, 252; derisive use of, 199;

dialect, 206; first recorded usage, 250; as regional term, 212; stereotype, 201–2, 250

"Hillbilly Heartbeats" radio show, 211

Hilsabeck Hotel, 64

Himmelberger and Harrison Company, 118

Hitchcock Shoals, 144

Hobart and Lee Timber and Tie Company, 68, 231

Hogan, James, 226

hogs: diet mainstay, 81; free-range, 85

Hollars, Denver, 91

Hollister, Mo., 16, 50, 54, 68, 91, 113, 137, 148, 150, 153, 154, 156, 158, 163, 164, 168, 185, 189, 192, 194, 209, 241, 245; Chamber of Commerce, 155; road bonds, 174; transformation to resort town, 155

Homeland Farms, 248

homesteads, 109; cost, 78, 98, 106, 229; diary, 105; improvements, 106, 107; land available, 102; squatters, 109; Sylvester, *106*. *See also* government land

Hovey, Edmund, 44

Howitt, Dad, 250

Hunt, Bill, 228

Hunt, William F., 63

Hurley, Mo., 244

Hyde, Arthur, 73, 228

immigrants, 77, 82, 83, 113, 189, 236; Anglo-Celtic, 78, 101, 104; differing husbandry, 104–5; ex-Union soldiers, 116; German-American, 79, 83, 101, 102, 104; Great Plains, 81, 82; as investors, 167–68; mid-westerners, 79, 149; white settlers, 96

immigration: rural, 95; southeast Ozarks, 229

Indian Creek, 42, 54, 125, 137

Indian Ridge, 54

Ingenthron, Dominick, 101, 209

Ingerie, Rudolph F., 54, 55

Inspiration Point, *27*, 28, 34, 112, 132, 218, 234

isolation of area, 6

Izaak Walton League, 73, 139, 140; Kansas City, 167

Jack's Fork River, 142

Jackson Hollow, 134, 141

Jackson Shoals, 144

Jake Creek, 54

Jakle, John, 25

James River Club House, 124, 127, 134

Jasper County, Mo., 97, 101

Shepherd of the Hills: Bank, 249; Cemetery, 58, 218 (*see also* Evergreen Historical Cemetery); country, as place name, 7, defined by novel, 31; Estates, 249; Expressway, 218; Inn, 249; Museum, 218; National Park, proposed, 222; statue, proposed, 251; Taxi, 32, 57, 183;
Shepherd of the Hills, The, 8, 26, 28, 31, 32, 35, 36, 50, 53, 62, 112, 123, 132, 136, 144, 160, 161, 191, 196, 210
Short, Dewey, 144, 185, 210
Shumate, Fern Nance, 250
Shut-In Club, 228
Signal Tree, 57, 192, 224
Silver Dollar City, 36, 132
Simmons, Jude and Madge Milligan, 242
Sims, Nancy, 80
Skaggs, M. B., 74
Skaggs Community Hospital, 74
Skaggs Trust, 229
Smith family, 41
Smithsonian Institution, 44
Southern Missouri Trust Company, 68
Southwest Presbyterian Assembly, 155, 156
spa resort towns: founding, 120
Spokane, Mo., 92, 178
Sportsmen Protective Leagues, 140
Springfield, Mo., 1, 2, 3, 6, 37, 38, 40, 44, 48, 54, 55, 61, 62, 64, 67, 68, 72, 94, 116, 125, 192, 209, 246, 250; Chamber of Commerce, 182, 211; as tourist town and regional market center, 120
Springfield Club House, 165, 175
Springfield-Harrison Road, 87, 90, 92
Springfield Light Guards, 38
Springfield Normal School, 55, 56, 158
Springfield/Ozark Shepherd of the Hills Tourist Association, 182
Spurlock, Pearl, 32, 35, 57, 173, 183, 198
St. Louis, Mo., 3, 6, 12, 13, 22, 54, 55, 61, 68, 72, 78, 79, 137
Standish, William, 129
Star Tobacco, 62
state geological survey, 43
State Guard unit, 120
State Highway Commission: organization, 174
State park system, 228; proposed, 73
steamboat. *See* boats
Stephens, Lon, 72
Stevens, Walter, 83, 200, 204
Stewart, Ollie, 28, 250

St. Francis River, 235
St. Louis and Iron Mountain Railway, 6, 124, 235; towns, 61
St. Louis and San Francisco Railroad, 2, 37, 61, 90, 116, 234, 235, 239
St. Louis Game Park (St. Louis Park and Agricultural Company), 12, 13, 62, 67, 68, 69, 70, 71, 72, 121, 139, 140, 142, 220, 226, 235; addition of Drury ranch, 229; boat landing, 65; Democrats at, 64; fence, 63, 65, 74; hunting lodge, 66; sale to Clemens and Campbell, 72; sale to Skaggs, 74; source for restocking animals, 68, 73; species of animals, 63, 65, 66, 74
St. Louis Park and Improvement Company, 224
Stone, William J., 65, 72
Stone County Courthouse, 99
Stowe, Harriet Beecher, 198
streetlights, 245
Stults, Ben, 13, 97, 151, 209
subsistence lifestyle, 92, 112
Sunset Inn, 56
surplus products, 3
Swallow, G. C., 116
Swan Creek, 80, 101
Swan Creek road, 246
Swanger, John E., 126, 238
Sycamore Club, 224
Sylvester family: John and Malissa, 105; Nettie, 107; Pleasant, 105; Riley, 105; William David (W. D., Billy), 13, 105, 107, 108, 209

Table Rock, 141; bluff, 144; Dam 145, 183, 194, 242; Lake, 1
Tagg, Lawrence, 31
Taneycomo Club, 164, 168, 192
Taney County Court, 52
Taney District, 77, 78, 79, 83
Taney Vista, 186
Taneyville, Mo., 63
telephone service, 245
Thompson, James B., 117–18, 235
Thoreau, Henry David, 26
timber: camps, 117; cedar posts, 93; exploitation of, 110; lumber, 2; for market, 103, 119, 170; telegraph poles, 168. *See also* railroad crossties
tobacco, 15, 61; cultivation, 78, 247; market at Branson, 73

Photo Credits

Most individuals listed below have contributed to or have been members of the White River Valley Historical Society, Point Lookout, Missouri. Their efforts in the preservation of family collections over the years have significantly contributed to the imagination of the past for this book, in the publication of the *White River Valley Historical Quarterly*, in civic and educational work, and in the promotion of Ozarks tourism. Although several have passed on to their ultimate reward, their work continues to inform us about our Ozarks home.

Velma Bass: 11, 43, 45

J. Ross Baughman: 87

James Denny: 101

Robert Emerson: 171

Herbert Hadley Papers, WHMC-Columbia, University of Missouri: 71

Viola Hartman: 91

Mabel Hicks: 8

Kalen and Morrow Collection: 16, 27, 27, 55, 80, 131, 133, 143, 154, 156, 157, 158, 159, 163, 175, 205, 207

Keith McCanse, *Where To Go in the Ozarks,* 1929: 188

Douglas Mahnkey: 198

Mary Craig Mappes: 127

Maschino/Brown Collection: 195

Ed Miller: 21

M. F. Miller Papers, WHMC-Columbia, University of Missouri: 46, 153

Missouri State Archives: 4–5, 193

Carl Moore: 71

Museum of the Ozarks, Springfield, Mo.: 14

Linda Myers-Phinney Collection: 29, 209

Northwest Arkansas Regional Library, Harrison, Ark.: 82

Hobart Parnell: 30, 33, 69, 75, 129, 151, 197

Walker Powell: 39, 53, 99, 130, 203

Powers Museum, Carthage, Mo.: 176–77

Ripley County Museum, Doniphan, Mo.: 111

Dorothy Roden: 51

Walter Stevens, *Ozark Uplift,* 1900: 64, 65, 67

Robert Wiley: 117, 171, 186–87

Edna Williams: 106